CAMBRIDGE LIBRARY C

Books of enduring scholarly va

Travel and Exploration in Asia

This collection of travel narratives, mainly from the nineteenth century, records the impressions of Europeans who visited China, Japan, South and South-East Asia. Some came as missionaries, others as members of trade or diplomatic missions, or as colonial administrators. Some were straightforward tourists, and one or two arrived as prisoners or shipwrecked sailors. Such accounts of travellers' experiences in exotic locations were eagerly received by European readers.

The History of Kamtschatka, and the Kurilski Islands, with the Countries Adjacent

James Grieve (1703–63), physician to Catherine the Great of Russia, and translator of this book, published posthumously in English in 1764, apologises in his 'Advertisement' for the crudeness and rambling nature of Stepan Krasheninnikov's original work, which nevertheless contains 'many very useful remarks, greatly contributing to the improvement of the trade, geography, and natural history, of the country he describes'. In 1755, Krasheninnikov (1711–55) had published his account of an expedition to Kamchatka between 1733 and 1743, under Vitus Bering, to increase knowledge of regions to the east, in particular whether a sea route to North America could be established. Krasheninnikov was to serve as a naturalist on the expedition, but he also took a keen interest in the geography, history and people of the lands he passed through. His narrative is a fascinating and detailed account of a huge area virtually unknown to the western world.

Cambridge University Press has long been a pioneer in the reissuing of out-of-print titles from its own backlist, producing digital reprints of books that are still sought after by scholars and students but could not be reprinted economically using traditional technology. The Cambridge Library Collection extends this activity to a wider range of books which are still of importance to researchers and professionals, either for the source material they contain, or as landmarks in the history of their academic discipline.

Drawing from the world-renowned collections in the Cambridge University Library and other partner libraries, and guided by the advice of experts in each subject area, Cambridge University Press is using state-of-the-art scanning machines in its own Printing House to capture the content of each book selected for inclusion. The files are processed to give a consistently clear, crisp image, and the books finished to the high quality standard for which the Press is recognised around the world. The latest print-on-demand technology ensures that the books will remain available indefinitely, and that orders for single or multiple copies can quickly be supplied.

The Cambridge Library Collection brings back to life books of enduring scholarly value (including out-of-copyright works originally issued by other publishers) across a wide range of disciplines in the humanities and social sciences and in science and technology.

The History of Kamtschatka, and the Kurilski Islands, with the Countries Adjacent

Stepan Petrovich Krasheninnikov
Translated by James Grieve

CAMBRIDGE
UNIVERSITY PRESS

University Printing House, Cambridge, CB2 8BS, United Kingdom

Cambridge University Press is part of the University of Cambridge.
It furthers the University's mission by disseminating knowledge in the pursuit of
education, learning and research at the highest international levels of excellence.

www.cambridge.org
Information on this title: www.cambridge.org/9781108075428

© in this compilation Cambridge University Press 2015

This edition first published 1764
This digitally printed version 2015

ISBN 978-1-108-07542-8 Paperback

This book reproduces the text of the original edition. The content and language reflect
the beliefs, practices and terminology of their time, and have not been updated.

Cambridge University Press wishes to make clear that the book, unless originally published
by Cambridge, is not being republished by, in association or collaboration with,
or with the endorsement or approval of, the original publisher or its successors in title.

The original edition of this book contains a number of oversize plates
which it has not been possible to reproduce to scale in this edition.
They can be found online at www.cambridge.org/9781108075428

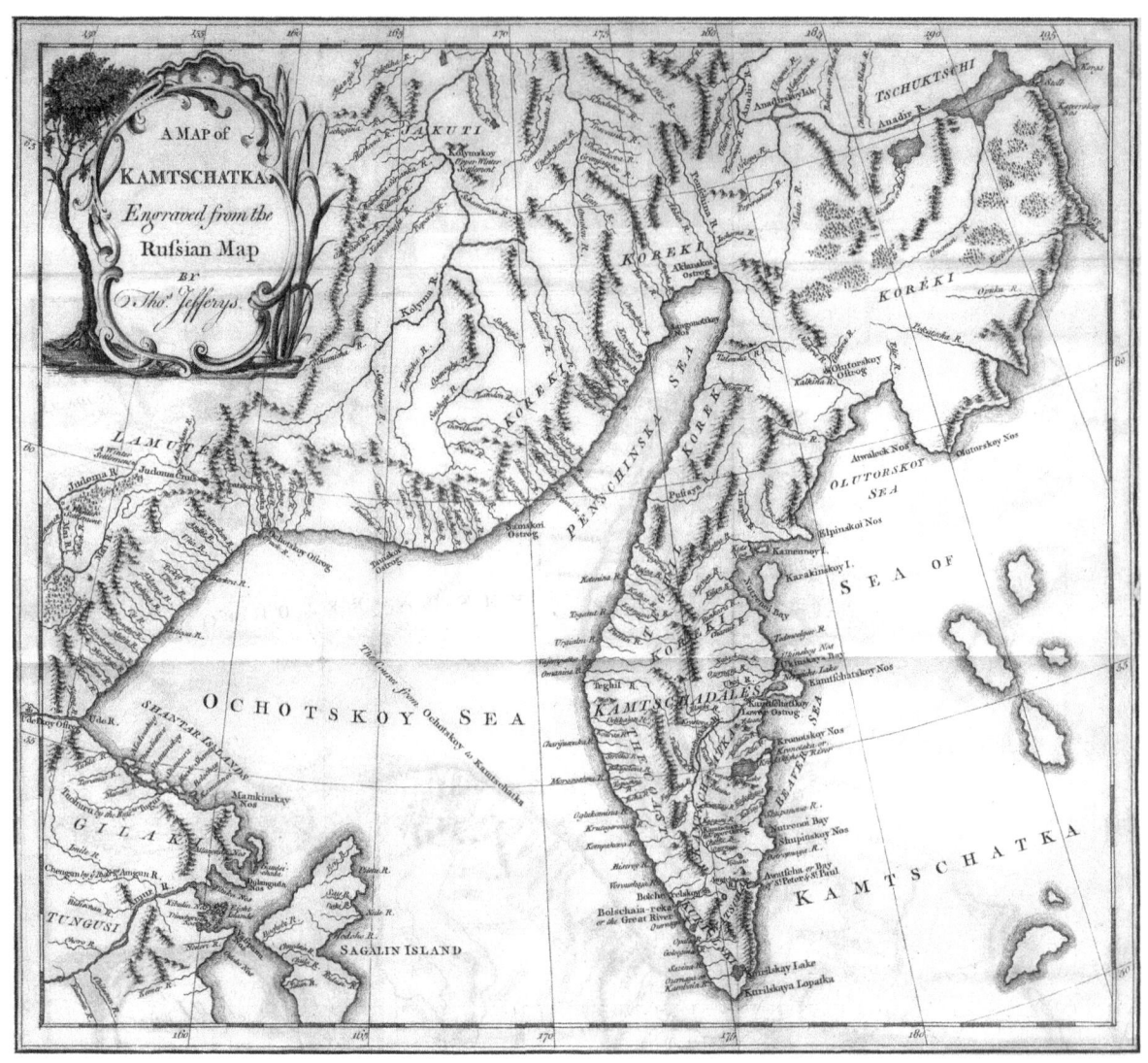

THE
HISTORY
OF
KAMTSCHATKA,
AND THE
KURILSKI ISLANDS,
WITH THE
COUNTRIES ADJACENT;
ILLUSTRATED WITH
MAPS AND CUTS.

Publiſhed at *Peterſbourg* in the *Ruſſian* Language, by Order of her IMPERIAL MAJESTY,

And tranſlated into ENGLISH

By JAMES GRIEVE, *M. D.*

GLOCESTER:
PRINTED BY R. RAIKES
FOR
T. JEFFERYS, GEOGRAPHER TO HIS MAJESTY, LONDON,
M.DCC.LXIV.

ADVERTISEMENT.

THE Russian language in which the Original of the following sheets was written, is rude and unpolished: other nations have with great care improved and refined their languages by giving proper encouragement to men of learning and genius, but in that country literature has, on the contrary, been 'till very lately rather discouraged.

Great indulgence should, therefore, be allowed the Author of this work: for though his manner is indigested, and his stile inelegant, abounding in digressions, and some uninteresting narrations, which obscure and confuse the more essential passages; yet he has communicated

ADVERTISEMENT.

nicated many very useful remarks, greatly contributing to the improvement of the trade, geography, and natural history, of the country he describes.

In order to render this piece more regular and perfect, it would have been necessary to new model the whole; but the gentleman, who undertook this Translation only for his amusement, was frequently interrupted in the course of the work by the necessary duty of his profession, and prevented from revising it before it went to the press by his sudden departure for Petersbourg. *Having been many years absent from* England, *and accustomed to write and speak in several different languages, he of course adopted their idioms, and, consequently, corrupted the phraseology of his own. Thus much it is thought necessary to say in justice to the Translator: and it must be confessed he has great merit with his countrymen; as it is entirely owing to his labours, hasty and imperfect as they may seem, that we have any knowledge of this remote, unknown, and very extraordinary country, since so few, and it may be said, scarce any* Englishman *is able to read the Original.*

This

ADVERTISEMENT.

This work is divided into four parts. The first, which is entirely Geographical, and in the Original makes eleven chapters, is here abridged, and reduced to four, as the Author had minutely described a great number of hills and rivers which did not serve to illustrate the subject. But it is hoped that nothing is omitted which may answer that end, or which might in any way entertain the reader, or help to ascertain the situations, measures, distances, and boundaries.

The second part contains the Natural History. This part has also been greatly contracted, from the design of offering to the reader nothing but what was really useful, curious, or entertaining; and in order to make it completely instructive, many notes have been adjoined, to explain some articles, or reconcile them with the accounts of former voyagers.

The third part of this work has been most considerably abridged, as in treating of the manners, customs, and religion of this barbarous nation, it was loaded with absurd practices, idle ceremonies, and unaccountable superstitions. Sufficient examples of all these have been retained

ADVERTISEMENT

retained to shew the precise state of an unpolished, credulous, and grosly ignorant people.

The fourth contains the first discovery, conquest, and planting of Russian *colonies in the country of* Kamtschatka. *This part is divided into eight chapters, giving a relation of several expeditions both by sea and land made into that country. It is also interspersed with a great many useful remarks relative to the geography, natural history, customs, manners, and civil and military policy, of the country. It likewise gives a particular account of the forts built there by the* Russians, *as well for the protection of their settlements, as to keep the natives in awe.*

THE

ERRATA.

For Fructicosa	*Page* 88, *Annot.*	*read*	Fruticosa
Chœreoptrylum	89,		Chœrophyllum
Autoris.	141,		Autorum?
Caudacuta	159, *Line* 29,		Caudâ acutâ
Self-murd	176, 26,		Self-murder
Dood. Append. 326, Ray Linn.	*Annot.* 192,		Doodij Raij Syn. II. Append. 329
Pentaphylladis fructicosus,	219, *Line* 1,		Pentaphylloides fruticosa
Chamaenchododendros	219, 18,		Chamœrododendron
Anemonides	220, 15,		Anemonoides

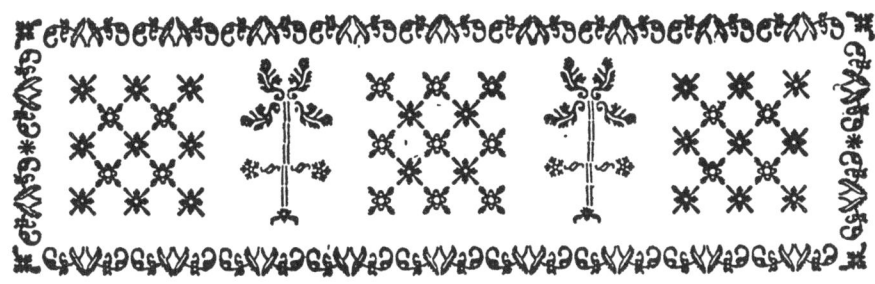

THE
RUSSIAN EDITOR's
PREFACE.

THERE is perhaps hardly any knowledge more pleasing than that which arises from accurate accounts of the variety of distinctions and divisions diversifying the face of the habitable globe, were we only to regard it so far as it gratifies our curiosity; but more noble purposes may be still effected by such informations. All who are employed in the management and superintendency of states and nations ought certainly to have an exact knowledge of those countries over which they preside, especially with regard to their soil and climate; what parts are proper for agriculture, or for pasture, and what are desert; what rivers are navigable, or may be rendered so; what communication there is already, or may be, made, between them; what beasts, birds, fishes, herbs, fruit-trees, and shrubs are found therein, and of what use they can be either in diet, medicine, dying, building, or any other part of œconomy; the inhabited and uninhabited parts, cities, forts, havens, mines, traffic, and manufactures; the particular commodities proper for home consumption, or for exportation; their imports from other countries; the situation and distances of places; their curiosities, whether natural or artificial; the condition of the public roads: they should likewise be acquainted with the customs and manners of the inhabitants, their number and language, religion, antiquity, and settlement; and also with the circumstances of the nations bordering upon them. All which knowledge may not only be serviceable to the people themselves, but likewise to neighbouring nations that are connected with them, either by trade or otherwise. The natural curiosity of man is not even satisfied with this: we frequently give ourselves a great deal of trouble in search of things that have no relation to us, especially if we have hitherto learned nothing, or at least nothing circumstantial and certain con-

cerning

PREFACE.

cerning them. For these reasons I hope readers of every denomination will favourably receive this description of *Kamtschatka*, designed both for use and entertainment. The author, if death had not prevented him, would himself have explained the occasion that gave him an opportunity of being informed of all these particulars; and, as such an account may be expected, I shall endeavour to do it for him in as few words as possible.

In the year 1733, her Imperial Majesty *Anne* ordered an expedition on foot to examine the coast of the Northern or Frozen Ocean, likewise that to the East about *Kamtschatka*, and from thence to *America* and *Japan*; and also at the same time to make out a description of *Siberia*, and particularly of *Kamtschatka*; to observe the situation of the places, their natural history and inhabitants, and whatever else might be necessary to a full knowledge of those people. To this end three professors of the Imperial Academy of Sciences were sent along with the sea-officers. These three gentlemen divided the task amonst them; one undertook to make the astronomical and physical observations; the second to remark whatever regarded natural history; the third to draw up a description of the people and country. To these members of the academy several other proper assistants were added: these were six *Russian* students, who had an opportunity to improve themselves while they

they were affifting the profeffors, and in time be qualified to fill up their vacancies. The author, *Stephen Krasheninicoff*, one of the above-mentioned fix, was born in *Mofcow*, and had his firft education in the Latin fchool of the convent of our Lord, where he learned the principles of rhetoric and philofophy, and excelled moft of his fchool-fellows, both in capacity and application to his ftudies. Though he was principally employed in the ftudy of natural philofophy, yet he fhewed fuch inclination to geography and civil hiftory, that in the Year 1735 he was employed in thefe different enquiries at fuch places as the profeffors themfelves did not vifit. In the year 1736 the members of the academy, being at *Yakutski*, were informed, that the sea-officers had made but a fmall progrefs in their difcoveries, and that they would not be able to reach *Kamtfchatka* in feveral years; the profeffors therefore having many ufeful obfervations to make in *Siberia*, thought proper to fend before them a perfon, on whom they could depend, to prepare for their reception at *Kamtfchatka*. To this truft Mr. *Krasheninicoff* was appointed, and at the fame time was furnifhed with proper inftructions and directions. Some accidents prevented the profeffors from arriving at *Kamtfchatka*, excepting the profeffor of aftronomy; the others were ordered by the fenate to return to St. *Petersbourg*, and in their way to make further obfervations in *Siberia*. Thus all enquiries

PREFACE.

quires into the state of *Kamtschatka* remained to be made entirely by Mr. *Krasheninicoff.* The professors furnished him with such assistances as they themselves had, by order of the senate. He travelled from one end of *Kamtschatka* to the other, accompanied by a guard and proper interpreters, being allowed to examine all the writings in the different forts and offices. The professors also, in the frequent accounts received from him, found that his observations in natural history and physics were just; and in any difficulties assisted him with their advice by letters.

In the mean time, the Imperial Academy of Sciences, sensible of the importance of pursuing their researches into the regions of *Siberia*, thought proper to send thither, in the year 1738, one of their adjuncts, *George William Steller*, who met the professors the following year in their return at *Yenefeisky*. This learned and curious gentleman had a great inclination to go to *Kamtschatka* by water. His desire was complied with; and the same instructions were given to him that were given to Mr. *Krasheninicoff.* They sent likewise along with him a painter, to delineate whatever might be found curious in natural history. They continued together at *Kamtschatka* 'till the year 1740, at which time Mr. *Steller* embarked in the voyage that was made in order to discover the coast of *America*; and Mr. *Krasheninicoff* was sent to *Yakutski*, which as soon as the professors

were

were informed of, they ordered him to join them, and return with them to *Petersbourg* in the year 1743. Mr. *Steller*, in his return from *Siberia*, died of a fever the 12th of *November*, 1745, in the town of *Toumen*.

When Mr. *Krasheninicoff* had given the Academy of Sciences a full report of all his observations at *Kamtschatka*, and had likewise received all Mr. *Steller*'s papers, it was thought proper to join these two works, and to commit their compilement to the person who had the greatest share in the merit of the discovery. This is the origin of the following description of *Kamtschatka*; a country never yet described by any author of credit, and where the manners and customs of the inhabitants are beyond measure singular and uncommon. It is to be wished that such writers as have hitherto given us accounts of new-discovered countries had taken the same pains to inform themselves that this writer hath. The author was advanced in the year 1745 to be an adjunct of the Academy of Sciences, and in the year 1750 was made professor of botany and natural history. He died in the 42d year of his age, when the last sheets of his book were printing off; and was one of those few whom personal merit alone, and no advantages of birth or fortune, contributed to raise.

For the better understanding of the geographical descriptions, it was thought proper to add two maps of of *Kamtschatka* and the neighbouring countries, between which and other maps of those countries, even such as the academy itself hath formerly published, the curious reader may observe a great difference. But the author asserts that every thing is laid down from the strictest inquiry, and had purposed to support the authenticity of his maps, by publishing such memoirs as would prove their accuracy beyond dispute.

A GEOGRAPHICAL DESCRIPTION OF

KAMTSCHATKA.

AND OF THE

COASTS and ISLANDS adjacent to it.

PART I.

CHAP. I.
Of KAMTSCHATKA.

THOUGH the country called *Kamtschatka* was long known to the geographers of former times, yet so little were they acquainted with its situation, that they believed it to be joined to *Yesso*; and this opinion was looked upon in those days as a very probable conjecture: but it has been since found that between the two countries there is a large sea, interspersed with many islands. The

Russians

Ruffians could form their maps of *Kamtfchatka* only from conjecture 'till it was brought under their fubjection; and then they could not immediately procure any accurate or fatisfactory knowledge of the country, for want of perfons properly qualified to make the neceffary enquiries.

The two late expeditions have greatly contributed to complete the geography of thefe parts; particularly the laft, in which the fea-officers delineated exactly all the eaftern coaft of *Kamtfchatka* as far as the cape of *Tchukotfkoi*, all the weftern to the *Penfchinfka* gulph, and from *Ochotfkoy* to the river *Amur*: they defcribed the iflands lying between *Japan* and *Kamtfchatka*, and alfo thofe which are between *Kamtfchatka* and *America*. At the fame time the gentlemen of the Academy undertook to determine the fituation of *Kamtfchatka* by aftronomical obfervations, and to remark every thing worthy of notice in the civil and natural hiftory of the country and places adjacent. In this chapter I fhall only treat of the geography of this country.

That great peninfula, which makes the boundary of *Afia* to the north-eaft, and ftretches itfelf from north to fouth about 7° 30', is called *Kamtfchatka*. I place the beginning of this peninfula at the rivers *Puftaia*, and *Anapho*, lying in the latitude of 59° 30'. The firft runs into the *Penfchinfka* fea, and the other to the eaftward. At thefe places the ifthmus is fo narrow, that I am credibly informed the fea may in fair weather be feen on both fides from the hills in the middle. As the country runs broader towards the north, I reckon this place the ifthmus that joins the peninfula to the main land. The government of *Kamtfchatka* extends no farther than to this place; and all the country north of this boundary is called *Zenoffe*, and is under the government of *Anadir*.

The fouthern part of this peninfula, which is called *Lopatka*, lies in 51° 3' north latitude. The difference of longitude from *Peterfbourg* is by the beft obfervations found to be at *Ochotfkoy* 112° 53'

112° 53' eaft longitude, and thence to *Bolfcheretfkoi* or the Great River 14° 6' eaft. The figure of the peninfula of *Kamtfchatka* is fomewhat elliptical, being broader towards the middle, and growing narrower towards both ends. Its broadeft place is between the mouth of the river *Teghil* and the river *Kamtfchatka*. Towards the fource they are joined by the river *Elouki*.

The *Elouki* runs in the fame latitude with thofe rivers for 415 verfts. They call the fea which feparates *Kamtfchatka* from *America* the Eaftern Ocean. On the weftern fide lies the *Penfchinfka* fea, which begins near the fouthern point of the cape of *Kamtfchatka* and the *Kurilfki* iflands, and runs northward between the weftern coaft of *Kamtfchatka* and the coaft of *Ochotfkoy* more than 1000 verfts. The northern part is called the bay of *Penfchinfka* from the river *Penfchina* which falls into it. The hills make one continued ridge from north to fouth through the peninfula, almoft equally dividing the country. From this ridge feveral others extend towards the fea, between which are the courfes of the rivers. Thefe ridges fometimes run a confiderable way into the fea, and are called Nofs, or capes. There are more of thefe upon the eaftern than the weftern coaft. All the bays between the capes are called, in general, feas; each having its particular name, as the *Olutorfky* fea, *Kamtfchatka* fea, &c. We fhall hereafter give our reafons for calling the whole peninfula by the name of *Kamtfchatka*, though in fact it hath in none of the different languages of the inhabitants any general appellation; but every part of the country receives its name from its inhabitants, or fomething remarkable obferved in it: and even the *Ruffian* Coffacks underftand *Kamtfchatka* to be only the country lying near the river of that name; and to the other parts of this peninfula they have given the following appellations:

Kurilfki Country is the fouthern part, fo named from the *Kuriles* that inhabit it.

The Coaſt extends from the *Bolſcheretſkoi* or Great River to the *Teghil*.

Awatſcha extends from the *Bolſcheretſkoi* to fort *Awatſcha*.

Bobrovoi or *Beaver Sea* is the diſtrict round *Kamtſchatka*.

Koreka, from the *Koreki* that inhabit it, extends from the north of the *Kamtſchatka* to the *Teghil*.

Ukoi is the eaſtern coaſt from the river *Ukoi*.

Teghil is the weſtern coaſt from the river *Teghil*.

Kamtſchatka is plentifully furniſhed with rivers; however they are ſo little that none of them are navigable by the ſmalleſt veſſels, except the river *Kamtſchatka*, which will carry ſmall veſſels 200 verſts upwards from its mouth. Into this river it is reported that ſome *Ruſſians* were brought by ſea, long before its ſubjection to *Ruſſia*. It is at preſent called *Theodotoſhine*, from the chief of thoſe people thrown a-ſhore, whoſe name was *Theodot*. Next to this, the moſt conſiderable rivers are, the *Bolſchaia-reka*, or Great River, *Awatſcha* and *Teghil*; upon which the *Ruſſians* have ſettlements. *Kamtſchatka* is likewiſe very well furniſhed with lakes, particularly about the river of that name, where they are ſo numerous that there is no paſſage over land in the ſummer-time. Some of them are very large: the moſt conſiderable are, the lake of *Nerpitche*, which is near the mouth of the *Kamtſchatka*; the *Kronotzkoy*, out of which runs the river *Krodakighe*; and the *Kurilſkoy*, out of which runs the river *Oſernoi*.

The river *Kamtſchatka* riſes in a marſhy ground, and firſt runs north-eaſt; then inclines more to the eaſt, and turning at once towards the ſouth-weſt, falls into the ocean in 56° 30' north latitude. From its ſource to its mouth, in a ſtrait line, is 496 verſts; but the length of its courſe, according to the exacteſt computation, is about 525 verſts; during which it receives into it many brooks and rivers. About two verſts from its mouth, upon the right ſide, are three deep bays. There are ſeveral forts built along the banks of this river by the *Ruſſian* Coſſacks, to awe

awe and keep in subjection the wild inhabitants. The *Elouki* may be reckoned the chief of all the rivers that fall into the *Kamtschatka* on the left side, and its head meets that of the *Teghil*.

The *Teghil* runs almost in the same latitude with the *Kamtschatka*; and the strait road from the one to the other is by the river *Elouki*. Some little forts and settlements of the natives are scattered here and there upon its banks.

The *Bolschaia-reka*, or Great River, called by the natives *Keeksha*, runs out of a lake 185 versts to the east from its mouth, and falls into the *Penschinska* sea in the latitude of 52° 45'. Its mouth is reckoned to be 555 versts to the south distant from that of the *Teghil*. It is called Great upon this account, that of all the rivers that fall into the *Penschinska* sea this is the only one which they can navigate from its mouth nearly to its spring, and this not without some difficulty, on account of its rapidity and the great number of islands. At the time of high water it is so deep at the mouth that large vessels may enter; for the water has been observed to rise at full and new moon very little less than nine *Paris* feet or four *Russian* yards. It receives a multitude of rivulets; the most considerable of which is the *Bistroy* or Rapid River, so called from the swiftness of its stream, caused by the many shoals and cataracts. You may go from the mouth of the Great River to that of the *Bistroy*, and up within 40 versts of its head; and from thence over a carrying place to the river *Kamtschatka*, that springs out of the same marsh, and runs quite to the Eastern Ocean. And though this passage must be laborious and tedious, upon account of the rapidity of the river, and the many shoals and cataracts, where every thing must be carried by land, and which would render it impossible to advance more than 10 versts in a day (as I found in my way to *Kamtschatka* in the year 1739, when the boats were carried over the marsh, about two versts from the head of the Rapid, to *Kamtschatka*); yet,

considering

considering that all sorts of carriages in the summer are worked from one settlement to another by men, the said passage by water would be a great help to the people of this country who are obliged to carry stores and baggage for the government: for, instead of employing 10 or 15 men about a carriage of 20 pood, the same would be performed with less trouble in a small boat by two; and to encrease the facility of commerce, there would at all times be a free road, which is the case now only in winter.

It may be hoped, however, that even without such a road this difficulty will be removed, when the new colony settled there shall have a sufficient number of horses for drawing those carriages. From the *Bolscheretskoi* to the upper fort you may travel in carts drawn by horses; but, in summer, this is practicable in no other part of the country by reason of frequent obstructions from rivers, marshes, lakes, and high mountains.

The *Baranew* rivulet is particularly remarkable for the number of boiling springs which are found near it. It falls into the *Keeksha*, on the south-east side, 44 versts from *Bolscheretskoi*; and upon the mouth of it stands the settlement *Kalickin*, or *Opachin*, which is about 70 versts distant from the boiling springs.

The river *Awatscha* rises from under a mountain about 150 versts from its mouth, and runs from west to east 'till it falls into the bay of St. *Peter* and St. *Paul* in the Eastern Ocean, almost in the same latitude with the *Keeksha*. This river is very near as large as the last, and of more utility.

The bay of St. *Peter* and St. *Paul*, or *Awachinskaya* bay, is 14 versts in length, and as many in breadth, of a circular form, and surrounded on all sides by high rocky mountains. Its mouth, considering the space of the bay, is very narrow, and so deep that ships of all dimensions may enter it without any danger. Upon its banks are built, by order of the navy, officers' apartments, barracks, magazines, &c. On the north side of the

Awachinskaya

Awachinskaya bay, almost opposite the *Kareemchin* fort, are two high mountains, one of which smokes almost continually, and sometimes burns.

The breadth of the cape of *Kamtschatka*, between the mouth of the *Keeksha* and the *Awachinskaya* bay, measures from sea to sea, by a strait line, only 255 versts; a distance much less than that between the *Teghil* and the *Kamtschatka*.

There are a multitude of rivulets which fall into the Eastern Ocean between the mouth of the *Awatscha* northward, and the river *Kamtschatka*, and from that again to the *Anadir*; but being of small note, we shall only remark any thing that may be curious relating to them; among which may be reckoned the mountain *Shupanoveskaya*, so called from *Shupanova* a stream near which it stands. This mountain is a volcano, and has smoked at the top in several places for many years, and sometimes rumbles, but does not flame. The *Camel's Throat*, a rivulet near this hill, is remarkable for the danger of its passage through a very narrow valley, between high and steep mountains, from whence the snow is apt to tumble upon the slightest accident, even, it is said, from a strong exertion of the voice; and, falling down in vast heaps, sometimes buries passengers under it; for which reason the natives make it criminal to speak aloud as they pass through the valley: in other respects the road is very convenient. On the south side of the river *Shophead*, or *Shupanova*, near the sea shore, are a great many pillars or rocks, which appear above water, and make its entrance very dangerous; a little beyond this to the south is a bay, called *Nutrenoi*, surrounded by rocky mountains, about four versts in length and breadth; and near it, about the head of a rivulet, called *Shenmeek*, are large wells of boiling water. Out of a mountain near these springs, in many places, proceeds a steam, and the bubbling of boiling water is heard, but no springs have made their way through yet, though there are considerable fissures here and there, and the steam issues forth with the same rapidity as out of the *Eolipile*, and is so hot that the hand cannot bear it. After passing through a very woody and mountainous country, we come to the remarkable stream *Krodakighe*, or the Larch-Tree River, which rushes out of the great lake *Kronotzkoy*, in such a cascade that one may walk under it: this lake is in length about 50 versts, reckoned to be 40 in breadth, and is near 50 from the sea. Around it are high mountains, two of which about the sides of the upper mouth of the rivulet *Krodakighe*, rise above the rest. Multitudes of rivulets empty themselves into the lake *Kronotzkoy*, whose springs are near those rivers which run into the *Kamtschatka*.

From this place, nothing worth remarking occurs till we come to the *Kronotzkoy* Noss; and here begins the Beaver Sea, which extends to the *Shupinskoy*. The coast from the *Kamtschatka* to the *Kronotzkoy* Noss is every where sandy; and near the bay, called *Ukinskaya*, begin the habitations of the settled *Koreki*; but the *Kamtschadales* inhabit all the country to this place.

The river *Nungeen*, which falls into *Nutrenoi* bay, is called, by the Cossacks, *Pankara*, because there was formerly on the south side of the bay a small *Koreki* fort of the same name; but the inhabitants having built a small fort on a high hill on the northern side of the bay, which they called *Gengota*, abandoned it: this fort is surrounded with a wall of earth about a fathom high, and a yard thick, having within it a double pallisade, and on each side are two bastions raised. It has three gates to the east, west, and north. The *Koreki* purpose to leave their old fort, and to remove into the new one, which they have built about the inward point of the above-mentioned bay, and call it *Ueackang-Atenum*: this was the first place that I found fortified by the natives; for the others were nothing more than habitations dug in the earth, surrounded with huts, as with so many towers without any outward fortifications;

fications; but, on the contrary, further to the north, there is not one settlement of these people which has not, besides its natural strength of situation, a wall to cover it. The *Koreki* in those places say, that they thus provide for their defence against the incursion of the *Tchukotskoi*: but as that people have never invaded these places, some other cause must be sought for this precaution of the *Koreki*; and we can account for it only from their apprehensions of the Cossacks, who usually travel this way.

Upon the north point of a bay which receives the *Kitkitannu*, a rivulet, there is a small fort built on a high rock, and fortified by a wall of earth about 10 feet in height. Its gates are on the east and south sides. The inhabitants of it are under the commander of the small fort *Keemgu*, whom the Cossacks call a *Russian*, he being of that extraction. From this fort there is a low cape that projects into the sea; beyond this cape there is a deep bay of about eight versts in breadth, and equally as broad at its mouth as in the middle; but all the rest of the bays which I have seen are narrow at their mouths. Into this bay the river *Karaga* enters by two mouths, and almost meets near its head with the *Lesnaya* river, to which they usually go from the *Karaga*. On the north shore of the bay there stands, on a high hill, the small fort *Keetalgeen*, in which every hut is inclosed with a palisade. Besides this small fort on the river *Karaga*, there are two other settlements of the *Korcki*. Over-against the mouth of the *Karaga*, 20 versts from the shore, is an island, called *Karaginskoy*, the lower end of which is opposite to *Nungeen*, and the upper end to *Kute* cape. *Koreki* inhabit this island; but those on the continent do not allow them to be of the same race with themselves; and it must be observed, that the manners of the *Karaginskoy* appear as barbarous to the *Koreki*, as those of the *Koreki* do to more civilized nations. Their number is reckoned to be 100 men or more, but not above 30 of them pay any tax, the reft, at the time of its gathering, hiding themfelves in the mountains. They go to this ifland in the fummer in their little boats; but in the winter they have no communication with it.

There is little worth notice after you pafs the above-mentioned ifland, 'till you come to the *Uyulen* or *Olutora* river. Upon this river the *Ruffians* twice built the *Olutorfkoy* fort. The firft was built by a native of *Jakutfki*, called *Athanafey Petrove*, upon the fouthern fhore, very little above the mouth of the *Kalkina* rivulet which falls into the *Olutora* from the fouth; and the fecond a great deal below that place under the direction of Major *Paulutfkoy*, who was fent there on account of the rebellious *Tchukotfkoi*; but both of them were forfaken and burnt down by the *Olutores*. The laft fort is about two days' voyage from the mouth of the *Olutora*.

The *Atwaleck* cape, which extends 80 verfts into the fea, begins near the river *Elir*, and points towards the *Govyannoy* cape. The fea between thofe capes is called *Olutorfkoy*. The *Pockatska* rifes in the fame plain with the river *Glotova*, which runs from the north-eaft into the *Olutora*. From the *Kalkina*, where was built the firft *Olutorfkoy* fort, to the river *Pockatska*, is five days' journey with rein-deer, reckoning for each day between 30 and 40 verfts. Between the *Katurka* and the land oppofite to *Anadir*, there projects into the fea a rocky cape, called *Kateerfkoy* in 64° 15' north latitude. The diftance from the *Petropaulauskaya* haven to the mouth of the *Anadir*, as obferved by the fea-officers, is 19° 20'; and the fea coaft from the *Kurilskaya Lopatka* to the *Tchukotskoi* cape, north eaft, which lies in 67°, is for the moft part mountainous, efpecially in thofe places where the capes project into the fea.

We

KAMTSCHATKA.

We now come to consider the rivers that fall into the East Sea from the mouth of the *Awatscha*, towards the south, to the *Kurilskaya Lopatka*; and from the *Kurilskaya Lopatka* into the *Penschinska* sea to the *Teghil* and the *Pustaia* rivers.

There are but few rivulets that intersect the country between the mouth of the *Awatscha* and the *Lopatka*. The ridge of mountains, which divides *Kamtschatka*, extends to the East Sea: the declivity is steep and craggy; and the gulphs and bays, which are formed by these mountains, afford a safe harbour for vessels of any burthen in the worst weather.

The *Kurilskaya Lopatka*, which by the natives is called *Kapoore*, is the southernmost point of the cape of *Kamtschatka*, and divides the eastern from the *Penschinska* sea: it takes its name from its resemblance to a man's shoulder-blade. Mr. *Steller*, who has been upon the *Lopatka*, says, that the place is not more than 10 fathoms above the surface of the sea, and for that reason is subject to great inundations, so that for 20 versts from thence no-body lives, except those who come there in the winter to catch foxes; and when the ice is carried thither with the beavers on it, then the *Kuriles*, who follow this ice along the shore, assemble here in great multitudes. Within three versts from the *Lopatka* nothing grows except moss; and there are neither rivers nor springs, only a few lakes and pools. The soil consists of two layers, the lower is strong, and the upper spongy; and its surface is full of hillocks, and useless. The first rivulet falling into the *Penschinska* sea, is called the *Utatumpit*; two versts from the *Utatumpit*, the rivulet *Tapgutpan* runs into the sea; upon which stands a small fort called *Kochinskoy*; and three versts from thence is the *Pitpuy*, or *Ozernaya*, which runs out of a considerable lake divided from the sea by a mountain. The *Russians* call this river *Kambala*, or Flounder River, because great numbers of flounders are caught in the mouth of it.

The lake out of which it runs, and the mountains which lie between it and the sea, are called by the same name. Near the *Kambalinskoy* lake is built *Kamabalinskoy*, a small *Kurilskoy* fort. From the *Kurilskoy* lake, towards the ocean, strait to the *Awatscha*, is not above 19 *German* miles; but the road is excessively difficult; for you must pass over eleven high mountains, and some of them are so steep that travellers are obliged to let themselves down with ropes.

About this lake are several remarkable mountains; particularly two, one on each side of it, which emit smoke, and have done so many years; and which Mr. *Steller* says he saw in his journey from the *Yavina* to the *Ozernaya* river.

Though I went as far as the river *Ozernaya* in 1738, yet I did not see those mountains, and only observed hot springs in two different places. These springs run within 20 versts from its mouth, some of them into the river *Paustia*, and others into the river *Ozernaya,* both of them on the south side of it.

The river *Apanach* is reckoned the boundary of the province of *Kurilskoy*. It runs from under the mountain called *Opalskaya Sopka*, which is 85 versts from the sea, and excels all the rest of the mountains about the *Penschinska* sea both in height and fame; particularly on this account, that it can be seen by seamen from both seas, and serves them for a land-mark.

The shore from the *Lopatka* almost to the *Kambalina* is low. From the *Kambalina* to the *Ozernaya* is so mountainous and steep, that one cannot go near the sea.

From the *Ozernaya* to the *Opala* it is likewise mountainous, but more upon a level.

From the *Opala* to the Great River is an extensive plain, so that not one hill is to be observed near the sea. After passing a great number of rivulets, all of which arise out of a range of mountains,

called

called *Stanovoy* ridge, we come to the river *Geek*, called by the Coffacks *Vorovſkaya*, or Rogue's River, becauſe the *Kamtſchadales* who live upon it were frequently concerned in inſurrections, and uſed to kill the tax-gatherers treacherouſly. From hence we meet nothing worth notice 'till we come to a *Kamtſchatkoi* fort, called *Tackauta*, in which travellers uſually equip themſelves for paſſing the ridge. Here the common road lies near a rivulet, from the head of which it paſſes the *Stanovoy* ridge, 'till it deſcends to the heads of the river *Keergena*, which falls into the *Kamtſchatka*.

From the *Keergena* we paſs up the river *Kamtſchatka* to the *Kamtſchatkoi* fort. The country between the little fort *Tackauta* and the *Stanovoy* ridge is a deſert of 110 verſts in extent, and from the ridge to the upper *Kamtſchatkoi* fort is 65, the land equally barren.

The above road is very difficult and dangerous, for a great part of it lies on the river, which, from the rapidity of its current, in many places never freezes. Travellers are obliged, therefore, in ſome parts to keep cloſe to the ſides with great care; for if the ice breaks nothing can ſave them, the rocks on the banks in ſeveral places being ſo ſteep that it is impoſſible to get on ſhore, and the river runs ſo ſwiftly that you are immediately driven under the ice. The ridge is paſſable only in calm and fair weather, for which we are obliged to wait ſometimes ten days or more; at other times it is impoſſible to find the way, and we muſt inevitably fall down the precipices, and be loſt. The propereſt time to paſs is when no clouds are to be ſeen on the top of the ridge, for even the leaſt cloud is a ſign of a great ſtorm there. To croſs over this ridge takes up a whole winter's day. The greateſt danger is in paſſing over the very top, which is called by the Coſſacks, *Greben*, or a comb. Its breadth is 30 fathoms; it is like a boat with the bottom upwards, the aſcent on both ſides being

very

very steep. The paſſage is troubleſome even in the calmeſt weather, for the road falling off leaves nothing but ice: the *Kamtſchadales*, therefore, in order to paſs it in ſafety, have under their ſnow-ſhoes, two nails; yet theſe are of ſmall ſervice if the wind overtakes them there, for they are frequently carried from one ſide to the other to the great hazard of their lives, or at leaſt of their limbs. Beſides which, this paſſage is attended with the danger of being ſmothered in the ſnow, the narrow path lying between high, and almoſt perpendicular, mountains, from which the ſnow falls in heaps upon the leaſt motion. This is a danger, indeed, unavoidable in every place where the road lies in narrow and deep vallies.

In mounting the ridge all muſt walk, for the dogs can hardly aſcend it even with the light baggage; but in deſcending it is otherwiſe, for then they only leave a ſingle dog in the ſledge: the reſt are taken out, it being impoſſible to manage them all in ſuch a road. Although this paſſage of the ridge be ſo difficult, yet, as it is the uſual road to *Kamtſchatka*, one may conclude that any other paſſage from ſea to ſea muſt be ſtill more difficult and dangerous.

The coaſt from the mouth of the Great River to the river *Puſ-taia*, as far as the *Shahack*, is ooze and ſoft mud, ſo that many veſſels have been thrown upon it without receiving any hurt. From the *Shahack* the ſhore begins to be bolder, though not rocky; but from the *Tulahan* river it is mountainous, rocky, and dangerous to ſeamen.

The late deſcriptions of the ſhore of the *Penſchinska* ſea, from the *Leſnaya* to the *Penſchina* and to the *Ochotska*, are more particular than the former: for in the year 1741 a high road was eſtabliſhed to *Kamtſchatka* with poſt-houſes at proper ſtations; yet, with regard to the diſtances of places, they are not much more accurate; ſince there were no aſtronomical obſervations

vations made, nor the diftances meafured: nor are there any hopes of its being foon done, as travelling in thofe parts is very dangerous; the wild *Koreki* oppofing the *Ruffian* government, and frequently committing murders upon fmall parties that pafs that way; and though fometimes they appear friendly, yet travellers are always obliged to be fo much upon their guard againft the deceit and cruelty of fuch a barbarous race, that they have no time to make accurate furveys. Beyond the *Puftaia* is the river *Talouka*; 50 verfts from which is the river *Penfchina*, remarkable for giving name to the *Penfchinfka* fea. Thirty verfts from the fea is built a fmall fort, called *Acklanfkoy*, from the river *Acklan*, which falls from the right fide into the river *Penfchina*. Here fome *Ruffian* Coffacks live for the difpatch of the poft, and to bring into fubjection the *Koreki* that refufe to pay taxes. The firft houfe was built there in the year 1679, fince which certain foldiers were fent there to gather the taxes; but afterwards, on account of the great diftance and danger of the place, it was abandoned. This fpot has been made remarkable by the murder of two commiffaries, with a party of Coffacks, many years ago, who conveyed the tribute from *Kamtfchatka* to the *Anadirfk* fort.

From the river *Talouka* to the mouth of the *Penfchina* the fea coaft lies north-eaft; thence it turns fouth-weft as far as the rivulet *Gogulan*; after which the coaft turns to the eaft, 'till we approach the river *Ochotfka*: the interval between which laft and the *Penjchina* is watered with feveral rivulets that run into the *Penfchinfka* fea, for whofe names we refer to the map. The *Cuchtai* river falls into the *Ochotfka* very near the fea: between them is a confiderable bay, in which veffels may anchor. The river *Cuchtai* is particularly remarkable for its port, and for the great quantities of Larch trees, and other forts of wood fit for building veffels for navigation, which grow on its banks, and which are not found in fo great plenty along the river *Ochotfka*. The river

river *Ochotſka* has three mouths; the New mouth, the Old mouth, and the *Bulginſkaya* out-let.

The New mouth is dry, except at the time of a great inundation; and even then veſſels cannot enter it. The preſent *Ochotſkoy* fort is built between the New and Old mouths, almoſt upon the beach; and the former, which is now called the old fort, was ſix verſts from the ſea. This place is called *Ochotſkoy* poſt, and commonly *Lama*; and has under its juriſdiction all *Kamtſchatka*, and the coaſt of the *Penſchinska* ſea to the frontiers of *China*. For which reaſon the tax-gatherers are all ſent out from hence; and the tax, when gathered, is immediately brought from all other places hither, where it is firſt appraiſed, and then ſent into *Jakutzk*. Formerly the *Ochotskoy* fort was poorly inhabited, and under the juriſdiction of *Jakutski*, but it is much increaſed ſince the *Ruſſians* have made this the port for their paſſage by ſea to *Kamtſchatka*.

This place is better built than any of the other forts, the houſes being good and regular, particularly thoſe belonging to the government, in which the officers of the *Kamtſchatka* expeditions reſided. In my time there was neither a church nor a fortification, but they were building both. Though the country be as barren as *Kamtſchatka*, yet its inhabitants are better furniſhed with every thing, becauſe goods and proviſions brought from *Jakutski* are ſold here cheaper by one half. Though plenty of corn is brought here, yet no freſh meat is to be got, except wild fowl and veniſon, and that ſeldom. Fiſh in this place is almoſt as plenty as in *Kamtſchatka*, except the *Chaveccha*, which they bring hither from thence. The greateſt want in this place is that of good paſturage near them; therefore the inhabitants cannot breed cattle. They have tried many times to keep them upon the river *Avi*, but with great loſs, moſt of them dying for want of ſuſtenance. Time will ſhew whether the *Jakutski* people, that are ſettled along the rivulets which fall into the

Ochotska,

The Harbour of S.t Peter and S.t Paul. See Page 14.

The Harbour of Ochotsky. See Page 24.

Ochotska, be more fuccefsful. The want of cattle, in fome meafure, is made up by the deer, which the natives have in greater plenty than in *Kamtfchatka*; but thefe are more ufed for carriage than food. They alfo travel with dogs, but not fo commonly as in *Kamtfchatka*.

There were four tranfport-veffels built here: namely; the Fortune, in which in the year 1737 I went to the Great River, and which was loft foon after; the boat Hauriel, which was ufed alfo in long fea voyages for fome time; the Galliot *Ochotska*; and a fmall veffel, which was not then launched. The paffage by fea ufed formerly to be only once a year; namely, in the autumn, when the tax-gathers went from *Ochotsky* to *Kamtfchatka*, and brought back the tax the next year: but now they go oftener.

The paffage from the *Ochotska* to the Great River is directly fouth-eaft. Between the fort *Ochotskoy* and the river *Amur*, whofe heads are in the *Ruffian* dominions, the following rivers run into the fea: the firft is *Urack*, 24 verfts from the *Ochotska*. It is to be obferved, that in the time of the *Kamtfchatka* expeditions the provifions were ufed to be fent down this river upon flat-bottomed boats to the *Ochotska*; for which reafon they built a dock 50 verfts from its mouth, where the failors and the *Ochotskoy* Coffacks ufed to build veffels for the above expeditions, and fend the faid provifions from the *Iudomskoy* Kreft, or crofs, to that place over land by horfes or deer in fledges. But this way of carriage by water was attended with great trouble, lofs of time and people; for the river is very rapid, rocky, and full of cataracts, and not always deep enough, except in the fpring, or after great rains: and as thefe additional waters run foon off, they are obliged to watch every opportunity of fending down the loaded veffels; which if they omit, they muft often wait a long time.

There never was a fleet fo happy in this navigation as not to lofe fome veffels either by rocks or cataracts, many of which are fo

dangerous,

dangerous, that a *Siberian* foldier, who ventured to be a pilot there, was made a ferjeant for it. One may judge of its great rapidity by this, that captain *Walton* went down the river from the *Urackſkoi* dock to the mouth in 17 hours, notwithſtanding the many ſtops he met with in paſſing the cataracts, and relieving the other veſſels which had ſtruck on the ſhoals.

Thirty verſts from the *Urackſkoi* dock, up the river *Urack*, is built a ſmall cuſtom-houſe; at which all paſſengers are ſearched for brandy, china, tobacco, and other contraband or ſmuggled goods.

The river *Urack* falls into a bay called by its name, which extends along the ſhore two verſts: its breadth is 200 fathoms. From hence, 'till we come to the *Ude*, nothing of moment occurs; on the nothern bank of this river ſtands the fort *Udeſkoy*, about ſeven days' voyage by water from its mouth, and we may reckon 10 or 12 verſts for each day's journey, as is generally allowed. The buildings in it are a church of St. *Nicholas*, the tax-office, and 10 houſes of the inhabitants. This fort is under the juriſdiction of *Jakutſki*, from whence the tax-gatherers are ſent.

The *Tunguſi*, who pay their taxes in here, are reckoned ſix nations; and their taxes amount every year to 85 ſables and 12 foxes' ſkins. Formerly only people that were in the ſervice of the government lived in this fort; but in the year 1735 a colony of 10 families of boors were ſettled there to eſtabliſh agriculture. But it is ſaid there are no hopes that corn will grow in theſe places, the ſoil being quite improper for cultivation.

Near the *Mamkinſkay* Noſs, and oppoſite to a large bay which abounds with whales and ſeals, lies *Medveſhuy*, or the Bear's iſland: it is about 10 verſts in length, and ſix in breadth, at about a day's ſail on the eaſt. South of the Noſs lies the iſland *Theocliſtove*, which uſed formerly to be reſorted to in winter by the hunters. This iſland abounds with rocks and woods, in which are ſables and foxes.

The *Shantanskoy* island is larger than *Theocliſtove*. *Shántura* is three day's journey by land from north to ſouth; and the boats are three days and a half in coaſting it.

The former of theſe iſlands abounds not only in wood, but alſo in different ſorts of animals; particularly foxes, ſables, ermines, and bears. The principal birds are ſwans, ducks, and geeſe. Several ſorts of fiſh are found in the bay; and different kinds of berries in the fields. Half a day's ſailing ſouth from the *Shantanskoy* is an iſland, in length and breadth about 12 verſts, called *Hoodee Shantar* (that is, unprofitable); ſo named, becauſe there grows no ſort of wood upon it, though it has not been long in this ſtate, for formerly there was wood enough, and many ſables were caught there; but being burnt through the negligence of the *Gilijacks*, who left their fires unextinguiſhed, it is now nothing but a bare mountain, and all the animals have left it. South from the *Hoodee Shantar*, in half a day's time, they go in boats to the *Belochay* iſland, which is equal in ſize to the former. This iſland abounds in woods, ſtocked with many animals, eſpecially ſquirrels, from whence it took its name.

The reſt of the coaſt has nothing worth remarking, 'till we come to the river *Amur*, or, as it is called, *Sagalin Ula*, being the laſt great river which comes within our notice.

This river riſes in the *Ruſſian* territories, and, according to the *Chineſe* maps, falls into the ſea, at the point of a large bay, in 52° 50' north latitude. This bay lies between the *Dulangada* Noſs and the *Vaſipunu* Noſs. From the *Vaſipunu* Noſs is the neareſt paſſage to a great and inhabited iſland, which extends from the north-eaſt to the ſouth weſt 4° 30': the channel is 30 verſts over. The coaſt from the river *Ude* to the *Amur*, excepting the capes and promontories, lies almoſt directly north and ſouth.

Having described all the coast and principal rivers on the continent, we shall now proceed to describe the principal roads through this country.

CHAP. II.

Of the ROADS *in* KAMTSCHATKA.

FROM the *Bolscheretskoi* to the upper *Kamtschatkoi* fort are three principal roads: the first, along the *Penschinsky* sea; the second, by the Eastern Sea; and the third, by the *Bistroy*.

By the first they go up the river *Ohlukomina* to the ridge *Ohlukominskoy*, and over the ridge to the river *Keerganick*, along which almost to the river *Kamtschatka*, and from thence up the river to the upper *Kamtschatkoi* fort.

By the second they go from the *Bolscheretskoi* up the Great River to the *Nachikin* fort, and cross a small ridge to the river *Awatscha*, to the haven of *Petropaulauskay*, or of *Peter* and *Paul*; and from thence along the coast of the Eastern Sea north to the river *Shupanova*, and up that river to its head; from whence over the ridge to the river *Poweecha*, and down the mouth of that river, which is over-against the upper fort.

The third road lies from the *Bolscheretskoi* up the Great River to the *Opachin* fort; from thence through plains to the Rapid River, up to its head; and thence, down the river *Kamtschatka*, to the upper *Kamtschatkoi* fort.

They travel the two first roads chiefly in winter; the third, on foot in summer. The first and the last roads are measured, but the second is only measured half way; and the particular distances are here adjoined.

KAMTSCHATKA.

First road from the *Bolscheretskoi* fort, by the *Penschinsky* sea.

	versts	fathoms
From the *Bolscheretskoi* office to the *Zaeemka*, or the estate of Mr. *Trapeznicoff*,	2	100
From thence to the river *Utka*,	21	200
From thence to the *Kiechchiek*, to the *Akaheeshevo*,	42	250
From thence to the *Nemtick*	25	0
From thence to the *Kole*	22	0
From thence to the *Vorovskaya*	51	0
From thence to the *Brewmka*	24	0
From thence to the *Kompucovoy*	13	0
From thence to the *Krootohorova*	36	0
From thence to the *Oblukomina*, to the settlement of *Tarein*,	24	0
From thence to the *Oblukominskoy* ridge	110	0
From thence to the upper *Kamtschatkoi* fort	65	0
	486	50

Second road from the *Bolscheretskoi* fort, by the Eastern Sea.

	versts	fathoms
From the *Bolscheretskoi* fort to the small fort *Opachin*	44	0
From thence to *Nachikin*	74	0
From thence to the *Awatscha* and the *Paratunka*	68	0
From the *Paratunka* to the *Petropaulauskaya* haven	16	0
From thence to the rivulet *Calahturka*	6	0
From thence to the fort *Nalacheva*	34	0
In all from *Bolscheretskoi* to the small fort *Nalacheva*	242	0

From the river *Nalacheva* they in six days arrive at the upper fort.

Third road from the *Bolscheretskoi* fort, by the Rapid River.

	verfts	fathoms
From the *Bolscheretskoi* fort, up along the Great River, to the *Opachin* small fort	44	0
From thence to the upper ford	33	0
From thence to the settlement of *Ahanichevo*	22	0
From thence to the settlement of *Ganaline*	33	0
From thence to the head of the *Kamtschatka*	41	0
From thence to the upper *Kamtschatkoi* fort	69	0
In all from the *Bolscheretskoi* to the upper *Kamtschatkoi* fort	242	0

In all the places expressed in the tables the travellers take up lodgings at night, except where the distance is only five or six verfts. Notwithstanding the great distance between the *Oblukominskoy* and the upper *Kamtschatkoi* fort, in good weather they travel it in three days, lying two nights in desert places.

There are other roads from the *Bolscheretskoi* to the upper fort, both from the *Penschinska* sea and from the Eastern; for every river there that falls into either of those seas has a passage to *Kamtschatka*: but, as nobody except the *Kamtschadales*, and sometimes the Cossacks, in great necessity, travel them, it was not thought material to describe them; nor can one well ascertain the distances by their journeys.

They go from the *Bolscheretskoi* to the lower *Kamtschatkoi* fort, either through the upper *Kamtschatkoi* fort, or by the coast of the Eastern Sea. From the upper *Kamtschatkoi* fort the way is along the river *Kamtschatka*, except where the river makes great windings.

windings. The distance from the upper to the lower *Kamtschatkoi* fort is laid down in the following table.

	versts	fathoms
From the upper *Kamtschatkoi* fort to the river *Keergena*	24	0
From thence to the small fort *Mashurin*	32	0
From thence to the small fort *Nachikin*	87	0
From thence to *Golka*	33	0
From thence to the small fort *Talecheva*	26	0
From thence to the *Ushky*	16	0
From thence to the *Krewky*	25	0
From thence to the *Krestee*	25	0
From thence to the *Gorboon*	26	250
From thence to the *Harchin*	11	0
From thence to the *Camenoy* small fort	27	0
From thence to the *Cavanackey*	16	0
From thence to the *Kamack*	6	0
From thence to the *Hapick*	8	250
From thence to the *Schockey*	9	0
From thence to the *Oboohoffs* settlement	17	250
From thence to the lower *Kamtschatkoi* fort, to the church of St. *Nicholas*,	7	250
In all from the upper to the lower fort	397	0
And from the *Bolscheretskoi*	833	50
	1230	50

The other road from the *Bolscheretskoi* to the lower *Kamtschatkoi* fort being measured only to the *Nalacheva* fort, it cannot exactly be known which is the nearest way; but one may imagine that there is not much difference between them.

The chief places on that road where they ufually lodge at night are the fmall forts of *Opachin, Nachiekiek,* and the *Tarein;* the haven of *Peter* and *Paul,* which was formerly called the fmall fort *Auftin;* the *Oftrovenaya* river, *Supanova,* and the *Chazma;* upon all which rivers there are *Kamtfchatkoi* habitations.

From the *Chazma* to the river *Kamtfchatka* the road lies over defolate mountains; and they come upon the river juft by the village *Oboohoffs,* feven verfts and a half above the lower *Kamtfchatkoi* fort, lodging but one night in a defert place.

From the lower *Kamtfchatkoi* fort to the northern parts two roads are made, the one is by the *Elouki,* to its head; and from thence over a ridge to the head of the river *Teghil,* along which they go quite to the fea; and from thence, not far off from the fea, to the rivers *Lefnaya* and *Podkargirnaya.*

In a moderate way of travelling, when there is no hindrance from bad weather, they go from the lower *Kamtfchatkoi* fort to the lower *Teghilfkoy* fmall fort, called *Shipin,* in 10 days.

By the fecond road they may travel in the fame manner to the river *Karaga* in ten days, whofe head is near the river *Lefnaya.*

From the upper *Kamtfchatkoi* fort to the *Teghil* the common road is by the river *Elouki:* firft, over the ridge to *Ohlukominfkoy* fort, and from thence north by the *Penfchinsky* fea; and another road is by the river *Kreftovaya* to the *Harhoofova.*

By the firft road they may reach *Teghil* in 10 days; but they very often lodge the tenth night on the road, not fo much on account of the diftance as the badnefs of the roads, and the very mountainous places over the *Utkolotskoy* cape. The fecond road requires 11 or 12 days.

The paffage along the *Elouki* to the *Teghil* is the longeft of all, for that requires above 14 days' journey.

From the *Bolfcheretskoi* fort fouthward to the *Kurilskaya Lopatka* the ufual paffage is nine days. The diftance from the

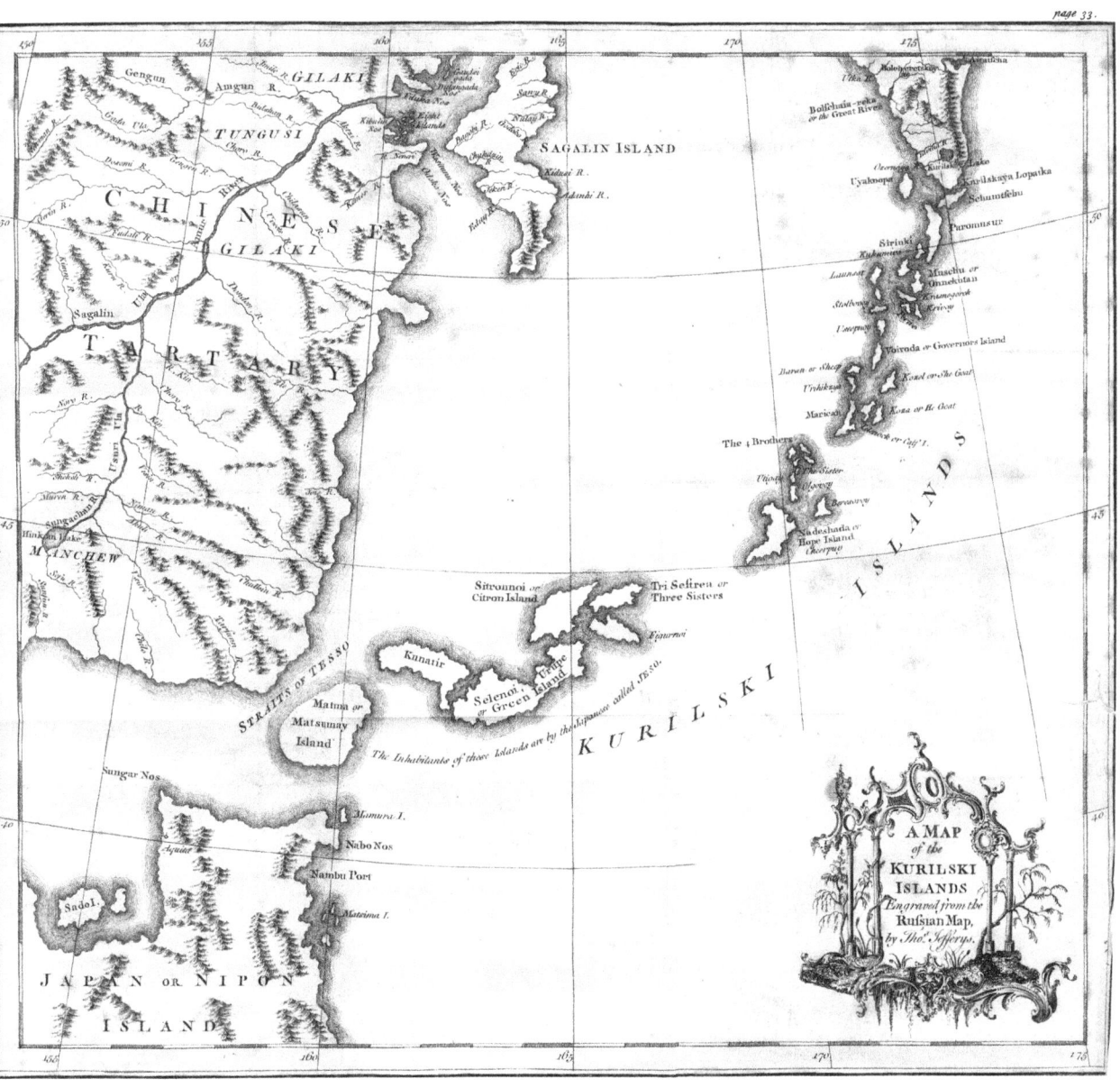

Bolscheretskoi fort to the *Kurilskaya Lopatka* is 210 verfts 300 fathoms, which fpace may be eafily travelled, even in four days; but the Coffacks of thofe places have a cuftom of ftopping at any fmall fort, under pretence of fome bufinefs there, though their moft probable motive is to refrefh their dogs. At a middling rate I have travelled in three days from the *Kamtf-chatkoi* to the *Bolfcheretskoi*, which is near 150 verfts.

	verfts	fathoms
From the *Bolfcheretskoi* fort to the mouth of the Great River	33	0
From the mouth, along the fea-fhore, to the river *Opala*	85	0
From thence to the *Kofhuhochiek*	18	0
From thence to the *Yavina*	15	0
From thence to the river *Ozernaya*	15	0
From thence to the *Kambalina*	36	300
From thence to the *Lopatka*	27	0
In all from the *Bolfcheretskoi* to the *Kurilskaya Lopatka*	210	300

CHAP. III.

Of the KURILSKI ISLANDS.

UNDER the name of *Kurilski* iflands are underftood all thofe iflands which extend from the *Kurilskaya Lopatka*, or the fouthern end of *Kamtfchatka*, in a row fouth-weft quite to *Japan*. They derive their names from the inhabitants of thofe iflands which lie neareft to *Kamtfchatka*, who are called by the natives *Kuſki,* and by the *Ruſſians Kuriles.* The exact number of thoſe iſlands cannot be aſcertained; but, according to the verbal accounts which were gathered from the *Kuriles,* and the natives of the ſouthernmoſt iſlands, and from the *Japaneſe,* who were driven by diſtreſs of weather upon the coaſt of *Kamtſchatka,* they are reckoned to be twenty-two. Perhaps they do not take the ſmall ones into this number: for by the account of captain *Spanberg,* who went as far as *Japan,* there appears to be a great many more; but as the ſaid captain found it difficult to give them *Ruſſian* names, all of them that had any relation to the *Kurilskoy* names, except the two that lay neareſt to *Matma Kunatin,* were allowed to keep their former appellations.

Schumtſchu is the neareſt iſland to the *Kurilskaya Lopatka,* and extends in length from the north-eaſt to the ſouth-weſt 50 verſts, and in breadth about 30. This iſland is full of mountains, out of which, as alſo from the ſmall lakes and marſhes, many little rivers run into the ſea. In ſome of them are found different kinds of ſalmon, and ſeveral other fiſh, but not in ſuch plenty as to furniſh the inhabitants with proviſions for a winter. Upon the ſouth-weſt point, near the ſtreight that is between this and the ſecond *Kurilskoy* iſland, are three *Kurilskoy* ſettlements, that contain only 44 inhabitants; ſome of whom pay the taxes in ſables and foxes, but the majority pay them in ſea-beavers' ſkins.

The inhabitants of this iſland, as well as thoſe of the *Kurilskaya Lopatka,* are not the right *Kuriles,* but are of the race of the *Kamtſchadales:* for ſome diſſentions having ariſen between the inhabitants of that nation, ſoon after the *Ruſſians* entered the country, a large party of them retired here and to the *Lopatka;* where they became connected, by mutual inter-marriages, with the people of the ſecond iſland, whoſe particular cuſtoms they have adopted, and from thence have received the name of *Kuriles.*

The channel between the *Kurilskaya Lopatka* and this island is 15 versts in breadth; over which they pass in small boats, when the weather is fair, in three hours. This passage requires not only fair weather, but likewise a flowing tide. In the time of the ebb, the waves spread for some versts, are rapid and white, and so large that even in calm weather they rise two or three fathoms high. Both the Cossacks and *Kuriles* have a superstitious awe and veneration for these waves; and when they row over them, offer them a sacrifice by throwing chips made on purpose, imploring a safe passage; the pilots also use conjurations the whole way.

The second *Kurilskoy* island, *Paromusir*, is twice as large as the first. It lies north-east and south-west, and is separated from the first by a channel two versts broad, where one vessel may lie in time of necessity, but not without danger, there being no proper place for anchorage: and if a vessel parts from her anchor, she will be in very great danger; for the shore here being steep and rocky, and the channel narrow, it is next to impossible for her to escape. There was a melancholy example of this in the year 1741, when one of our vessels was cast away here. This island is also mountainous, and has as many lakes and rivulets as *Schumtschu*; and on both of them, there is no other timber than *Slanetz* and *Ernick* which are used by the inhabitants for fuel, and they build their huts of different kinds of wood which they find thrown on the shore by the waves from *America* and *Japan*; among these are sometimes found pieces of ranfarn wood, of which several large one's were brought thence to me. The inhabitants of this island are right *Kuriles*, who came there from the island *Onneckoot*; but upon what account is not known. All affirm, that between the inhabitants of the two above-mentioned islands, and the most remote, commerce was formerly established: those of the remote islands brought to them all sorts of lackered wooden ware, scymitars, silver rings which they wear in their ears, and cotton stuffs; and from them in return, they used to take chiefly, eagles' feathers, which are used in ornamenting their arrows: this seems very probable; for I had from this island a lackered waiter, a bason, a *Japanese* scythe, and a silver ring; all which I have sent to the *Imperial* Chamber of curiosities. These articles the *Kuriles* could have from no other place than from *Japan*.

The *Kuriles* of this island have their habitations near the south-west point, upon a lake five versts in circumference, out of which a small rivulet, called *Petpu*, runs into the sea.

Both these islands are subject to frequent and terrible earthquakes, and inundations: one of these calamities happened in the year 1737, about the time of my coming to *Kamtschatka*; and another in *November*, 1742. We shall relate the first circumstantially in its proper place; but as for the second, though it was great, yet I have not been informed of the mischief and destruction it occasioned; for it happened after my departure from *Kamtschatka*; and Mr. *Stëller* makes no mention of it in his account.

The third *Kurilskoy* island is called *Sirinki*, and lies southwest of *Paromusir*. The fourth island is called *Onnecutan*. This island is less than *Paromusir*, and lies from north-east to south-west, as that does, from which they row to it in one day. It has many inhabitants of the same origin with the *Kuriles* of *Paromusir* island, as was said before, out of which some families go over to visit the inhabitants of *Paromusir*, and voluntarily pay a tribute in beavers and foxes. The author concludes from this, that the rest of these islands would not refuse to pay the tribute, if proper persons were sent to bring them under subjection; and give them assurances, by
kind

kind reprefentations, of the clemency of her Imperial majefty, with promifes that she would protect and defend them from their enemies.

Neither I nor Mr. *Steller* could have an oppportunity to inform ourfelves particularly of the reft of the *Kurilski* iflands; therefore we shall give the accounts of them that were communicated to me by Mr. *Muller*, which he had from the *Japanefe*, who were fhipwrecked upon the coafts of *Kamtfchatka*.

Between Mr. *Muller*'s account and our's, there is fome difference; for in his, *Onnecutan* is called the fixth ifland. However this might happen only on account of his reckoning the fmall iflands alfo, which the *Kuriles* do not. According to his defcription, beyond the *Paromufir*, or the fecond *Kurilskoy* ifland, there are three more iflands; *Sirinki* is reckoned the third; *Uyakoopa*, the fourth; and the *Kukumita*, or *Cucumiva*, the fifth; the *Sirinki* and *Kukumita* are fmaller than *Uyakoopa*, which ifland is remarkable for a high mountain. The faid iflands are placed in a triangle; the *Uyakoopa* lying moft north, and fartheft weft; and the *Sirinki*, with regard to the former, fouth-eaft, and in the fame longitude with *Paromufir*; and the *Kukumita* a little farther fouthward than the *Uyakoopa*. It feems that thefe iflands in the General *Ruffian* map are expreffed under the names of *Diacon*, *St. Iliah*, and *Galanta*, which are placed in a triangle, though their fituation is not exactly the fame as in the above defcription. The fixth *Kurilskoy* ifland, according to Mr. *Muller*, is called *Muska* and *Onnecutan*. The feventh is *Araumakutan*, is uninhabited, and there are fome burning mountains as in *Kamtfchatka*. On the eighth ifland *Sujaskutan*, which is as large as the former, fome few people inhabit who are not taxed. From this ifland to the weft lies the ninth called *Emarka*; and thence on the fouth-weft fide is the tenth ifland *Mafhachu*, which is fmall and uninhabited; and on the fouth-eaft fide from the *Sujaskutan* there is a fmall ifland *Ehachu*, which is reckoned the eleventh.

The

The twelfth island *Shockoeki* lies on the south side, and so distant from the *Suiaskutan*, that they can hardly row to it in half a day, even when the days are longest, in the lightest boat. It is said, that the *Japanese* carry ore from it in large vessels; but what ore is not known. The thirteenth island, and the following to the seventeenth, are called *Motogo, Shatovo, Utitir, Kituy,* and *Shimutir.* The *Utitir* lies somewhat to the east, and the rest in one line south. The channels are crossed in light boats, in less than half a day, but the passage is excessively difficult, because the tide runs very rapid in all of them; and, when it happens to be a side wind, these small vessels are driven into the sea, and lost; and for this reason the inhabitants of all these islands pass and repass these places early in the spring in calm weather. The *Motogo, Shatovo,* and the *Utitir* islands have nothing remarkable in them. On the island *Kituy* grow the reeds of which they make their arrows. The *Shimatir* is larger than the rest, and has many people on it, who resemble the *Kuriles* of the first three islands in all respects, but are not under the *Russian* government, nor any other foreign power. The navigators who were sent by *Peter the Great*, only saw this island, beyond which no *Russians* ever were until the second *Kamtschatkoi* expedition.

The *Cheerpuy* is reckoned the eighteenth of the islands. It lies west at the mouth of the channel. On this is a very high mountain, but no inhabitants. Some people come there from the other islands to catch fowls and dig roots. The people of *Kituy* have sometimes heard firing of cannon on this island, as they relate, but on what account they know not. They likewise report, that formerly a *Japanese* vessel was lost upon it, whose people were taken by the inhabitants of the next island, and were sent to *Japan* to be redeemed.

The channel which divides the island *Shimutir* from the nineteenth island *Eturpu* is so broad, that one cannot see one ifland from the other; but from thence to the twentieth ifland *Urupe*, and from that again to the twenty-firſt *Kunatir*, the channels are much narrower.

The twenty-ſecond and the laſt ifland near *Japan* the *Japaneſe* uſed to call *Matma*, but how broad the channel is between that and the former ifland *Kunatir* is not mentioned in Mr. *Muller*'s account; but one may judge that it is not very wide, eſpecially to the weſt, for reaſons to be given hereafter. The ifland *Matma* is larger than any of the reſt, and next to it in ſize is the *Kunatir*.

The natives of the *Eturpu* and the *Urupe* iflands call themſelves *Keek-Kuriles*. They have a particular language of their own, and reſemble the natives of the ifland *Kunatir*, but we do not know whether their language is the ſame or not; neither are we aſſured whether the language of the *Keek-Kuriles* has any affinity with that of the *Kuriles* of *Kamtſchatka* and the iflands near it. This is to be obſerved that the *Japaneſe* ſay they call the natives of the laſt four iflands by the common name of *Jeſo*; from which we may conclude that the inhabitants of *Matma* are of the ſame race with the natives of the former iflands, and the language is the ſame on all theſe four iflands. Thus we may correct the errors of former geographers, who give the name of *Jeſo* to a large country lying north-eaſt of *Japan*, which now we find is made up of the above-mentioned iflands. In this there is nothing contrary to the accounts that we meet with in the voyages of the *Europeans*, particularly of the *Dutch*, who in the year 1643 were ſent to diſcover the land of *Jeſo*. Some of the inhabitants of the iflands of *Eturpu* and *Urupe* (which had a commerce with the natives of the iflands near *Kamtſchatka*, about 25 or 30 years ago) were taken captives on the ifland *Paromuſir*, and were brought to *Kamtſchatka*; and this probably put an end to their communication and traffick by ſea. However theſe captives were uſeful; for the accounts received from the *Japaneſe* were explained

plained and corrected by them, and some new information obtained. According to them those *Keek-Kuriles* on the islands *Eturpu* and *Urupe* are under no foreign subjection; but *Matma*, both by the account of *European* travellers and of the *Japanese*, has been for many years subject to *Japan*. They say also, that upon these islands are a great number of the *Kuriles* and *Kamtschadales* in slavery, who had been formerly carried off. It is worthy of observation throughout all these islands, that such as lie more westernly have no wood, but those that lie to the eastward have it in abundance, and consequently there is great plenty of game. There is safe anchoring in the mouths of the rivers for large ships, in the island *Eturpu* particularly. The *Japan* silk, cotton stuffs, and all sorts of iron houshold furniture also, are brought to the islands *Eturpu* and *Urupe* by the natives of *Kunatir*, who purchase them from the inhabitants of *Matma*.

The inhabitants of *Eturpu* and *Urupe* make stuffs of nettles, which they sell to the *Japanese*: they likewise sell to them all sorts of furrs, which they have among themselves, and which are brought to them from the islands near *Kamtschatka*; also dry fish and whale's fat, which is used in victuals by the natives of the island *Matma*. By the accounts of travellers, these things are carried even into *Japan*.

The island *Matma* lies from the south-west to the north-east. The *Japanese* have a strong guard upon its south-west point, perhaps with a view to defend the country from the *Chinese* and *Koreans*. Not far from thence, upon the shore of the channel, which divides the island *Matma* from *Japan*, stands a *Japanese* city of the same name with the island, where are kept all sorts of ammunition, muskets, and guns for defence, and in which where lately built new fortifications. Most of the *Japanese* settlements upon *Matma* were made by people banished thither. The *Japanese*, who were brought to *Kamptschatka*, give us the same accounts of the channel between *Matma* and *Japan*, which

we

we find in the *European* voyages; namely, that this channel is very narrow in several places, and very dangerous, on account of several rocky capes projecting into it from both sides. At ebb and flow the sea is so rapid that if the least time is lost the vessels will be either dashed against the capes, or carried into the sea. The Dutch relate that they have found a small island eastward of these, which they named the States' Island; and farther towards the east, they saw a great land, which they named the Company's Land, and imagined it to be part of the continent of *North-America*. We can give no satisfactory information of these things from any accounts received from the *Japanese*, but the Company's Land seems to be the same with the land discovered by *De Gama*, and it ought to be considered rather as an island than the main land; because *America*, by all the observations made between *Japan* and *New Spain*, cannot extend so far to the west. In these accounts collected by professor *Muller*, we have only to correct the general situation of the *Kurilski* islands, which do not extend to the south, as he was informed, but lie in a row to the south-west, as I have shewn above, and as they are laid down in the General *Russian* Map: for it is well known by the new maps, and from the verbal accounts of the *Japanese*, who have been there, that the channel *Tessoy*, which reaches along the *Chinese* coast, S. S. W. is only 15 versts broad; but, according to his account of the situation of the islands, it ought to be considerably wider to the south. In short, if captain *Spanberg*'s description of the *Kurilski* islands to *Japan* could be reconciled with Mr. *Muller*'s, then the exact situation of each of them would be known, and their distances from each other ascertained; of which we can only now judge by conjecture.

Mr. *Spanberg* gives only two of the islands which constitute *Jeso* their proper names; namely, *Matma* and *Kunatir*; but he distinguishes the islands *Eturpu* and *Urupe* by the names of the Green and the Orange islands: and as those islands, except *Matma*, are described, and both their size and situation laid down, there seems to be no doubt but that the cape *Tessoy* is the north-west point of the island *Matma*, which was observed by the *Russians* only from the east side of *Japan*; and though in the above accounts of Mr. *Muller*, it, being said to lie from south-west to north-east, may occasion some doubt, yet we may reconcile it in this manner; that the nearest point of *Matma* to *Japan* extends towards *China* from the S. E. to the N. W. and to the *Kurilski* side from the S. W. to the N. E. as it is expressed in the *Chinese* maps, in which are only wanting the divisions between the islands of *Jeso*. The channel between *Japan* and the island *Matma*, according to the new maps, in some places is 20 versts, and in others much less. The north part of the island *Japan*, or *Niphon*, is a little above the 40th degree of latitude.

The accounts of the great plenty of wood on the islands nearest to *Japan* are confirmed by Mr. *Steller*, who says, that, in general, the islands lying farthest to the west from *America* are the most fruitful, and abound with trees of various kinds, among which are lemons, bamboe, *Spanish* canes or reeds, and poisonous herbs, whose roots are as yellow as saffron and as thick as rhubarb, and are well known to the inhabitants of the first *Kurilskoy* island, for they formerly bought them from the natives of those islands, and used to poison their arrows with the juice. Vines also grow there; and I have tasted some grapes which Lieutenant *Walton* brought from those islands in his return from *Japan*. Upon the island *Kunatir*, there are great numbers of pine, larch, and fir trees, but a scarcity of good water. Wild animals they have in abundance, particularly bears, whose skins the inhabitants use for their cloaths. The natives of this island, by his account also, wear long silk cloaths like the *Chinese*, have long beards, pay no regard to cleanliness, and feed on fish and whale's fat. Their bedding is of wild goats' skins, of which there

there are plenty. They acknowledge no sovereign, though they live near *Japan*. The *Japanese* come to them every year in their small craft, and bring all sorts of iron ware, brazen pots, wooden lackered waiters and bowls, leaf of tobacco, and silk-and-cotton stuffs, which they exchange with them for whales' fat and the skins of foxes; but they are not so good as those of *Kamtschatka*. The natives of the island of *Kunatir* told the *Russians* to beware of those of the island of *Matma*, because they had cannon, asking our people at the same time, whether they came from the North, and if they were those who are famous for their armies, and able to wage war with, and conquer, every nation. The language of the island *Kunatir* is almost the same with that spoken in the island *Paromusir*: from hence we may conclude, that the natives of *Eturpu* and *Urupe* differ little in their language from the *Kurilski*. The inhabitants of these islands are said to call themselves *Keek-Kuriles*; but the word *Kuriles* being corruptly used by the *Cossacks* for the word *Kushi*, (which is a common name for the natives of the *Kurilski* islands) it is more probable, that, if the natives of *Eturpu* and *Uturpe* do distinguish themselves by the addition of the word *Keek*, they are called *Keek-Kushi*, and not *Keek-Kuriles*.

CHAP. IV.

Of AMERICA.

THE following accounts of that part of *America* which lies directly east from *Kamtschatka*, are collected from notes taken out of Mr. *Steller*'s journal.

The main land of *America*, which is now known from 52 to 60 degrees of north latitude, extends from the south-west to the north-east side, at almost an equal distance from the coast of *Kamtschatka*; namely, about 37° in longitude: for the coast of *Kamtschatka* also lies in the same direction, in a strait line from the *Kurilskaya Lopatka* to the *Tchukotskoi* Nofs, excluding the gulphs and capes; insomuch that it may be reasonably concluded, that these lands were once joined, especially at the *Tchukotskoi* Nofs; for between it and the land, which lies east over against it, it is not above two degrees and a half. Mr. *Steller* offers four reasons to prove the same. 1st. The appearance of the coast which, both of *Kamtschatka* and *America*, seems to be tore off. 2d. Many capes project into the sea from 30 to 60 versts. 3d. Many islands are in the sea which divides *Kamtschatka* from *America*. 4th. The situation of the islands, and the small breadth of that sea. But, however, this is left to the judgment of the learned; it is enough for us to relate facts. The sea that divides *Kamtschatka* from *America* is full of islands, which extend from the south-west point of *America* to the channel of *Anianova*, one following another, as the *Kurilski* islands are to *Japan*. The islands lie in a row from 51° to 54° of latitude, to the east, and begin a little above 5° from *Kamtschatka*. Mr. *Steller* thinks, that between the *Kurilski* and *American* islands is to be found

the

the company's land, but several doubt this; for, according to his opinion, that land ought to be the base of the triangle of the *Kurilski* and the *American* islands; this would be probable, if the company's land should be rightly laid down in the maps.

America enjoys a much better climate than the coast of the north-east side of *Asia*, although equally near the sea, and every where full of high mountains, which are continually covered with snow; but they have greatly the pre-eminence when we compare their qualities with those of *Asia*. The mountains of *Asia* being every where rocky and ragged, they lose their compactness and internal native heat; for which reason they have no valuable metals, nor any trees or herbs, and in the vallies there grows only small shrubby wood and hardy herbs. The *American* mountains are close and their surface not covered with moss, but with a fruitful earth, for which reason they are cloathed from the bottom to their tops with a thick and fine wood. The herbs that grow at their feet are of that kind that grow in dry places, but not in marshes; and the same herbs grow in the vallies as on the very tops of the mountains, because there is every where an equal warmth and moisture. But in *Asia* it is quite different, for the same herb grows twice as high in the plain as in the mountains.

In *America* at 60° the coast is covered with wood; but at *Kamtschatka*, which is only 51° of latitude, the small willows and poplars do not grow nearer the sea than 20 versts, and birch wood not nearer than 30, nor the pitch wood along the river *Kamtschatka* nearer than 50 from its mouth: and in *Kamtschatka*, in 62°, not one tree is to be found. In Mr. *Steller's* opinion *America* extends from the before-mentioned latitude to 70° and farther, and is defended and covered from the west by the above wood; but on the coast of *Kamtschatka*, especially upon the *Penschinska* sea, it is quite barren, being open to the

violent

violent north winds, which blow here frequently; and we find that places lying farther north are more fruitful, as about the *Tchukotſkoi* Noſs, where they are covered from theſe winds.

It is likewiſe obſerved, that the fiſh enter the rivers in *America* earlier than in *Kamtſchatka*. Great plenty of fiſh have been ſeen there on the 20th of *July*, at which time in *Kamtſchatka* they only begin to appear. There are a ſort of raſberries of a very extraordinary ſize and fine taſte; beſides honeyſuckles, cranberries, blackberries, and bilberries in great plenty: as alſo ſeals, ſea-beavers, whales, dog-fiſh, marmotta-minor, red and black foxes which are not ſo wild as in other places, perhaps becauſe they are ſeldom hunted.

Among the known birds have been obſerved magpies, crows, ſea-gulls, water-cranes, ſwans, ducks, quails, plovers, *Greenland* pigeons, and fowls called northern ducks; and among the unknown, ten kinds diſtinguiſhable from any ſpecies of *European* fowl.

The natives there, who are as wild as the *Koreki* and the *Tchukotskoi*, are plump, broad ſhouldered, ſtrong boned, of a middle ſize, with ſtreight and black hair which hangs looſe. Their faces are ſwarthy and flat, their noſes ſomewhat pointed but very broad, with black eyes, thick lips, ſmall beards, and ſhort necks. Their ſhirts, which come lower than the knee, are girded about their bellies with leather ſtrings; and their breeches and trowſers are made of the ſkins of ſeals dyed with alder, and are like thoſe of the *Kamtſchatdales*. To their girdles they hang iron knives in caſes, like thoſe worn by the *Ruſſian* boors. Their hats are made of graſs, as thoſe of the *Kamtſchatdales*, without tops, in the ſhapes of umbrellos, dyed with green and red colours, with falcons' feathers before, or with graſs that is combed out, which looks like the plumage that the *Americans* uſe about *Brazil*. They feed on fiſh, ſea animals, and the ſweet herb, which they

prepare

prepare as the *Kamtfchatdales* do; befides they ufe the dry bark of the poplar and pine trees, which is eaten as food, not only here and in *Kamtfchatka*, but in all *Siberia*, and fome parts of *Ruffia*, even as far as the province of *Viatka*, efpecially in times of fcarcity; they ufe likewife fea-grafs laid up in heaps, which looks like, and is as tough as, leather thongs. Wine and tobacco they know not, which ferves as a real proof of their having had hitherto no communication with the *Europeans*. They efteem it a particular ornament to make holes on their faces in different parts, in which they place various ftones and bones; others wear in their noftrils feathers about two inches long; fome wear bones of the fame fort in their under lips, and others upon the forehead. The people who live on the iflands near the *Tchukotfkoi* Nofs, and who have a communication with the *Tfchuktfchi*, are certainly of the fame race, for among them it is always efteemed as an ornament to wear bones. The late major *Paulutfkoy* having had once a fkirmifh with the *Tfchuktfchi*, found among the dead two men of this country, under whofe nofes were placed two teeth of the fea-horfe, in holes made for that purpofe; for which reafon the natives call thofe iflanders *Zoobatce*, or large teethed; and, as the prifoners reported, they did not come there to affift them, but to fee their manner of fighting with the *Ruffians*.

It may be concluded from this, that the *Tfchuktfchi* and they have the fame language, or, at leaft, that there is fuch a near refemblance between their languages, as to enable them to converfe together without an interpreter. The language of the *Tfchuktfchi* is derived from that of the *Koreki*, and differ from it in dialect only; the *Koreki* therefore can converfe with them without difficulty. And Mr. *Steller*'s faying, that not one of our interpreters could underftand the *American* language, might arife from the great difference in the dialect, or from the particular pronunciation, which is obferved, not only between the

wild

wild natives of *Kamtschatka*, but also between the *Europeans* in different provinces. There is scarce one fort in *Kamtschatka* which does not differ in language from that of another; and those forts of some hundred versts' distance hardly understand one another. The *Americans* and the *Kamtschadales* agree in the following things: First, their features are alike. Secondly, the *Americans* prepare the sweet herb in the same manner as the *Kamtschadales* do, which has never been observed any where else. Thirdly, they both use wood in striking fire. Fourthly, it has been observed, from many instances, that their hatchets are made of stone or bone; and Mr. *Steller* thinks, not without reason, that the *Americans* had formerly a communication with the people of *Kamtschatka*. Fifthly, their wearing apparel and hats are the same. And, sixthly, they dye the skins of beasts with alder, as the *Kamtschatdales* do: from whence it appears probable, that they are of the same race. These particulars may help to answer the question, Whence was *America* peopled? for though we should grant, that *America* and *Asia* were never joined, yet these two parts of the globe lie so near each other, that the impossibility of the inhabitants of *Asia* going over to *America*, (especially as the number of islands lying between them made the passage more easy) cannot be maintained.

Their arms are the bow and arrow; but what sort of bows we cannot tell, for our people saw none of them. Their arrows indeed are longer than those of the *Kamtschadales*, but resemble intirely those used by the *Tunguski* and *Tartars*, which our people found were dyed of a black colour, and scraped smooth. The *Americans* use boats made of skins, as the *Koreki* and the *Tschuktschi* do. Their boats are 12 feet long and two broad, the head and stern sharp, and the bottom flat. The inside is made of poles joined at both ends, which are kept extended by a proper piece of wood; and the skins sewed round seem to be those of seals dyed of a cherry colour: the seat is round,

two

two yards from the stern, and sewed about with guts, which, with the help of leather thongs laced round the edges, can be drawn together and opened like a purse. The *American* sitting in this place stretches out his legs, and draws the skin tight about his body. These boats will live in the most stormy sea, though they are so light that they may be carried with one hand.

When the *Americans* see any strangers they row towards them, making a long speech; but whether this be some conjuration, or a ceremony at receiving them, we cannot certainly say; for both the one and the other is in use among the *Kuriles*: but, before they approach them, they paint their cheeks with a black pencil, and stop their nostrils with grass. They seem to receive strangers very kindly, converse in a friendly manner, with their eyes fixed upon them, treat them with great civility, and make them presents of whales' fat, and of those pencils with which they daub their own cheeks, not doubting but such things are as acceptable to others as to themselves.

It is very safe sailing in those parts in the spring and summer; but in the autumn so dangerous, that there is not a day on which they dare venture out for fear of perishing; the winds and storms being so violent, that the *Russians*, who have used the sea for forty years, declare they have never seen any thing equal to them. The following are looked upon here as signs of the land being near: When many different sorts of sea-cabbage appear floating on the sea; when they observe that sort of grass of which cloaks, carpets, and little bags are made at *Kamtschatka*, for it grows only upon the sea shore; and when sea-gulls and sea animals, such as seals and the like, appear in great numbers; for though, the seals have an opening in their hearts, called the *Foramen ovale*, and a passage called *Ductus arteriosus botalli*, which are both open, and therefore can keep under water for a long time, and may go far from the shore without danger, as they can find proper food at a great depth; yet, notwithstanding all this, they seldom go out above ten miles to sea. But the most certain sign of the land being near, is, when they see *Kamtschatkoi* beavers, which feed only upon lobsters and crabs, and, by the formation of their hearts, cannot continue under water above two minutes.

We must yet mention some islands, which lie near to *Kamtschatka*, though not in a strait line with those above described, but north of them, particularly *Bering*'s island, which is now so well known to the *Kamtschatkoi* inhabitants, that many go thither for the trade of sea beavers and other animals. This island extends between 55° and 60° of latitude from the south-east to the north-west. Its north-east end, which lies almost directly opposite to the mouth of the river *Kamtschatka*, is about two degrees from the eastern shore of *Kamtschatka*, and its south-east point is about three degrees from the *Kronotskoy* Nos. The length of this island is 165 versts, but its breadth is unequal, being from the south-east point to the steep and unpassable cliff, which lies fourteen versts from the point, between three and four versts in breadth; from this to the *Seepucha* bay about five versts; from the *Seepucha* bay to the *Beaver* cliff, six versts; and thence to the small river *Kitova*, five versts. Farther on it grows broader and broader; and its greatest breadth is opposite to the northern cape, where it is twenty-three versts. One may say in general, that there is so little proportion between the length and breadth of this island, that our author doubts whether its equal is to be found in any other part of the world; at least, he has neither read nor heard of such; and he says also, that the islands which he saw near *America*, and the whole range of them towards the east, have nearly such proportions.

This

This island consists of one rocky ridge divided by many vallies lying north and south; and the mountains are so high that, in fair weather, they may be perceived almost in the middle of the passage between the island and *Kamtschatka*.

The natives of *Kamtschatka* were of opinion for many years, that over-against the mouth of the *Kamtschatka* there ought to be land; because there was always the appearance of a fog or mist there, let the horizon be ever so bright. The highest mountains here are not higher than two versts perpendicular; the tops are covered for the thickness of half a foot with a common yellow clay; but below are hard yellow rocks. The *Stanovoy* ridge is hard and entire; and the mountains upon the sides are separated by vallies, through which run small rivers on both sides of the island. It is observable in this island, that the mouths of all the rivers lie either to the south or to the north, and from their springs they either run south-east or north-west.

There are no plains near the principal ridge, except the sea-shore, and even there are little mountains of half a verst, or a verst, in circumference. Such hills are observed near every rivulet, with this difference, that the flatter the capes are towards the sea, the larger are the plains behind. The very same thing is also observed in the vallies: if they lie between high mountains, they are less, and the rivulets in them also smaller; but in those vallies which are between low mountains, it is otherwise. On the *Stanovoy* or principal ridge, wherever the mountains are steep and full of cliffs, there are always found lakes half a verst, or a verst, from the sea-shore, which run by small outlets into the sea.

The mountains consist of one hard blue stone; but where they are parallel with the sea, there the capes are made up of a strong greyish clean stone, fit for polishing. This circumstance the author esteems worthy of observation, because he imagines the stone might obtain this change from the sea-water.

In many places of the island the beach is so narrow, that it is hardly possible to pass it at high water; and in two places there is no passage at all: one of these is near the south-east, and the other near the north-west point of the island.

It is remarkable, that wherever there is a bay on one side of the island, on the other, directly opposite to it, is a cape; and where the shore on one side is flat and sandy, on the other it is rocky and torn. Where the turning is sharp, either to one side or the other, there the shore is cliffy and stony about a verst or two from the turning. The mountains nearer the *Stanovoy* ridge are rather the steepest. There are many cracks which were occasioned at different times by earthquakes; and it has been observed, that in the highest mountains something sticks out like kernels, ending as cones; which, though they seem to be of the same substance with the mountain itself, yet are somewhat softer and clearer, and have a particular figure. Such kernels are found on the mountains of *Baykal*, and on the island *Olehon*. Mr. *Steller* received from *Anadirsk* stones of a green colour somewhat resembling these kernels, and was informed that they were taken from the top of the mountains; and that whenever they are broken off, others grow in their places. It is thought that these stones are formed by some internal motion of the earth, particularly by its pressure towards the center; from whence these kernels may be reckoned a species of chrystal, or the purest stony matter, which is first pressed from the center in a liquid state, and afterwards hardened by the external air.

On the north-east side of the above-mentioned island is no haven, even for the smallest vessel, except one place which is in breadth 80 fathoms, where a vessel may anchor in calm weather. There are shoals that lie off as far as four or five versts from the shore, which are laid with stones as if done by design, and on which you may walk at low water to the deep places without wetting your feet.

North

North of the haven is a large bay, in which are such stones and pillars as are found on the shore. The south-west side of the island is quite different; for though the shore is rocky and more torn, yet in two places there is a passage for flat-bottomed boats, not only to that, but even into the lakes. The first place is 50, and the second is 115, versts from the south-east point of the island. This last is easily known from the sea, for the land turns there from north to west; and in the very cape runs a river, which, though small, is the largest in that island, and the depth of it at high water is seven feet. It runs out of a great lake, which is a verst and a half from its mouth; and as the river is deeper when they have passed the bar, the sailing to the lake in small vessels is very easy and safe. The principal mark by which they can know this river is an island seven versts round, and it lies seven versts south from the mouth of it. The shore from thence to the west, for five versts, is sandy and low, and there are no rocks. From the high mountains of this island are to be seen the following places: in the south, two islands; one of them in circumference seven versts, as was said before; and the other is in the south-west, opposite to the very point of *Bering*'s island, and at the distance of 14 versts. It consists of two high and split rocks, about three versts in circumference. From the very north-west point of *Bering*'s island, in clear weather, are seen mountains covered with snow; and the distance of them from thence may be reckoned about 100 or 140 versts. These mountains were taken by the author for a cape of the main-land of *America*, for the following reasons: first, because the mountains, as he judged by their distance, were higher than those of the island: secondly, because within the same distance on the east from the island there were plainly observed such other white mountains; from the height and direction of which, all were of opinion that

it

it was the main land of *America*. From the south-east point of *Bering*'s island they saw lying south-east some other islands, but not so plainly; and their situation was thought to be between *Bering*'s island and the continent. It has been observed, that above the mouth of the river *Kamtschatka*, towards the west and south-west, in clear weather, there is always a fog; and from that, in some measure, it was known that *Bering*'s island was not far from the country of *Kamtschatka*. To the north part of *Bering*'s island there is another, in length from 80 to 100 versts. The channel betwixt these islands, towards the north-west, is about 20 versts, and towards the south-east, about forty. Near the points of both are many rocks and pillars in the sea.

The weather differs from that of *Kamtschatka* only in being more severe and sharp; for the island has no cover from any point, and is narrow and without wood. The wind is so strong in the low and narrow vallies that a man can hardly keep his feet, and it was observed to be highest in the months of *February* and *April*, when it blowed from the south-east and the north-west; when from the former, the weather was clear and tolerable, and, when from the latter, it continued clear, but was very cold. The highest tides were in the beginning of *February*, when the wind was north-west; and in the middle of *May*, from the great rains and the melting of the snow, another flood happened; yet both these floods were moderate, compared to those which, undoubtedly, have been formerly in those islands; for thirty fathoms higher than the sea-mark, lie wood and whole skeletons of sea animals, which have been left by the sea; and it is probable that in the year 1737, the flood was as great here as at *Kamtschatka*. Earthquakes happen frequently. The greatest here, which lasted exactly six minutes, was felt in the beginning of *February*, when the wind was westernly; a great

great noife, which preceded the fhock, was heard under ground, attended with a whiftling wind, which went from fouth to north.

The water here is remarkable for its lightnefs and purity; and its medicinal virtues have been experienced by the fick. Every valley has its rivulet, and the number of them all is above fixty. By reafon of the great declivity of the vallies they are very rapid; and, near the fea, divide themfelves into many ftreams.

THE NATURAL HISTORY OF

KAMTSCHATKA.

PART II.

CHAP. I.

Of the SOIL.

UPON the banks of the river *Kamtschatka* is found plenty of roots and berries, which in some measure supply the want of corn. There is also wood sufficient not only for building houses, but even for ship-building; and Mr. *Steller* is of opinion, that near the head of this river, both summer and winter corn would grow as well as in any other places in the same latitude, the soil being deep and rich; and though snow falls in very great quantities, yet it thaws early enough, and the spring is not so rainy, nor have they such damps, there as in many other places. Several tryals of summer-corn have been actually made both in the upper and lower *Ostrog* * of *Kamtschatka*; in which both barley and oats have succeeded. At the monastery of our Lord of *Jakutski*, they have

---

* *Ostrog* is a little town fortified with pallisades, where the *Russian* Cossacks, and other inhabitants live.

several

several years paft fown feven or eight poods † of barley, which yielded a crop not only fufficient for groats and meal for their own ufe, but even enough to fupply their neighbours, though they are obliged to plough their land with men.

All garden ftuff thrives not alike; the moft fucculent produce only leaves and ftalks. Cabbage and lettice never grow to any head, and the peas continue in flower until late in the harveft without yielding fo much as pods; but garden roots which are full of juice, fuch as turnips and radifhes, grow very well. Thefe tryals, however, were only made upon the banks of the Great River and *Awatfcha*. Such things as require a hot foil, grow very well every where, but ftill beft upon the *Kamtfchatka*. Upon the Great River I never faw any turnips larger than three or four inches diameter; but upon the *Kamtfchatka*, I have feen them four or five times as big.

The grafs grows here fo high, and is fo full of fap that one fcarcely fees any thing like it in all the empire of *Ruffia*; near the river and lakes, and in the opening of the woods, it rifes to above the height of a man, and fo faft that it may fometimes be mowed thrice in a fummer; fo that few places can be more proper for breeding of cattle; and although the blades are thick and high, and make but a coarfe fort of hay, yet the cattle are large and fat, and give plenty of milk both fummer and winter, which I attributed to the richnefs of the foil and the fpring rains. The grafs continues full of juice, even to the beginning of winter, which being condenfed by the cold prevents the grafs from turning hard during that feafon. As the grafs is fo high and thick, a great deal of hay may be made upon a fmall fpot; and the cattle can find food in the fields all the winter. The places where the grafs thus grows are never fo much covered with fnow as the bogs and fwamps, and for this reafon it is difficult to travel over them in the winter.

† A pood is a *Ruffian* weight of 40 lb.

In other places lying upon the Eastern Ocean, either to the N. or S. of *Kamtschatka*, there is no land fit for culture; for all that is near the shore is either sandy, stony, or boggy, and the banks are so narrow, that if the ground was good, yet there is not enough for agriculture; and there are but very little hopes of the land about the *Penschinska* sea answering better, especially for winter-corn, it being all marshy and boggy. At some distance from the sea are found woody places which are dry and high, and appear not improper for corn; but the snow which falls in the beginning of the harvest before the earth is frozen, and lies generally deep upon these places 'till the middle of *May*, both prevents the sowing of the summer-corn, and destroys the winter-corn; and, because at the thawing of the earth the corn would be blasted by the evening frosts, it is impossible to sow any before the middle of *June*; after which time to *August* are continual rains, so that sometimes the sun is not seen for fourteen days together: this would cause the corn to grow very high and full of juice; but, for want of warm and dry weather, it would never ripen. Notwithstanding, Mr. *Steller* thinks, that if the ground was properly prepared, oats and barley might ripen there; but this is much to be doubted, until, at least, further tryal can be made; for I have myself several times sown barley upon the Great River, and it grew well in thickness, height, and strength of blade 'till the beginning of *August*, when, just as the ear was putting forth, all of it was destroyed by the frost.

All these barren places, not only near the *Penschinska* sea, but even within the land, appear to be composed of earth brought from other parts. This one may discover by the different strata, and perceive how they have encreased yearly on the banks of the rivers, which are high, and on the cliffs that are bare. I have seen hanging out of the earth, trees which are not to be found in that country, more than seven feet deep under the surface. Hence it may be concluded, that all these barren, boggy places, where at present

present are no woods, but only shrubs, and stunted sallows, and birches, were formerly covered with water, which has decreased by degrees here, as it has upon the north-eastern coast. Below the earth lies a bed of pure ice, extremely hard; and under that a soft waterish clay, with gravel; this continues from the sea up to the very mountains, and will sufficiently account for the barrenness of these parts. But, though the land is not every where fit for agriculture, yet some places upon the river *Kamtschatka* (which have been already mentioned) and along the *Bistroy* river, are sufficient to furnish with corn, not only the inhabitants, but also the neighbouring parts. It is however to be feared, that the burning of the woods, in order to clear the lands, may drive away the sables, who have a particular aversion to smoke: this happened upon the river *Lena*, formerly the best hunting country, but now deserted by these animals. The scarcity of wood is a great inconvenience, both the *Russians* and natives being obliged to fetch it twenty or thirty versts with great trouble and loss of time, for the necessary uses of boiling their salt and curing their fish: and it is very difficult to bring it down in floats, because the current is rapid and so shallow, that they can bring only two little bundles on each side of a small fishing-boat; otherwise they would obstruct themselves in the management of their boat, and thereby run the risk of being driven upon the rocks, sand-banks, and trunks of trees, where not only their boat and wood, but frequently the people themselves are lost. Sometimes the scarcity of wood is supplied by such as is thrown up by the sea, which the inhabitants gather upon the shore; but this wood that has been soaked in the water, although they are at great pains to dry it, never burns clear, but smothers away with a continual smoke very hurtful to the eyes.

At the distance of 30 or 40 versts from the sea, and near the heads of the rivers, grow birch-trees, alder, and poplar; of which the people build their houses and make their boats. But this

this they bring down with great difficulty, using the method above mentioned: for which reason a very poor house will cost here 100 rubles and more, and a small fishing-boat five rubles. In other places, where the hills are nearer the shore, and the water-carriage easier, wood for firing and building is much cheaper.

Upon the *Biſtroy* river, which falls into the Great River below the *Bolſcheretſkoi Oſtrog*, grows the best wood that is in these parts; even the birch-trees are so large, that captain *Spanberg* built a sloop with their wood, in which he made several distant voyages to sea.

It is very remarkable, that when this vessel was launched she lay as deep in the water as a vessel full loaded; and it was believed, that she never would be fit to go to sea, but that the smallest loading would sink her. But, when she was laden, she drew very little more water, and few vessels sailed better or lighter, or could go nearer the wind: the reason of which may be, that as this wood has not so much rosin, it sucked a greater quantity of water at first, but so soon as its parts were once filled, it then sucked very little more.

There is great plenty of wood upon the eastern coast of *Kamtſchatka*; from the hills down to the very shore grow very fine birch and alder trees. Beyond the river *Jonpanoba*, and towards its head, begin the woods which continue to the *Kamtſchatka*, *Lopatka*, and along the river *Kamtſchatka* to the mouth of the river *Elouki*. Up the river, almost to its head, grow likewise pines, but not large enough for buildings. About the neck of land which joins the peninsula of *Kamtſchatka* to the continent, the wood begins again to fail.

The changes of the weather and air are commonly in the following order: harvest and winter make up more than one half of the year; and the spring and summer cannot be reckoned

above

above four months: the trees commonly begin to bud about the end of *June*, and some of them to lose their leaves in the month of *August*.

The winter is moderate and constant, so that there are neither such severe frosts nor sudden thaws as in *Jakutski*. The mercury in *de l' Isle*'s thermometer was between 160 and 180 degrees. From the severe frosts that we had two years following in the month of *January*, it fell to 205 degrees. The month of *January* is always their coldest month; and at that time the mercury was between 171 and 200 degrees.

The spring weather is pleasanter than the summer; when, although it sometimes rains, yet now and then there are fine clear days. The snow lies to the end of *May*, which with us is reckoned the last spring month.

The summer is for the most part very disagreeable weather, rainy and cold*; the reason of which is the continual damps from the neighbouring mountains being covered with snow that never melts. It frequently happens, that for a week or two the sun does not appear: and during all the time that I was there we had never one whole week of fair weather, never one day so clear but the mornings were foggy; and there fell, as it were, a small drizzling rain, which continued 'till twelve o'clock. From this moist air and the neighbouring hills it is so cold, that one can never be without warm cloathing.

I never observed either violent rains or loud thunder; for the rains are small, and the thunder resembles some rumbling noise under the earth. The lightning is also very weak.

In the *Ostrog* upon the Great River, where the air is warmer, the mercury in the thermometer changed from 130 to 146 degrees; and by an extraordinary heat, that happened two different years in the month of *July*, it rose 118 degrees.

---

* This is to be understood of the country about the Great River and the *Penschinska* sea; in other places the summer is tolerable, as will be mentioned hereafter.

The

The inconstancy of the summer weather not only occasions the unfruitfulness of the land, but is likewise a great hindrance to the people in preparing their fish against the winter; so that, although there is vast plenty of fish, they are not able to prepare so much as to prevent a scarcity before the winter is over; nor can they preserve one fish out of ten which they hang up to dry, the continual wet breeding worms which consume it; so that the fish which the dogs and bears catch themselves and lay up, sells very dear in the spring.

In the more distant places from the sea, and especially about the upper *Kamtschatka Ostrog*, the weather is very different; it being fine and clear from the month of *April* to the middle of *June*. The rains begin after the summer solstice, and continue to the end of *August*. Deep snows fall in the winter; but high winds seldom happen, and, when they do, are but of short continuance: and although there does not, perhaps, fall more snow than upon the Great River, yet it is deeper, as it lies lighter.

The harvest weather is generally agreeable and clear, except at the end of *September*, when storms frequently happen. The rivers are generally frozen over in the beginning of *November*; for their swift current prevents their freezing in moderate frosts. Upon the *Penschinska* sea the winds are generally in the spring south-south-east and south-west; in the summer, west; in the autumn, north and north-east; in the winter before the solstice, uncertain; but after that, to the month of *March*, the north-east and east winds prevail. From these winds the spring and summer, before the solstice, are generally thick and heavy; but the weather in the months of *September*, *October*, *February*, and *March*, is more agreeable, and is the time for trade and long journies. In *November*, *December*, and *January*, there is little clear good weather, but heavy snows and great drifts, which in *Siberia* they call *Pourgami*. The east and south-east winds blow long and most violently, sometimes for two days together, and with such vehemence,

that

that a man cannot stand upon his feet. These winds, which generally rage the three last-mentioned months, bring a great quantity of ice upon the shore of the *Lopatka* and *Awachinskaya* bay, with a multitude of sea-beavers: about this time, therefore, is their best season for catching these animals. The north winds, either in summer or winter, bring agreeable clear weather; but the south and south-west winds in summer are attended with rain, and in winter with snow. And although the cold is not so great, yet the air is always heavy and thick, and at sea generally attended with great fogs, as our people, who went upon the *American* and *Japan* expedition, experienced: therefore sailing in such weather is as dangerous as living upon the land is disagreeable; and this agreement of the weather of *Kamtschatka* with what is found far out at sea is to be attributed not only to neighbouring countries, but likewise to the great and extensive Southern Ocean. Hence the northern parts of *Kamtschatka*, that are sheltered from the south wind, are both more fertile and enjoy a better climate; and the nearer one comes to the *Lopatka* the moister and thicker is the air in summer, and the winds more violent and of longer duration in winter. It frequently happens, that about the Great River the weather is very calm and agreeable, while at the *Lopatka* the inhabitants cannot stir out of their huts; because it is a narrow point of land, and exposed to every wind, except in the bay. All along the *Penschinska* sea, the more northernly any place lies, the less rain have they in summer and wind in winter. The winds and weather about the mouth of the *Kamtschatka* river, and near to the upper *Ostrog*, are very changeable. From the east and south-east they have as violent storms as about the *Penschinska* sea; but yet, compared with this, the weather is more frequently fair than rainy. The difference between the eastern and western parts of *Kamtschatka* is plainly to be seen in travelling from the head of the *Bistroy* river: for towards the *Penschinska* sea the air appears always thick and hazy,

hazy, the clouds heavy, and always dark; while *Kamtfchatka* appears like another world, where the land lies higher, and the air is clear and ferene.

The fnow lies always deeper upon the *Lopatka* than upon the northern fide of *Kamtfchatka*; fo that, if it be twelve feet in depth about the *Lopatka*, upon the *Awatfcha* and the Great River it is not fo deep by one third, and at the fame time lies lighter and more equal, by reafon that the winds are not fo high there. About *Teghil* and *Karaga* the fnow is feldom deeper than a foot and a half: hence the reafon appears why the *Kamtfchadales* do not keep rein-deer as well as the *Koreki*, but depend upon the fifh for their nourifhment, which upon the north-eaft and north-weft coaft from the Great River is fo fcarce, that unlefs thefe barbarous creatures could digeft every thing they can get down, they would not be able to fupport life; for, though throughout the country of *Kamtfchatka* there would be food enough for rein-deer, yet the depth of the fnow renders it impoffible to maintain a number of them; and what rein-deers we had occafion for in the expedition were never kept here in the winter, the depth of the fnow making it hard for them to dig down to their food.

The force of the fun reflected from the fnow in the fpring is fo great, that the inhabitants are as tawny as *Indians*; nay, they have their eyes fpoiled and blinded thereby: therefore the natives generally wear covers pierced with fmall holes, or nets of black hair, to leffen the number of rays which would otherwife fall upon their eyes. This is occafioned by the great winds, which drive the fnow fo clofe together that it is almoft as hard and folid as ice, and will not allow the rays of the fun to penetrate, but reflects them with greater force upon the very delicate and fenfible nerves of the retina than they are able to bear. Mr. *Steller* fays, that neceffity forced him to find out a remedy for the pain and inflammation of the eyes, which generally gave relief in fix hours'

hours' time. It was the white of an egg, with some camphire and sugar, which he rubbed 'till it foamed upon a pewter plate, then tied it in a handkerchief, and bound it upon the forehead. This he found to succeed in every inflammation of the eyes.

It hails frequently both in summer and harvest; but I never saw the hail bigger than pease. It seldom lightens but at the summer solstice. The thunder is also but seldom heard, and then seems to be at a great distance. We have no instance of any one killed by thunder: the natives say, indeed, that before the arrival of the *Russians* they had a great thunder, and some were killed by it; but this is to be questioned, since for so long a time we have had no instances of it. As to fogs, it is impossible that there should be greater any where than at *Kamtschatka*; and it is to be questioned whether deeper snows fall any where between 55 and 52 degrees north latitude than here, from the melting of which the rivers swell so much as to overflow their banks, and the earth in the spring is entirely covered with water. The cold in winter is most intense about the Great River and the *Awatscha*; but in the lower *Kamtschatkoi Ostrog* it is much warmer than in any other place of *Siberia* in the same latitude.

The greatest inconveniency arises from the violent winds and storms, concerning which the following remarks may not be improper. Before a great wind, which generally comes from the east, the air is always thick and dark; but, as I had not a thermometer, I cannot be certain if it is warmer then than at other times. The east winds coming from the *Lopatka*, where are burning mountains and warm springs, I imagine that they not only arise from the narrowness of the land, but also from subterraneous fires and vapours.

With regard to other advantages or disadvantages of this country, one may say in general, that its greatest riches consist in plenty of good furs and fish, and its greatest inconveniences in the want of iron and salt. The first they are supplied with from
other

other places, and the second by boiling sea water into salt; but the troublesome distant carriage of the iron, and the boiling of the salt, are attended with such expence and difficulty, that they are both sold at a most intolerable price. One cannot buy a common ax under two rubles, and a pound of salt costs four rubles.

CHAP. II.

Of the VOLCANO's *or* BURNING MOUNTAINS.

THERE are three burning mountains in *Kamtschatka*, the *Awachinsky*, the *Tulbatchinsky*, and the *Kamtschatka*.

The *Awachinsky* mountain stands upon the north side of the bay of *Awatscha*, at a good distance indeed, but its bottom reaches to the very bay; and all the high mountains, near one half of their height, are made up, as it were, of rows of hills set one upon another, and the top they call the *Shatse*, or tent, which is always naked, but the lower parts are generally covered with wood.

These mountains for many years throw out a continual smoke, but flame only at times. The most terrible fire happened, as the *Kamtschadales* say, in the summer of the year 1737; but this lasted no longer than 24 hours, and concluded by throwing out a vast cloud of ashes, which covered the adjacent parts the depth of a vershoke *.

* A vershoke is the $\frac{1}{16}$ of the *Russian* arshia, which contains 27 inches.

After this, in *Awatscha* and the islands near the *Kurilskaya Lopatka* they felt a terrible earthquake and motion of the waters, which was observed in the following manner. The earthquake began about three o'clock in the morning the 6th of October, 1737, and continued about a quarter of an hour, and many of the *Kamtschatkoi* huts and tents were overturned. At the same time the sea was driven upon the shore, and rose about 20 feet; immediately after all the water was carried back to a great distance from the shore, and then it returned again higher than before, and afterwards retired so far that one could not see it from the shore. At that time, in the passage between the first and second of the *Kurilski* islands, they observed clusters of rocks in the bottom of the sea that had never been seen before, although they formerly had great earthquakes and extraordinary agitations of the sea. A quarter of an hour after this the earthquake returned with most terrible waves, and the sea overflowed the shore 200 feet high, which, as formerly, immediately retired. This rolling motion continued for a long time, the sea frequently approaching the shore and departing from it. Before every earthquake a great, heavy, rumbling noise was heard from this overflowing of the sea. The inhabitants were all ruined, and many of them miserably lost their lives. In several places the meadows, little hills, and fields, were turned into salt-water lakes. This was not so violent upon the *Penschinska* sea as upon the Eastern Ocean; and the people about the Great River suffered very little.

At this time we sailed from *Ochotska* to the mouth of the Great River; and when we came on shore the 14th of *October*, the earthquake was still perceptible, which was sometimes so strong that we could not stand upon our feet; and this continued to the spring of the year 1738: however, it was more upon the *Kurilskaya Lopatka* and the coast of the Eastern Ocean, than in those places that were more remote from the sea.

The Coſſacks of the great river, who were then upon the *Kurilſki* iſlands, told me, that upon the beginning of the earthquake they ran with the natives up to the tops of the mountains, and left all their goods, which were deſtroyed, as well as the habitations of the *Kuriles*.

The *Tulbatchinſky* mountain ſtands upon that neck of land which lies between the rivers *Kamtſchatka* and *Tulbatchik*: it has ſmoked for many years. In the beginning of the year 1739, for the firſt time, it threw out a ball of fire which ſet the woods on fire. After this fire-ball aroſe a thick cloud, which increaſing gradually at laſt fell down and covered the ſnow 50 verſts round with aſhes. I was going at this very time from the upper to the lower *Kamtſchatkoi* fort, and was obliged to wait a new fall of ſnow, as we could not travel upon this ſooty matter.

Nothing extraordinary happened upon this conflagration, except ſome ſmall ſhocks of an earthquake, which were felt both before and after. The great ſhock was about the middle of *December*, which I felt when I went to the upper *Kamtſchatkoi* fort from the Great River. We were then not far from the *Hrepta*, or *Ogulminſky* ridge. When we ſtopped about noon, the diſmal ſound in the woods that we heard at firſt ſeemed as an approaching ſtorm; but our kettles being thrown from the fire, and we ourſelves rocked in our ſledges, we were ſoon convinced of our miſtake. This earthquake had only three vibrations, which ſucceeded each other at about a minute's diſtance.

The mountain of *Kamtſchatka* is higher, not only than the two laſt mentioned, but than any other mountain in that part. Two thirds of its height are made up of rows of hills, as I mentioned, of the *Awachinſky*; the *Shatſe*, or top, making alone one third of its height. The circuit round the bottom of the mountain is near 300 verſts. The *Shatſe*, or top, is very ſteep on every ſide, and has ſeveral deep openings lengthways: the very ſummit turns gradually broadest from the falling in of the earth into the mouth of the burning gulph. It is so high, that in a clear day it is to be seen from the upper *Kamtschatkoi* fort, which is about 300 versts; and one cannot see other mountains; the *Tulbatchinsky* for instance, although they are much nearer. Before a storm the summit appears surrounded with three girdles; the highest seems in breadth about the fourth part of the height of the mountain, from whence arises a continual thick smoke. The inhabitants say that it throws out ashes twice or thrice yearly, and sometimes in such quantities, that for 300 versts around the earth is covered with them the depth of a vershoke. From the year 1727 to 1731 the inhabitants observed that it burnt almost without interruption, but they were not under such apprehensions as in the last conflagration in the year 1737. This terrible conflagration begun the 25th of *September*, and lasted one week with such violence, that to the people who were fishing at sea near the mountain it appeared one red-hot rock, and the flames, which burst through several openings, sometimes shewed like rivers of fire with a shocking noise. Within the mountain were heard thunderings, crackling and blowing like the strongest bellows, which shook all the neighbouring country: the nights were the most terrible. This conflagration ended as usual, with throwing out a vast quantity of cinders and ashes, of which however little fell upon the land, the whole cloud being almost carried by the wind to the sea. It throws out porous stones and glass of different colours, which are frequently found in the brook *Boukosse*, which rises out of this mountain. The 23d of *October* following at the lower *Kamtschatkoi* fort happened such a violent earthquake, that most of the houses and stoves were thrown down, the bells of the churches rang, and the new church, which was built of thick balks of larch wood, was so much shaken that the joinings of the balks were all loosened. Some shocks were felt at times until the spring of the year 1738;

however

The Burning Mountain named Kamtschatka. See Page 70.

The Lower Kamtschatka Fort. See Page 265.

however the agitation of the waters was less than what had been formerly observed. The earthquakes are said to be more violent near a mountain that burns, than near one that has left off burning, or is not quite kindled.

Besides these mountains, I heard of two other gulphs where smoke arises: one is called *Joupanosky*; the other, *Shevelitche*; but there are several places farther north than the river *Kamtschatka*: some of which emit smoke, and some fire: and there are in the *Kurilski* islands, one upon the *Paromusir*, and another upon the *Alaide*; concerning which Mr. *Steller* observes, that it is only one hill which burns, not a whole ridge; all these mountains have outwardly the same appearance, and it is, therefore, probable that their contents are much the same; that from the external appearance, one may judge of their internal contents, and of their aptness to take fire and burn; and that in all these which have smoked or burned formerly, but have been extinguished, lakes are always found; whence he concludes, that as these were burnt down to the bottom, the waters rushing through the opened passages, filled the empty space; and hence an account may also be given of the cause of the hot springs.

There are two hills which have left off burning; the *Apalsky*, out of which rises the river *Apala*; and the *Biloutchinsky*, from which comes the river *Biloutchik*. At the bottom of this hill is a lake, where vast numbers of herrings are caught in the months of *March*, *April*, and *May*.

CHAP. III.

Of the HOT SPRINGS.

I Found the following hot springs: 1ſt, Upon the river *Oſernoi*, which runs out of the *Kurilſkoy* lake. 2d, Upon the river *Paudche*, which falls into the *Oſernoi*. 3d, Upon the river *Baano*, which is reckoned a branch of the Great River. 4th, Near the fort *Natchikute*. 5th, Near the mouth of the river *Shematchinſki*. 6th, Near the head of the ſame.

Theſe waters, which are upon the river *Oſernoi*, run in little ſprings from the ſouth bank; ſome fall directly into the river: others keep their courſe parallel to the river, and, joining after at ſome diſtance, fall together into the *Oſernoi*. Theſe ſprings are not conſiderable, nor very hot, only raiſing the thermometer (*Farenheit's*) which in the open air was at 45° to 145°.

The ſprings upon the *Paudche* are four verſts and a half diſtant from the firſt, and riſe out of the ground, upon the eaſt bank of the river in an open high hill which has a plain at the ſummit of 350 fathoms* in length, and 300 in breadth. This hill goes in a promontory towards the river, where it makes a a ſteep bank; but on the other ſide the deſcent is eaſy.

Several of theſe ſprings throw out their waters, like artificial water-works, about a foot, or a foot and a half, high, and with a great noiſe. Some of them ſtand in large pools like little lakes, and ſend out ſmall ſtreams, which, joining upon the plain, divide it, as it were, into ſo many iſlands, and at laſt fall in a conſiderable ſtream into the *Paudche*. That little lake marked by the letter ⌐ is remarkable for having an opening two fathoms deep.

---

* The *Ruſſian* fathom is ſeven feet.

In the ifland are a great many openings, fome very fmall, and others above a foot diameter; but from thefe large openings iffues no water, though the fmall ones fend out fometimes water and fometimes vapour with a very great force.

All thofe places from which formerly iffued out water, may be known by a various coloured clay which is found round them, for this clay is commonly thrown up by the waters. Sulphur is alfo found there, efpecially about thofe openings which emit vapours only.

Some fprings likewife flow from that fteep bank which we mentioned, two fathoms or more higher than the river. It is remarkable, that the ftones of which this bank, and perhaps all the hill, is formed, are round, outwardly very dry, but within fo foft that they may be rubbed between the fingers like clay: hence it has been conjectured, that the various coloured clay, which is found about the mouths of the fprings, is nothing but thefe ftones foftened by the moifture and heat. The clay in tafte is four and aftringent; and if a piece of it, or a ftone, is broken, there appears an efflorefcence of alum, like a mofs, with the colours blue, white, red, yellow, green, and black, which are fo mixed as to refemble marble; and when the clay is not quite dry, the colours are pretty bright.

Oppofite to the promontory of the hill is an ifland in the river *Paudche*, where there are likewife fprings of hot water, but fmaller than thofe before mentioned.

A more diftinct idea may be had of thefe hot fprings from the fubjoined plan, in which each fpring is marked with a particular letter, with the different degrees of heat.

A Table *of the different degrees of heat which were found in each spring, by* De l'Isle's *and* Farenheit's *thermometers.*

	De l'Isle's	Farenheit's
The lake at the head of the stream	80	116
The eye which is in the corner of that lake	65	134
The little lake into which the stream falls	115	74
The spring out of which the stream 1 runs	50	152
The mouth of that stream where it falls into the lake	106	87
The mouth of the stream E where it comes out of the lake	95	98
The spring of the stream 2	20	188
The little lake at the head of the stream 3	60	140
In the same lake at the mouth of the stream 3	80	116
Where this stream joins the stream 2	93	108
At the head of the stream N	10	200
The mouth of this stream	55	146
The head of the stream K	80	116
Where this stream joins the stream N	95	98
Where both these streams fall into the *Paudche*	110	80

De *l'Isle*'s thermometer stood at this time, in the open air, at 136°, and that of *Farenheit*'s at 49°.

The springs which are upon the river *Piaana* are not very different from those of *Paudche*. They rise upon both sides of the river; and as upon the south bank there is a high plain, and upon the north a cliff of rocks, the springs on the south bank fall into the river in little streams; but those upon the north side run along the cliff, except one which rises about 80 fathoms from the rest, and where the cliff is more distant from the river, which has a course of 40 fathoms.

Amongst

KAMTSCHATKA. 75

Amongſt the ſprings upon the ſouth bank it is to be remarked, that one place is full of openings of very different diameters, where the water is thrown up two feet and a half with a great noiſe. The thermometer, which in the open air ſtood at 185 degrees, roſe to 15 degrees.

The ſprings of the Great River fall into it in one conſiderable ſtream, which runs between ſtony hills in a narrow channel. The banks are boggy, and the bottom ſtony, covered with moſs. From its ſpring to the place where it falls into the Great River is 261 fathoms. At the ſpring the mercury roſe in *De l' Iſle*'s thermometer to 23, and *Farenheit*'s to 185, degrees; thence to where it falls into the River it grew cooler gradually, ſo that at the mouth *De l' Iſle*'s thermometer only roſe to 115, and *Farenheit*'s to 74, degrees; in the open air the one ſtood at 175, and the other at 14, degrees.

The hot brook, that is near the river *Shematche*, and falls into the Eaſtern Ocean, is much larger than any of the abovementioned. At its mouth it is three fathoms broad, and in ſome places near four feet deep, and its length is three verſts * and 88 fathoms. It runs between high ſtony hills with a ſtrong current: its bottom is a hard ſtone covered with green moſs, which in ſtill places ſwims upon the ſurface. Near the banks at its mouth, the heat is like that of ſummer water; and towards the head the graſs and plants upon the banks were green and ſome of them flowered in *March*. In going from this river to the laſt hot ſpring that lies upon the river *Shematche* one muſt paſs a great ridge of hills. Upon the eaſt ſide of this ridge, near the ſummit, is an even plain covered with round grey ſtones, without any plants growing upon it. Upon this plain in ſeveral places a vapour aſcends with great force, and a noiſe reſembling the

---

* A *Ruſſian* verſt is 500 fathoms, or 3500 feet.

bubbling

bubbling of water is heard. Here I dug, expecting to find water; but I found a stratum of such hard stone that we could not dig through it. It is probable that the waters of the warm brook, that falls into the Eastern Ocean, have their origin from this place, for it is directly opposite to the rise of that brook: and the last stream that falls into the river *Shematche* is likewise thought to derive its source from the same place, as it rises from this ridge, upon the west side, in a deep hollow, surrounded with smoking hills. The very bottom itself is full of boiling springs for near a verst and a half; all which join at last in one stream.

In this bottom are two large wells, that deserve particular notice; one is five, the other three fathoms' diameter; the first one and a half, the other one fathom deep. In these the water boils up with white bubbles, and makes such a noise, that one person cannot hear another in the common way of speaking; nay, scarcely when he cries aloud. The vapour is so thick, that one cannot see a man at seven fathoms' distance; and the boiling of the water is only to be observed by lying down upon the ground. The earth between these wells yields like a bog, so that one is in continual fear of sinking in. The water of these springs is distinguished from all others by a black matter, like *Chinese* ink, that swims upon the top, which sticks so to the fingers that one cannot without difficulty wash it off. They have, in common with other hot springs, clay, lime, alum, and sulphur, of various colours. In all the above-mentioned springs the water is thick, and stinks like rotten eggs.

The *Kamtschadales* esteem all the burning mountains, and places where hot springs arise, as the habitations of spirits, and approach them with fear; but, as the latter are the most dangerous, they are under the greatest awe of them; and therefore they never willingly discover them to any *Russian*, lest they should be obliged to accompany him near them. It was by chance that I heard of them after I had travelled 100 versts from the

the place; but this natural phænomenon appeared so curious that I returned to examine it. The people of *Shematchinski* village were obliged to declare the true reason why they had not formerly discovered them, and much against their will were forced to shew me the place, but would not go near it: and when they saw that we lay in the water, drank it, and eat things boiled with it, they expected to see us perish immediately; but when they perceived this did not happen, they told it in the village as an uncommon wonder, and looked uqon us as very extraordinary people, since even the devils could not hurt us.

This is remarkable, that north from the mouth of the river *Kamtschatka*, and west along the coast of the river *Osernoi*, there are no hot springs, although it abounds in Pyrites sulphur, iron ore, and stones that yield alum and vitriol. Mr. *Steller* observes, that the appearance of the country of *Kamtschatka*, and the frequent earthquakes there, give reason to think that it is full of caverns replete with combustible matter, which taking fire in the bowels of the earth produces earthquakes, and makes those vast alterations of which we see numerous instances in rocky shores being torn off both upon the *Beaver* sea, and in the islands which lie between *Asia* and *America*. The combustible matter, he tells us, is kindled by the rushing of the salt water into those subterraneous caverns, through their apertures towards the sea; which hypothesis is strengthened by his observation, that earthquakes are most frequent about the equinoxes, when the waves of the sea are driven by the great storms with uncommon violence upon the shores; and especially about the spring equinox, at which time the water always rises higher than at any other: and the inhabitants of *Kamtschatka* and the *Kuriles* know this so well, that they always fear the beginning of *March* and the end of *September*.

It is very extraordinary, that no iron has been discovered here, although some ore is observed mixed with clay and earth, to
which

which sulphur being added the subterraneous fires may easily be accounted for; nor do we yet know of any salt springs, although the narrowness of the isthmus of the peninsula of *Kamtschatka*, and so many subterraneous caverns under the rocky hills which have communication with the sea, should give us reason to conclude that there must be some.

After the hot springs we ought to take notice of the rivers which never freeze. These are so common in *Kamtschatka*, that there is scarcely one river which has not some very large openings, even in the most severe frosts; and the plains under the hills are so full of springs that one cannot go dry any where in the summer. These springs, which joining make a little rivulet, and fall into the *Kleutchova Kamtschatka*, never freeze, and yield fish almost the whole winter, which gives an advantage to the *Kleutchova*, as it furnishes not only the *Kamtschadales*, but all the people of the *Ostrog* of *Nishnishantalsky*, with fresh fish, which is generally esteemed, on account of its scarcity at that time, as a very great delicacy. This may also account for the wholesomeness of all these waters, which the inhabitants drink after eating the fattest fish without the least harm, although, in other places, cold water drunk upon fat fish produces the bloody flux.

CHAP. IV.

Of the METALS and MINERALS.

ALTHOUGH the peninsula of *Kamtschatka* is hilly, and the ground such as might naturally be supposed to produce metals and minerals, especially iron and copper, with which *Siberia* abounds; yet hitherto little has been discovered. This is no proof that such ores are not in *Kamtschatka*; for, besides that the *Kamtschadales* are entirely unexperienced, the *Russians* who live here have as yet given themselves no trouble in the search after metals; as they have such large quantities of iron and copper instruments brought to them, that they have not only sufficient for themselves, but are also enabled to furnish the *Kamtschadales* and *Kuriles* with them at a very considerable profit. It is also to be considered, that the providing for their subsistance takes up so much of their time, that they can spare but little for any thing else; and moreover, the places proper for such tryals are very difficult of access: to which it may be added, that the frequent storms and general inclemency of the weather are great hindrances to such tryals; especially when every necessary for the undertaking must be carried upon men's backs, for in the summer they can carry nothing upon dogs. It is reasonable to presume that ore might be found in *Kamtschatka*, if it was worth while to search for it. Copper ore has been found about the *Kurilskoy* lake, and the *Ivovoy* bay; and a sandy iron ore upon the banks of the several lakes and rivers; whence it is expected that there is iron ore in the hills from which these lakes and rivers rise. Native sulphur is gathered about the rivers *Kambalinskoy* and *Osernoi*, and the *Kronotzkoy* cape. The sulphur

phur which they bring from *Olontoſki*, where it drops from the rocks, is quite fine and pellucid; and in the Pyrites upon the coaſt it is to be found every where.

The following kinds of earth are common. Great quantities of white chalk are found about the *Kurilſky* lake; tripoly and oker about the Great River, and the villages of *Nachikin* and *Koutchinuhiff*; and a purple-coloured earth about the hot ſprings, and ſometimes a hard ſtony oker. Among the ſtones in the mountains are found, but rarely, ſmall cherry-coloured chryſtals; and near the river *Charious* are found pieces of fluſſe, which is like a coarſe green glaſs, of which the inhabitants formerly made knives, axes, lancets, and darts. It is called by the *Ruſſian* natives glaſs, and by the *Kamtſchadales*, *nanagy*. This fluſſe is alſo found in the copper mines about *Ecatherinenbourg*, where it is called a topaz. There is likewiſe here a ſort of light ſtone, white like chalk, of which the inhabitants make plates, and lamps wherein they burn their fiſh oil; and every where upon the ſhore is found an iron-coloured hard ſtone, porous as a ſpunge, and eaſily turned by the fire.

The inhabitants find pellucid ſtones near the ſprings of the river, which they uſe inſtead of flints. Some of theſe ſtones are ſemi-pellucid, whitiſh and milky, and reckoned cornelians by the *Ruſſians*. Some ſmall pellucid ſtones of a yellowiſh colour, like corals, are found upon the banks of ſeveral rivers; and plenty of hyacinths near *Tomſkoy*.

Hitherto they have diſcovered no precious ſtones here. The hills are firmer than thoſe in *Siberia*, and do not fall away like them; but when the earth falls off they find much *lac lunæ*; and a ſoft kind of bolus, of a fattiſh creamy taſte, is found near the *Penſchinſka* ſea, *Kurilſkoy* lake, and the *Olutorſkoy*: this is uſed as an excellent remedy in fluxes. I ſent ſpecimens of moſt of the above things to the Muſeum of the Imperial Academy of *St. Petersbourg*. I muſt not forget to mention that

that amber is gathered here, near the *Penschinska* sea, upon the river *Teghil*, and farther north.

CHAP. V.

Of TREES and PLANTS.

THE most useful wood is the larch*, and the white poplar †, which serves for building their houses and forts; and they are fit, not only for such boats as the inhabitants use, but even for the building of ships. The larch-tree, indeed, only grows upon the river *Kamtschatka*, and such other rivers as fall into it: in other places they make use of the white poplar. The pine-tree ‖ and the black poplar ‡ are no where to be found upon the *Kamtschatka*; and the pitch-tree ** only in one place, and there in small quantities. Although there be many birch-trees ††, yet they make little use of them, unless in their sledges, having none near their houses but what are crooked and useless; and it is very troublesome to bring the better sort from the distance at which it grows.

They make great use of the birch bark, which they strip from the trees while yet green; and cutting it in small pieces, like vermicelli, eat it with dried caviar. In the winter, whenever you enter any of their villages, you find the women employed in hacking this green bark with their bone or stone axes. They also ferment this bark with the juice or sap of the birch, which makes an agreeable drink. The birches of

---

* Larix.   ‖ Pinus.   ** Picea.
† Populus alba.   ‡ Populus nigra.   †† Betula.

Kamtfchatka are much fuller of knots and hard excrefcences than thofe of *Europe*; but of thefe knots they make very ufeful plates, fpoons, and cups. Mr. *Steller* obferved, that the white poplar near the fea was quite porous and light, which he attributed to the falt water; that the afhes of this wood, laid out in the open air, turned into a ftony fubftance heavy and hard, which, the longer it lies, the harder and heavier it grows. This ftone, when broken, fhews fome fpecks of iron in its fubftance. Sallows * and alders † are the common fire-wood in *Kamtfchatka*. The bark of the fallow is ufed for food, and that of the alder in dying their leather; as fhall be related more at large in another place. They have the tree tcheremough ‖ and the hawthorn ‡ of two fpecies, one yielding a red, and the other a black fruit; of thefe they lay up a great quantity againft winter: they have likewife the fervice-tree ** in great plenty, whofe fruit is efteemed amongft their moft delicate confections.

Their principal nourifhment is from the nuts of the flantza, which grows every where, both in hills and dales. This fhrub, or tree, is truly of the cedar kind, only it is much lefs; and inftead of growing ftraight, it creeps along the ground. Its cones and nuts are not half fo large as thofe of the cedar: the *Kamtfchadales* eat them with the fhells. Thefe, as well as the tcheremough and the hawthorn berries, are very aftringent, especially if eaten in any quantity. The greateft virtue of thefe nuts is, that they are a good remedy againft the fcurvy, as all our feamen can witnefs: for in the moft fevere fcurvy this is, as one may fay, almoft their only medicine; and from the tops of the flantza and cedar was their common drink made, fometimes fermented, at other times drunk warm like tea; and orders were given by

---

* Salices.
† Alni.
‖ Padus foliis annuis. Linn.
‡ Oxyanthus fructu rubro et nigro.
** Sorbus.

the commanding officer that the kettle with flantza and cedar tops should never be taken from the fire. Red currants, rasberries, and kneshnitza are very rare there, or grow at such a distance from their houses that no one cares to go in search of them. The blackberries of the gimoloft * are of great use, being of an agreeable taste, something like new-fermented beer. The bark of this shrub is useful in distilling brandy, giving strength and sharpness to the spirit.

The juniper † grows every where; but they do not use the berries, as they lay up great store of morosky ‖, pianitza ‡, brushnitza **, klioukva ††, and vodinitza ‖‖ : and when they have great plenty of these berries they not only use them as confects, but distil brandy from them, except from klioukva and vodinitza, which yield no spirit. Mr. *Steller* writes, that the vodinitza is no bad remedy for the scurvy; and the inhabitants dye any old cloaths with it that have lost their colour, to which it gives a cherry-colour. Some boil it up with train-oil and alum, and dye the beaver and coarse sables with it well enough to deceive the unwary or ignorant. In many places they content themselves with roots and herbs, and make them supply not only their want of bread, but of fish also. The principal of these is the saranne, which serves instead of groats. It belongs to the class of the lillies ‡‡ ; but as this sort is never seen any where but in *Ochotskoy* and *Kamtschatka*, I shall give description of it. It grows about half a foot high; has a stalk near the thickness of a swan's quill, red below and green above. Its leaves grow in two

---

* Lonicera pedunculis biflorio, floribus infundibuli formis, bacca solitaria, oblonga, angulosa. GMEL. flor. Sib.

† Juniperus.

‖ Chamemorus RAII Syn.

‡ Vaccinium Spec. 2. LINN. Bilberry.

** Vaccinium Bilberry Spec. 3. LINN.

†† Vaccinium Red Crowberry Spec. 4.

‖‖ Empetrum.

‡‡ Lillium flore atro rubente.

rows upon the ftalk; the lower row having three leaves, and the upper four, placed crofsways: the form of the leaves is oval. Sometimes above the fecond row one leaf grows juft under the flower. Upon the uppermoft part of the ftalk grows one dark cherry-coloured flower, rarely two, fomething lefs than that of the common lilly; and this is divided into fix equal parts. The pointal in the center of the flower is triangular, at the top flat, and in three different cells contains flat reddifh feeds. Round the pointal are fix white ftamina with yellow heads. Its root, which is properly the faranne, is about the bignefs of a root of garlick, made up of many little cloves, whence it acquires a round form. It bloffoms in *June*, at which time one can fee no other flower over the whole fields.

The natives of *Kamtfchatka*, and the wives of the *Ruffian* Coffacks, dig up the roots in the harveft, or take them out of the nefts of the field-mice, dry them in the fun, and fell them for five or fix rubles the pood. The faranne half boiled, and beat up with brambleberries, cranberries, or fuch other of this kind, makes one of the moft agreeable confections, being of a fharp fweetnefs; and if one had enough for every day's ufe, the want of bread would be tolerably well fupplied. Mr. *Steller* reckons five fpecies of this plant: 1ft. the kimtchiga, which grows near *Teghil* and *Harioufkovoy*, in appearance like a large fugar-pea, and if boiled taftes much the fame; but neither he nor I ever faw this plant in bloffom: 2dly, the round faranne, which I have defcribed above: 3dly, ovfenka *, which grows every where in *Siberia*, being roots of red lillies, whofe flowers are all turned up in curls; the bulb is compofed of an infinite number of fmall cloves: 4thly, titichpa,

---

* Lilium radice tunicata, foliis fparfis, floribus reflexis, corallis revolutis. GMEL. flor. Sib.

which grows upon the Great River; but neither he nor I ever saw this in the flower: 5thly, matifta fladka trava*, or the sweet plant, is as useful in their oeconomy as the faranne; for the *Kamtfchadales* use this not only as a confection in tarts and broths, but in all their superstitious ceremonies this is absolutely necessary. The *Ruffians* were no sooner settled there, than they found that brandy was to be distilled from it; and at present this is the only brandy that is publickly sold. The root of this herb is without yellowish, within, white; and of a bitter, spicy taste. The stem is fleshy, of three or four joints, and about a man's height. Its flower is a reddish green, with short white hairs, longest near the root. The leaves upon the stem nearest the root are five or six, and sometimes even ten: they grow upon thick, round, fleshy, green, rough stalks, marked with little red spots. Upon the main stem, at every joint, arises one such leaf, but without a stalk. The flowers are small and white, like fennel, or other herbs of that sort; and consist of five leaves, of which the innermost are largest, and the outward smallest. It has two ovaria upon every flower, upon short small necks; and round them are five white stamina with green points, which rise higher than the flower. The flowers, taken all together, resemble a plate; while the stalks which support the umbella are longest without, and in the middle shortest: stalks arise from every joint, upon which are flowers.

This plant abounds every where in *Kamtfchatka*, and the inhabitants gather and prepare it in this manner: they cut off the stalks of the leaves which grow nearest the root, and with a shell

---

* Sphondylium foliolis pinnatifidis. Linn. Cliff.

scrape off the skin; and then bind up ten stalks together. When it begins to smell a little, then they put it in a bag to sweeten; where it yields a sweet dust, which perhaps sweats out from the pith of the plant. This herb-sugar, as they call it, has something the taste of liquorice, and is not very pleasant. A pood of the plant does not afford above a quarter of a pound of this dust.

The women, when they gather this, must wear gloves; for the juice is so sharp or caustic, than whenever it falls upon the flesh it raises swellings and blisters. For this reason, when in the spring the *Russians* eat it fresh, they only bite it with their teeth, taking care not to touch it with their lips. I have seen instances of some that were unacquainted with this, who rashly chewed it as they would do any other herb; upon which, not only their lips, but their chin, nose, and cheeks, and also wherever the juice of this plant had touched, was immediately swelled up and full of blisters; and although these burst, yet the swelling continued for a whole week.

The manner of distilling spirits from it is as follows:--- They lay several bundles of this plant in a small vessel, upon which they pour hot water; and to make it ferment, they put in some berries of honey-suckle or cranberries, and binding the vessel close up set it in a warm place, where they leave it until the liquor ceases to make a noise; for during the time of fermentation, it cracks and bounces so much as to make the vessel shake. In the same manner they prepare more wort in a large vessel, and add to this, which now generally ferments in 24 hours, as above. They throw both the fermented herbs and liquor into the kettle, and cover it close with a wooden cover; and instead of a pipe they take the barrel of a gun. The first running is as strong as brandy; which, if they distil a second time, produces a spirit so strong that it consumes even iron. But it

is

is only the richer sort of people that use this brandy; and what they sell is only the first running, which makes a very good dram.

Two pood of herbs generally render one vedro * of the first running, and the pood costs four rubles or more. The herbs that remain in the still after drawing off all the spirit, are made use of as a yest, instead of berries, to ferment other infusions or wort; and what they cannot use thus the cattle eat very greedily, and it fattens them much. It is remarkable that brandy distilled from the plants from which the skin has not been clean scraped, it causes melancholy and perturbation of mind. Mr *Steller* made the following remarks upon this brandy: 1st, that it is very piercing, and contains a good deal of a sharp acid, which coagulates the blood and makes it black: 2dly, that a small quantity of it makes people drunk and quite senseless, and causes their faces to turn black: 3dly, that if a person drinks a few drams of it, he is plagued the whole night with disagreeable dreams, and next day is uneasy and disturbed as if terrified with the apprehension of the greatest misfortune: and, what is very extraordinary, he has seen some people the day after they have been drunk with this spirit, from one draught of cold water, become again so drunk that they could not stand upon their feet. They wet their hair with the juice, which they squeeze out of this herb in the spring, as a preservative against lice, and find it to be their only relief. Many of the *Kamtschadales*, who desire to have children, will not eat this herb, green or dry, imagining that it impairs the generative faculties.

The herb kipri †, which grows in all *Europe* and *Asia*, has the third place in the food of the *Kamtschadales*. They

---

* Vedro is a *Russian* liquid measure containing 25 pints.
† Epilobium. LINN. Succ. Spec. 1. French willows.

boil it with their fish, and use the leaves as tea; but the greatest use is made of its pith, which, after having split the stalks, they scrape out with shells, and, tied up in bundles, dry it in the sun. It is then very pleasant, and in taste resembles dried *Persian* cucumbers. The *Kamtschadales* use it in several dishes, and serve it up green as a desert. The kipri boiled gives a thick sweet wort, that makes the best quasse * imaginable: it also affords them a very strong vinegar, if to six pounds of the kipri they add a pound of the sweet herb of sphondilium, and ferment it in the usual way: they get a great deal more brandy, when they use the infusion of the kipri, instead of water, to prepare the sweet herb for distillation.

They cure the navels of their children with this herb, chewing it, and laying it upon the part. They grind the roots and stalks, and use them instead of green tea, to which the flavour has some resemblance. The same use the *Kuriles* make of another shrub †, which has flowers like the strawberry, only yellow, and produces, no berries. This is called *Kurilskoy* tea, and has great virtue in fluxes and gripes.

The wild garlick ‖ is not only useful in the kitchen, but also in medicine. Both the *Russians* and *Kamtschadales* gather great quantities, which they cut and dry in the sun for their winter provision; at which time boiling it in water they ferment it a little, and use it as an herb soup, which they call *shami*. They esteem the wild garlick so efficacious a remedy against the scurvy, that they think themselves in no danger so soon as it begins to

---

* Quasse is a *Russian* drink made of rye-malt, and flower, and very little fermented. Sometimes they add mint to it, and it makes no disagreeable drink.

† Potentilla caule fructicosa. LINN. Cliff.
‖ Allium foliis radicalibus petiolatis floribus umbellatis. GMEL. flor. Sib. tom. 1. p. 49.

shew itself under the snow: and I have heard an extraordinary account of its virtues from the Cossacks that were employed with captain *Spanberg* in building the sloop Gabriel: they were so ill with the scurvy, that scarce any were able to work, or even to walk, so long as the ground was covered with snow; but as soon as the high lands began to appear green, and the wild garlick to sprout out, the Cossacks fed upon it greedily. Upon their first eating it, they were covered over with scabs in such a manner, that the captain believed they were all infected with the venereal disease. In about a fortnight, these scabs fell off, and they were perfectly recovered of the scurvy.

We must reckon amongst the food of the *Kamtschadales* the shelmina *, and the morkovai †, which is the stalk of a plant that is hollow and juicy, such as the angelica. The shelmina is a species of the ulmaria. Its root is blackish without, and white within: it sends out from one root two or three stalks about a man's height; which, near the root, are about a finger thick, but above, somewhat thinner. The leaves shoot out from long branches which grow all over the stalk. Their upper part is green and smooth; and their lower rough, with high reddish veins. Where the branch springs from the root there are two leaves like those above described, but somewhat less. The stalk is triangular, reddish, hard, and rough. At the top of the plant is a flower resembling that of the service-tree. It has four oval pistils, flattened in the sides, with downy edges; in each of which are contained two longish seeds. They are surrounded by ten white stamina, rising above the flower; the anthera being likewise white. It flowers about the middle of *July*, and the seeds are ripe about the middle of *August*. The root, stalks, and

---

* Ulmaria fructibus hispidis. STELLER. † Chæreoptrylum seminibus levibus nitidis, petiolis ramiferis simplicibus. LINN. Cliff. p. 101.

leaves of this plant are very aftringent: both the *Ruſſians* and *Kamtſchadales* eat it in the fpring. They preferve the root for winter, which they ftamp and boil for a gruel. It has fome refemblance in tafte to the Piftacho nut.

The morkovai poufhki, or carrot bunches, are fo called becaufe they are like carrots in their leaf as well as in tafte. They likewife eat this green in the fpring, but they oftener four it like four crout, or make a liquor with it.

The kotkonia * grows upon the banks of the rivers of *Kamtſchatka* in great plenty. Its root is about the thickneſs of one's finger, bitter and aftringent, black without, and white within. Sometimes five, but always more than two ftalks arife from this root, about ten inches high, of the thickneſs of a goofe-quill, and of a yellowifh-green colour. At the top are three oval leaves fpread like a ftar, from the middle of which rifes a ftalk half an inch high, which fupports the flower. The cup of the flower confifts of three oblong green leaves, and the flower itfelf of as many white ones. In the middle of the flower is the piftil, of fix fides, a yellow colour, with a red top: it contains three cells, and is furrounded with fix equal yellow-coloured ftamina; the anthera is alfo yellow. When the piftil is ripe it is as big as a walnut, is foft, flefhy, and of an agreeable tafte, like a pleafant apple. It flowers about the middle of *May*. The *Kamtſchadales* eat the root of this plant both frefh and dried, with caviar; but the fruit muft be eaten as foon as gathered, for it is fo delicate that it fpoils if it be kept one night.

The ikoume ‡, or biftort, grows in plenty both on the hills and in the vallies. The *Kamtſchadales* eat it frefh or dried, and

---

* Tradefcantia fructu molli eduli.
‡ Biftorta foliis ovatis oblongis acuminatis. LINN. Cliff.

pounded

pounded with caviar. It is far from being so astringent as that in *Europe*, is juicy, and tastes like a nut.

Utchichlcy † is a plant that has leaves like hemp, but flowers like the ragwort. When the leaves are dried, and boiled with fish, they make the broth taste as if the flesh of the wild goat was boiled in it.

The root called here mitoui, and at *Jakutski* sardan, they fry in the fat of fish, or seals, and esteem it a delicate dish.

These are the principal plants which they make use of in their kitchens; however there is a great number of others, and also of plants thrown out by the sea, which the *Kamtschadales* eat both fresh and dry in the winter: for, as Mr. *Steller* observes, they refuse nothing, but eat every thing they can get down, even the driest plants and nastiest rotten mushroons, although one would imagine the consequence dangerous, as indeed it sometimes happens. However, he tells us the natives have obtained such a knowledge of plants, and of their use both in food and medicine, that he is surprised; and that one shall not find so much knowledge of this sort among any barbarous nation, nor even, perhaps, amongst the most civilized. They give a name to every one of their plants, and know all their properties, and the different degrees of virtue which they derive from the various soils and expositions in which they grow; and so accurate are they in these distinctions, and also in the proper time of gathering the several fruits and other produce, that it is truly wonderful. Hence the *Kamtschadales* have this advantage above other people, that they can find food and medicine every where; and, by their knowledge and experience, are in little danger from the noxious plants.

† Jacobea foliis cannabis. STELLER.

Amongst the medicinal plants we must mention the following: 1st, Kailoun, a plant which grows in all the swamps near the rivers. The inhabitants use this as a cataplasm in all boils to make them suppurate; and taken in decoctions, they imagine it produces sweat, and drives away every infectious humour. 2dly, The tchaban*, which grows in plenty through all *Kamtschatka*, they use in decoctions for all pains and swellings of the legs. 3dly, Katunatch †, or wild rosemary, is not so strong as in other parts. The inhabitants have thought it beneficial in the venereal disease, but in this are deceived. 4thly The sea oak ‖ is thrown out by the waves; and being boiled with the sweet herb, a decoction of it is given in fluxes. 5thly, The sea rasberry is given to women in labour, to promote the birth. 6thly, There is yet another sea plant, called yachanga ‡, which the sea throws out near to the *Kurilskaya Lopatka*, resembling the whale's beard. This the inhabitants use in cholic pains, infusing it in cold water. 7thly, The omeg**, or water hemlock, grows upon all the rivers, and almost all the shore of *Kamtschatka*. This plant is made use of against pains in the back in the following manner:---They put the patient into a hut made exceedingly warm; and when he begins to sweat profusely, they rub his back with the cicuta, being careful not to touch the loins, for, what is very extraordinary, that would occasion sudden death: however from this practice they generally obtain great relief. 8thly, The zgate †† must not be omitted, whose dreadful qualities are but too well known in all this part of the world. They anoint the points of their darts and arrows with the juice which is squeezed from the

---

* Dryas. Linn.
† Andromeda foliis ovatis venosis.
‖ Quercus marina. Clus. et Lob.
‡ Species fuci.
** Cicuta aquatica.
†† Anemonoides et ranunculus.

root

root of this plant, and the wounds which they give are incurable unless the poison be sucked out. This is certainly the only method, and, if this be neglected, the wound immediately turns blue and swells, and in two days the patient dies. The very largest whales when they have received a slight wound from such a poisoned weapon, cannot bear the sea for any considerable time; but throwing themselves upon the shore, expire most miserably, with terrible groans and bellowing.

The following are very serviceable for cloathing, and other household purposes.

There grows upon the sea-shore a whitish high plant, resembling wheat. I have seen it at *Strelinimuise*, the palace below *St. Petersbourg*, upon sandy ground. Of this they make mats, which serve them as coverings and curtains; the best of these are made of different colours, with the beards of the whales split very small and dyed. They also make clokes of it, like the old *Russian* milled clokes, smooth within, and rough without, which makes the rain run more easily off them. The prettiest of this kind of work is their little bags and baskets, in which the women keep their trinkets. These are so neat, that one would take them to be made of split canes; and they are ornamented with the hair of whales' beards and horse-hair, dyed of different colours. When this plant is green they make large bags of it to contain their fish or different herbs and roots, which they provide against the winter: besides it serves also to thatch their houses or huts. They mow it with a scythe, made out of the shoulder-blade of a whale; which they whet so well by grinding it upon a stone, that they bring it to a very good edge.

In the marshes there is found a plant resembling the cyperoides. This they dress with a double-toothed comb of bone, and use it to wrap their children in instead of shirts or swaddling cloaths, to keep them clean and sweet. They also roll

roll it about their legs, and it serves for stockings. The women wrap it round their bodies, from an opinion that the warmth promotes fruitfulness. It serves to light their fires, being easily kindled. On great holidays they bind garlands of it about the heads and necks of their idols; and when they make any sacrifice, or kill any wild beast, they offer some of this plant as an atonement, that the relations of the beast which is killed may be appeased. Formerly they did the same by the heads of their enemies: after having adorned them with these garlands, they performed several sorceries, and then stuck them upon poles. The Cossacks call this plant *tontchitze*.

Few plants are of more general use than the nettles; for being without any kind of hemp, they would have no materials to make nets of for fishing, which is absolutely necessary for the support of life. They pull them up in the months of *August* or *September*, and binding them in bunches lay them to dry in the shade. When they dress them, they first split them with their teeth, then peel off the skin, and beat them. After this they comb them, then spin them between their hands, and wind them up upon spindles. The thread of the first spinning, they use for sewing, but to make their nets they double and twist it; which, after all, never last above one summer. The truth is they are very ignorant and unskilful in this manufacture; and moreover they neither steep their nettles, nor boil their yarn.

CHAP.

CHAP. VI.

Of the LAND ANIMALS.

THE principal riches of *Kamtſchatka* conſiſt in the great number of wild beaſts: among which are foxes, ſables, ſtone foxes, hares, marmottas, ermins, weaſels, wolves, rein-deer wild and tame, and ſtone rams. Their fox ſkins in the thickneſs, length, and beauty of their hair equal, if not excel, all the foxes of *Siberia*; beſides there are in *Kamtſchatka* almoſt all the different ſpecies of foxes which are to be found in other places, ſuch as the red, fiery, blue-breaſted, or marked with a black croſs, the cheſnut, black cheſnut, and the like; and ſometimes white foxes are found there, but theſe very ſeldom. It is remarkable, that the more valuable foxes are the moſt cunning; ſuch are the black cheſnut, the blue-breaſted, and the fiery coloured; ſo that not only the *Kamtſchadales*, but even the *Ruſſians* find it difficult to catch them. It happened while I was at *Kamtſchatka*, that the Coſſacks tried for two winters to catch one black fox which frequented the Great River, without being able to effect it. The moſt uſual method of taking them is either by poiſon, traps, or bows. The poiſon is thrown in lumps in the freſh tracts; the traps are ſet upon the ſides of hills, baited with a live animal; and for the greater ſecurity two or three of the traps are placed upon one hillock, that whatever way the foxes approach they may fall into one of them; and this is found neceſſary, for thoſe, which have been once in danger from the ſtroke of this trap, proceed afterwards ſo cautiouſly, that they eat the bait without being ſeiſed; but, with all their cunning, it is difficult for them to eſcape the

ſeveral

several traps, which seize them sometimes by the head, and sometimes by the foot. The method of killing them with the bow is thus: the hunters must know exactly how high to place it; when the bow is bent, it is fastened to a stake driven into the earth near which the fox's tract is observed, and then a cord drawn from the bow-string, is stretched very tight over his ordinary path; and so soon as this cord is touched with the foot of the fox, the bow is discharged, and the arrow pierces the very heart. These are the inventions of the *Russian* Cossacks; for formerly the *Kamtschadales* gave themselves no trouble about the foxes, not valuing their furrs much more than dogs' skins. They pretend they could have killed as many as they wanted with sticks, and that foxes were formerly so numerous in *Kamtschatka*, that when they fed their dogs, they were obliged to drive them away from the trough: and though this may seem improbable, yet it is certain, that even now they are in great plenty near the forts, which at night they enter without any seeming apprehension of danger from the dogs of the country, which either cannot catch them, or, not being bred to it, do not mind them. It happened when I was there, that one of the inhabitants catched several of them in the pit where they keep their fish. The best time to hunt foxes is, when the earth is hard frozen, before the snow falls, as it is then difficult for them to dig out the rats' nests, which they do when the earth is thawed, the rats being their chief support. The *Kuriles*, who live upon the *Lopatka*, catch foxes in a manner peculiar to themselves. They have a net made of the hair of whales' beards, composed of several rings; this is spread upon the ground, and to a ring in the middle they bind a magpye; round the net is drawn a cord, the ends of which are held by a person concealed in a pit near at hand, who, when the fox springs upon the bird, draws the cord and gathers together the net, which surrounds the fox as the drag net does a fish.

The

The fables of *Kamtfchatka* excel all other fables of *Siberia*, both in largenefs, thicknefs of hair, and brightnefs; but in point of blacknefs they do not come up to thofe of *Olekmine* and *Vitime*: however their other properties are fo valuable, that the *Kamtfchatka* fables have by much the preference; and in *China*, where they know how to improve the colour, fetch fo great a price that few of them are brought into *Ruffia*. The fables of *Teghil* and *Oukine* are moft efteemed, and are fometimes fold for thirty rubles a pair. Mr. *Steller* fays, that the worft are hunted about the *Lopatka* and *Kurilfkoy* feas. It often happens that the worft kind of fables fhall have their tails fo black and thick haired, that they will fell dearer than any other.

Before the conqueft of *Kamtfchatka* there was fo great a plenty of fables that one hunter would kill feventy or eighty in a year; and that not for the fake of the furr, but the flefh, which they efteem very delicious. The inhabitants at that time willingly agreed to pay their tribute in fables; and were glad to receive a knife for eight, and an ax for eighteen. Some merchants have gained in one year by furrs only more than thirty thoufand rubles. The fables are ftill in much greater plenty here than in any other country, as is obferved by every one who has been upon the fpot, and compared their tracts upon the fnow with what are feen either upon the rivers *Lena* or *Beloy*, and this even in the neighbourhood of the forts. And if the people of *Kamtfchatka* were as induftrious in hunting as thofe about the *Lena*, they could fell a great many more than they; but fuch is their natural lazinefs, that they never kill more than what they muft pay in tribute, and what will pay their debts. They look upon him as an extraordinary good hunter that kills fix or feven fables in a winter; and feveral are not able to furnifh their tribute furrs, but muft borrow either from the *Ruffian* Coffacks, or fome more induftrious hunter of their own country, to whom for payment they are bound to work the whole enfuing fummer. Their baggage when they go to hunt confifts of a net, a bow and arrows, a fire-fteel with flint and tinder. When they find a fable concealed either in the earth or under the root of fome tree, they throw the net over the place, in which he entangles himfelf when he comes out. With the bow and arrows they fhoot them when they fly to the trees; and the fteel and flint are to ftrike fire, by which they fmoke them, and drive them out of their holes. The beft hunters, to be nearer the game, go out with their whole families to the hills, where they build huts and live the whole winter.

Although the ftone foxes, and hares, abound in *Kamtfchatka*, yet hardly any one thinks it worth his trouble to hunt them, their furrs being of fmall value; and when they fall into the fox traps, they ufe their fkins as coverings in their beds. The *Kamtfchatka* ftone foxes are little better than the hares of *Tourouchan*, which are very bad, the hair eafily falling off. *Steller* relates, that fome ufed to few the tails of the ftone foxes to the hare-fkins of *Tourouchan*, and impofe them upon the ignorant as true ftone fox-fkins, the thicknefs of the fkin and furr making it difficult to difcover the cheat.

Marmottas * abound every where in *Kamtfchatka*. The *Koreki* ufe their fkins for cloaths; and, indeed, they are reckoned no ordinary drefs, being both light and warm. *Steller* compares the furrs made of the backs of the marmottas to the fpotted feathers of birds, efpecially if feen at a diftance; and he alfo fays, that this animal is found both upon the continent and the

---

* Marmotta minor. GMEL.

KAMTSCHATKA.

iflands of *America*. When they eat, they fit upon their hind legs like a fquirrel, and hold their food, which is roots, berries, and cedar nuts, with their fore feet. They are pretty to look at, and whiftle furprifingly loud. No body thinks it worth his while to hunt ermines *, weafels †, or common marmottas ‡, unlefs by chance they meet with them; fo that one cannot reckon ermines amongft the furrs of *Kamtfchatka*. But there is a creature of the weafel kind, called the glutton ||, whofe furr is fo greatly efteemed above all others, that when they would defcribe a man moft richly attired, they fay that he is cloathed with the furr of the glutton. The women of *Kamtfchatka* drefs their hair with the white paws of this animal, and reckon them a very great ornament. However, the *Kamtfchadales* kill fo few of them, that they not only have not enough for exportation, but even import fome from *Jakutfki* at a very great price. They put the greater value upon the furr of the glutton the whiter and yellower it is, although every where elfe this fort is defpifed: nay, they efteem it fo much, that they fay the heavenly beings wear no other garments than of this furr; nor can they make their wives or miftreffes a greater prefent than of one of thefe fkins, which was formerly fold for thirty, and even fixty rubles; and for the two paws which the women wear in their hair, they fometimes give one, and fometimes two fea beavers. The greateft number of thefe gluttons is found near *Karaga*, *Andirfka*, and *Kolima*. They have a furprifing dexte-

---

* Ermineum majus. GMEL.
† Ermineum minor. Ejufdem.
‡ Marmotta vulgaris. Ejufdem.

|| Muftella rufo-fufca, medio dorfi nigro. LINN.

rity in killing of deer, which they practife in this manner :—They climb up fome tree, carrying with them a parcel of fuch mofs as the deer ufe to eat. This they let fall from the tree, and if the deer comes to eat it, they throw themfelves down upon his back; then faftening themfelves between the horns, they tear out his eyes, and give him fo much pain, that the miferable animal, to put an end to his torment, or if poffible to free himfelf from the caufe of it by deftroying his enemy, ftrikes his head againft the trees, which generally kills him. No fooner is he brought down than the glutton divides his flefh carefully, and hides it in the earth, to fave it from being feized by any other creature; and never eats a bellyful before he has done this. In the fame manner, upon the river *Lena*, they deftroy horfes. They are eafily tamed, and are capable of learning feveral tricks. It has been faid, but we never heard it afcertained, that they carry their gluttony to fuch a degree as to be obliged to relieve themfelves by fqueezing their over-fwoln bodies between two trees to unburthen their bellies of the infufferable load. Thofe that are tamed are not fo voracious; but perhaps thefe animals are not alike in all countries.

Bears and wolves are fo numerous here, that they fill the woods and fields like cattle; the bears in fummer, and the wolves in winter. The bears of *Kamtfchatka* are neither large nor fierce, and never fall upon people, unlefs they find them afleep; and then they feldom kill any one outright, but moft commonly tear the fcalp from the back part of the head; and, when fiercer than ordinary, tear off fome of the flefhy parts, but never eat them. The people who have been thus wounded, are called *Dranki*, and are frequently to be met with. It is remarked here, that the bears never hurt women; but, in the fummer, go about with them like tame animals,

efpecially

especially when they gather berries. Sometimes, indeed, the bears eat up the berries which the women have gathered, and this is the only injury they do them.

In the season, when the fish enter the mouths of the rivers in vaft shoals, great numbers of bears come down from the hills, and settle in proper places for catching them; which they do in fuch plenty, that they only eat and fuck the bones of the heads, neglecting the bodies; but when this plenty is paft, they are glad to gnaw the bones which they formerly defpifed. They frequently fteal fish from the fishing huts of the Coffacks, although there is always a woman left to watch them. To her indeed they never do any hurt, fatisfying themfelves with what fish they can find.

Before the introduction of fire-arms, they ufed feveral devices for killing the bears. Cutting feveral billets of wood, they ftop up the mouth of the den with them, which the bear draws in, that his paffage may not be fhut up. This they continue until he is fo ftraitened in his den that he cannot turn himfelf; then they dig down from above, and kill him with their fpears. The *Koreki*, in order to catch the bears, feek out fome tree that is crooked above, upon which they faften a fnare, and behind it place fome proper bait; which the bear endeavouring to feize is held faft by the head or the paw. They place heavy logs of wood, in fuch a manner, that they will fall with the leaft touch and crufh them. Another method is to lay a board driven full of iron hooks in the bear s tract, and near to that they place fomething that eafily falls down; this frightening the bear by its fall, he runs upon the board with greater force; and finding firft one fore paw wounded and feized by the hooks, he endeavours to free himfelf by beating the board with the other; thus both being fixed, he refts on his hinder legs, which caufes the board to rife before his eyes,

eyes, and perplexes him in such a manner that he falls in a fury and beats himself to death. The people about the rivers *Lena* and *Ilime* have still a more odd way of catching them. They place a noose upon the bear's tract or entrance to his den, fastened at the end to a large log of wood; when the bear finds himself entangled, and that the log hinders his walking easily, he takes it up, and carrying it to some precipice, he throws it down with great force, which dragging him after it bruises him very much: however, he continues this 'till in the end he kills himself. This last method is somewhat like that which the *Russians* use to preserve their honey from the bears. They hang such a log at the end of a long string upon those trees where the bees are hived; and when the bear, climbing up to get at the hive, finds himself interrupted by the log, he shoves it away; but returning it strikes him again, and obliges him to toss it with greater force, which makes it revert with still greater upon himself. He continues this sport sometimes until he is killed, or falls from the tree.

The making bears drunk and killing them, or hunting them with proper dogs, is so common that I have no occasion to say more about it.

One method is yet to be mentioned, which I have heard from people of reputation; namely that one man will kill such bears as a whole company would be afraid to attack, and that without any other instrument than a stilletto, sharp pointed at both ends, fastened to a thong. The thong he wraps about his right arm up to the elbow; and taking the stilletto in this hand, and the knife in his left, he advances upon the bear, who, as usual, standing upon his hinder legs, and opening his mouth, attacks the hunter: but he, with great resolution and address, thrusts his hand into his throat; and placing there the stilletto, not only prevents him from shutting his mouth, but also gives him such
exquisite

exquisite pain that the bear can make no further resistance, and allows the hunter to lead him wherever he pleases, or stab him with his knife, without any danger.

The *Kamtschadales*, however, look upon it as an affair of such consequence to kill a bear, that whoever has this honour, is obliged to feast all his neighbours; at which entertainment the bear's flesh is the principal dish; and, as a trophy, the bones of the head and thighs are hung round about their huts.

Of the bears' skins they make their beds and coverings, caps, gloves, and collars for their dogs. The flesh and fat are their most delicate food; and the fat, when melted, is thin, and might be very well used with sallad. With the guts they cover their faces in summer to keep off the sun: sometimes they use their skins as shoe-soles, to prevent them from sliding upon the ice; and with their shoulder-blade bones, made sharp, they cut grass.

From the month of *June* to the end of harvest the bears are very fat; but in the spring they are lean and dry. In the stomachs of those killed in the spring nothing is found but a frothy slime: whence the inhabitants maintain the general opinion, that the bear has no food throughout the whole winter, but supports himself by sucking his paws.

Although, as has been related above, wolves abound in *Kamtschatka*, and their furrs are in great esteem for cloaths, yet few are caught there. They differ in nothing from the wolves that are found in other places. By their cunning and fierceness they do more hurt to the inhabitants than their furrs bring profit; for they kill not only the wild deer, but even herds of the tame, notwithstanding the latter have always a watch. Their favourite morsels seem to be the tongues of the deer, or even of the whales that are thrown upon the shore: they sometimes steal the hares and foxes out of the traps and snares. White wolves

wolves are very seldom seen here, and therefore they are much more esteemed than the grey. Although the *Kamtschadales* are called universal eaters, yet they never eat the flesh of either wolves or foxes. The deer and stone rams may be reckoned among the most useful of all the animals in *Kamtschatka*, because their skins are most used in cloathing. The inhabitants, however, kill but few in proportion to the great numbers that are in this country. The deer live in mossy places, and the wild rams upon the highest mountains; so that the hunters of the wild rams leave their dwellings in the beginning of harvest, and taking all their families with them go to the hills, where they are employed in this chase until the month of *December*. The wild rams resemble goats, but their hair is like the deers'. They have two horns that are twisted round like the *Ordinsky* rams, but much larger. The horns of those that are of full age weigh each of them from 25 to 30 pounds. They run very swiftly, throwing their horns back upon their shoulders; spring over rocks, and run upon the narrow ledges of the most dangerous precipices. Cloaths made of their skins are very warm. The fat upon their haunches is equal to that of the deer, and the flesh is a most delicious food. Of the horns they make ladles, spoons, and other small utensils; and the horn entire they carry upon the road at their girdles, and use it for a bottle.

There are three kinds of rats; the first of which is of a brown colour, as large as the greatest house-rats in *Europe*: but their cry is very different, resembling the squeaking of pigs; otherwise they are very like our common rats. Of the second kind there are but few, and these in the houses, where they run about without fear, and live upon any offals. The third sort have a disposition somewhat like the drones among bees, laying up no manner of provision, but stealing their food from the first kind, which live in the fields, woods, and high mountains, in great numbers.

numbers. The tegulchitch, or first kind, have nests very roomy, neat, and spread with grass, divided into different apartments; in some of which they lay up the saranne quite clean, in others rough; in others, again, several sorts of roots, which they gather in summer with great labour, and lay up against winter. In dry sunny days they drag these out of their nests, and dry them. During the summer they live upon berries, and what else they can find proper for their food; never touching their winter provision so long as they can find any food in the fields. Among the several things found in their nests, I observed the saranne, the anacampserus, bistort, goats-beard, burnet, and cedar nuts.

These rats change their habitations like the wandering tartars, and sometimes for a certain number of years they all leave *Kamtschatka*, and go to some other place. This retirement is very alarming to the *Kamtschadales*, who think it forebodes a rainy season and a bad year for the chace: but when these creatures return, they confidently expect a fine one and good hunting; so that, as soon as they begin to re-appear, expresses are sent to all parts to carry the good news. They always take their departure in the spring, first gathering together in vast numbers. They direct their course due west, crossing rivers, lakes, and even arms of the sea; and when, after long swimming, they reach the shore, they lie upon the banks, as if they were dead, 'till at length they recover their strength, and then set out again upon their march. Their greatest danger in the water is lest some ravenous fish should swallow them up: but upon the land they have nothing to fear; and the *Kamtschadales*, who are so greatly interested in their preservation, when they find them weak upon the banks of the rivers or lakes, they give them any assistance in their power. From the river *Pengin* they go southward, and about the middle of *July* they generally reach *Ochotska* and *Judoma*. Sometimes their troop is so numerous

merous that travellers muſt wait two hours before they paſs. They return commonly to *Kamtſchatka* about the month of *October*. It is ſurpriſing that ſuch ſmall animals, in one ſummer, can paſs over ſuch an immenſe tract of land; and one cannot but admire the order and regularity which they obſerve in their march, as well as the foreknowledge they have of the change of weather.

Some of the inhabitants aſſured me, that when they go out of their neſts they cover their proviſions with poiſonous herbs, to deſtroy other rats that may come to rob their ſtore; and that, if all their winter proviſion is taken away, and nothing left that they can eat, in the ſtead of their own ſtores, they ſtrangle themſelves for vexation, ſqueezing their necks between the forked branches of ſhrubs: for which reaſon the *Kamtſchadales* never take away all their ſtore, and even pay for what they take by putting in either dried caviar, or ſomething that will ſerve the poor creatures for ſuſtenance. Although all theſe circumſtances are related by the moſt ſerious of the *Kamtſchadales*, yet we muſt not implicitly rely on their authority, before the facts are better enquired into.

The dogs of *Kamtſchatka* are extreamly like the common village dogs, and are white, black, ſpotted white and black, or grey like the wolves; brown or other colours being very rare. They are eſteemed ſwifter and longer-lived than any other dogs; and this may be attributed to their light ſimple food, which is fiſh. In the ſpring, every one lets his dogs run at liberty, without taking any care about them; for they can be uſed for travelling only while the ſnow is on the ground. They then feed upon what they can get in the fields, where they dig for the mice; and in the rivers they, as well as the bears, catch fiſh. In the month of *October* the *Kamtſchadales* call them home, and tie them up near their huts, 'till they loſe a good deal of their fat, that they may be lighter for the road, and then one

hears

hears their continual howling night and day. In the winter they are fed with opana and fiſh-bones, which are laid up for them in ſummer. The opana is thus prepared :---As much water as they think their dogs want they pour into a large trough, and then throw in ſome ladlefuls of ſour or rather rotten fiſh, which is prepared in pits for this purpoſe, adding to this ſome fiſh-bones, and heating the whole with glowing ſtones until the fiſh and bones be boiled. This opana is reckoned the beſt and moſt agreeable food for the dogs, and they feed them with it only at night, which makes them ſleep well; but never give them any in the day when they deſign to travel, becauſe it would make them heavy and lazy: though they be never ſo hungry they will not touch bread; but rather than that, eat their own bridles, reins, or harneſs, if they can get at them. However fond they may be of their maſter, yet, if he happens to fall out of his ſledge, and loſe his hold of it, they run away without regarding him; and he muſt walk on foot until the ſledge be overturned, or catched and ſtopped by ſomething or other; and therefore he ought to be careful never to loſe his hold, but rather ſubmit to be dragged upon his belly until the dogs tire. Beſides, upon any ſteep deſcent, eſpecially the banks of rivers, one half of them muſt be unyoked, otherwiſe they are not to be managed; for thoſe that appear quite tired ſhew an uncommon vigour in ſuch places, and the more dangerous the deſcent is the more ſtrength they exert. They are in like manner unruly if they find the ſcent of the deer, or hear the howling of other dogs in the villages near at hand. But for all this, the dogs are, and always will be, abſolutely neceſſary in *Kamtſchatka*, even although there ſhould be plenty of horſes; for they could ſeldom be uſed in winter on account of the great depth of ſnow, and the frequency of hills and rivers; and in ſummer, the bogs are ſo frequent, that ſome places are impaſſable even for men. Beſides dogs have this advantage over horſes; that in the greatest storm, when a man cannot see the path, nor even keep his eyes open, they very seldom miss their way; and if they should, they go from one side to the other, 'till by the smell they find it again: and when it is absolutely impossible to travel at all, which often happens, then the dogs lying round their master defend him from all danger. They also give certain signs of an approaching storm; for, when they stop, if they scrape the snow with their feet, it is adviseable, without loss of time, to look out for some village, or other place of safety. And, it is said, the dogs here serve instead of sheep, because their skins are used for cloaths; particularly those of the white dogs, with which all their different sorts of garments are trimed.

The number of dogs they put to a sledge, how they break them, and what weight they carry, shall be mentioned hereafter, when we come to describe the manner of travelling with dogs.

Those which are bred up to hunt the deer and wild rams, sables, foxes, and the like, are sometimes fed with jackdaws, which, it is observed, make their scent the stronger for finding out birds and wild beasts.

Besides dogs, they have here cows and horses, but no other domestic animals. There is no fit place to feed sheep on, either upon the Eastern Ocean, or the sea of *Pengine*; for the wet weather and the strong juicy grass would soon rot and destroy them. Near the upper *Ostrog*, and upon the river *Kosireff*, sheep thrive; the weather being fairer, and grass less watry; but then there must be a good provision of hay made for them against the winter, the snow being too deep for them to find their food in the fields; for which reason, from the mouth of the river *Ilga* to *Jakutski*, very few sheep are kept.

CHAP.

CHAP. VII.

Of the VITIMSKY SABLES, *and the Method of hunting them.*

ALTHOUGH the sable-hunting of *Vitimsky* does not properly belong to the description of *Kamtschatka*, yet as in treating of the latter we have had occasion to mention the sable, I thought it might not be amiss to give an account of the various methods of this chace in different places. The *Kamtschadales* do not stir out for a fortnight or more after a piece of ill-luck, or having hunted one day without game; but the *Vitimsky* hunters spend almost the whole year in continual toil, and are very happy, if, in that time, they catch ten sables for each man in company. It is true indeed, that ten common *Vitimsky* sables are equal to forty of *Kamtschatka*: but, notwithstanding, if the inhabitants of *Kamtschatka* would take the same pains as those of *Vitimsky*, they might exceed them in the profits of hunting; for sables are as numerous in *Kamtschatka* as squirrels are upon the river *Lena*. The *Vitimsky* hunting is the more remarkable for being subject to many rigorous laws and superstitious observations, which the hunters bind themselves to observe.

Before *Siberia* was conquered by the *Russians*, it abounded with sables; but, at present, wherever the *Russians* are settled, none can be catched; for sables retire at a distance from all inhabited places, and live in desolate woods and mountains. The sable hunters go up by the river *Vitime* and the two rivers *Muma*, which fall into that river, as far as to the lake *Oronne*, which is upon the right hand, as high and higher than the great cataract, where the best hunting is. The finest sables are caught

upon

upon the little river *Kutomale*, which falls into the river *Vitime*, upon the right hand above the cataract and mouths of the lower *Mama* and the brook *Petrova*. Lower than these places the sables are considerably worse; and all the hunters agree that nearer the heads of the rivers the sables are better, and nearer the mouths still worse.

The sables live in holes, like other animals of their kind; such as martins, weasles, and ermines. The hunters also relate, that they build themselves nests upon the trees with rods and grass; that they sometimes lie in their nests and sometimes in their holes; that in summer as well as in winter they lie about twelve hours in their holes or nests, and in the other twelve they go about to seek their food. In the summer time, before the berries are ripe, they feed upon weasels, ermines, or squirrels, but chiefly upon hares; and in the winter upon birds. When the berries ripen, they eat cranberries and hurtleberries, but principally those of the service-tree, which causes them to itch and rub themselves against the trees, by which they wear off the hair from their sides. Hence it happens, when the service-berries are very plentiful, that the hunters lose their labour.

The sables bring forth their young in their holes or nests, about the end of *March* or the beginning of *April*; and have from three to five at a time, which they give suck to from four to six weeks.

They never hunt sables but in winter, for in the spring they cast their hair; which in the summer is very short, and even in the harvest does not come to perfection. Such sables are called *nedasobili*; that is, imperfect sables; and sell at a low price.

The sable-hunters, both *Russians* and natives, begin to set out for hunting about the end of *August*. Some *Russians* go themselves, and others hire people to hunt for them, giving them proper cloaths and instruments for hunting, and provisions for the time of their being out. When they return from the

chace

chace they give their masters all their game, and restore them likewise all that they received, except their provisions.

A company, that agrees to hunt together, assembles from six to forty men, though formerly there were sometimes even fifty. They provide a small boat for every three or four men, which they cover over; and take with them such persons as understand the language of the people amongst whom they go to hunt, and likewise the places properest for hunting. These persons they maintain at the publick charge, and give them besides an equal share of the game.

In the above-mentioned boats every hunter lays 30 poods of rye-flower, of wheat-flower one pood, of salt one pood, and of groats a quarter of a pood. Every two men must have a net, a dog, and seven pood of provisions for the dog, a bed and covering, a vessel for preparing their bread, and a vessel to hold leaven. They carry out very few fire-arms, as they only use them in the harvest, while they live in their huts.

The above-mentioned boats they draw against the stream of the *Vitime*, and out of the *Vitime* up the river *Mama*, or as far up as the lake *Oronne*, where they build huts for themselves if they find none ready. Here they all assemble, and live until the river be frozen over. In the mean time they chuse for their chief leader one who has been oftenest upon these expeditions; and to his orders they profess an entire obedience. He divides the company into several small parties, and names a leader to each, except his own, which he himself directs: he also appoints the places where each party must hunt. As soon as the season begins, this division into small parties is unalterable, even although the whole company should consist only of eight or ten, for they never all go towards the same place. When their leaders have given them their orders, every small company digs pits upon that road which they must go. In these pits they lay up for every two men three bags of flower against their return, when

they

they shall have consumed all their other provisions; and whatever they have left in their huts, they are obliged to hide also in pits, lest the wild inhabitants should steal it.

As soon as the rivers are frozen over, and the season is proper for the sable-hunting, the chief of the leaders calls all the huntsmen into the hut, and, having prayed to God, gives orders to every chief of each small company, and dispatches them the same road which was before assigned them. Then the leader sets out one day before the rest to provide lodging places for them.

When the chief leader dispatches the under leaders he gives them several orders; one of which is, that each should build his first lodging to the honour of some church, which he names, and the other lodging places to the honour of such saints whose images they have with them; and that the first sable they catch should be laid aside in the quarter of the church, and at their return be presented to it. These sables they call God's sables, or the church's. The first sable that is caught in the quarter of each saint is given to the person who brought the image of that saint with him.

On their march they support themselves with a wooden crutch about four feet long; upon the end of which they put a cow's horn, to keep it from being split by the ice, and a little above they bind it round with a with and thongs, to hinder it from running too deep into the snow. The upper part is broad like a spade, and serves to shovel away the snow, or to take it up and put it into their kettles; for they must use snow, as they have frequently no water. The principal chief, having dispatched the several small parties, sets out with his own. When they come to their places of lodging they build little huts of trees, and bank up the snow round them. They hew several trees upon the road, that they may the more easily find their way in the winter. Near every quarter they prepare their trap-pits, each of which

which is surrounded with sharp stakes, about six or seven feet high, and about four feet distant, and is covered over with boards to prevent the snow from falling in. The entrance through the stakes is narrow, and over it a board is hung so nicely, that by the least touch of the sables it turns and throws them into the trap; and they must absolutely go this way to reach a piece of fish or flesh with which the traps are baited. The hunters stay in one lodging until they have made a sufficient number of these traps, every hunter being obliged to make twenty in a day; and so many do they make at every lodging place where they expect sables. When they have passed ten of these quarters the leader sends back the half of his company to bring up the provisions that were left behind, and with the remainder he advances to build more huts and make more traps.

The people sent back for the provisions go with empty sledges to the places where they were hoarded. Every man is obliged to draw six poods of flower, and half a pood of flesh or fish, and to overtake the other hunters and their chief. These carriers must stop at all the lodging places to see that their traps are in order, and take out any sables they may find in them, and skin them, which none must pretend to do but the chief man of the company.

If the sables are frozen, they thaw them by laying them under the cloaths with themselves in bed. When the skin is taken off all present sit down and are silent, being careful that nothing be hanging on the stakes. The skinned body of the sable is laid upon dry sticks, which they afterwards light; and carrying them three times round the body, they smoke it, and then bury it in the snow or earth. And often, when they apprehend the *Tungusi* may meet with them and take away their booty, they put the skins into pieces of wood hollowed, covering the ends with snow, which being wetted will soon freeze. These they hide in the snow near their huts, and gather them up when they return in a body. When these carriers are come back with the provisions then the other half are sent for more; and thus they are employed in hunting, the leader always going before to build traps. When they find few sables in their traps they hunt with nets, which they can only do when they find the fresh track of a sable in the snow. This they follow until it brings them to the hole where the sable has entered; or if they lose it near other holes, they put smoaking pieces of rotten wood to them, which generally forces him to leave the earth. The hunter at the same time has spread his net, into which the sable commonly falls; and for precaution his dog is also near at hand: thus the hunter sits and waits sometimes two or three days. They know when the sable falls into the net by the sound of two very small bells that are fastened to it. Upon this the hunter runs himself, and puts on the dog, which seizes the sable and kills it: but they never put smoaky pieces of wood into those holes that have only one opening, because the sable will sooner be smothered than come towards the smoke; in which case he is entirely lost.

When they trace the sable to the root of some tree, they fasten their net about the tree, that, if after digging him out he should escape their hands, he may be taken in it. If the track goes towards some tree where they can see the sable, they shoot him with a blunt arrow: but if they cannot see the sable upon the tree among the branches, they cut it down, and placing their net where the top of the tree is to fall, which they can judge, stand themselves near the trunk; and the sable, jumping from it as it falls, drops into the net. Sometimes this does not happen, and then they search every hollow part of the tree. A sable that has once been in a net or trap is scarcely to be deceived a second time.

When the chief leader and all the hunters are gathered together, then the leaders of the small parties report to the chief

how

how many sables or other beasts their party has killed, and if any of their parties have done any thing contrary to his orders and the common laws. These crimes they punish differently: some they tie to a stake, others they oblige to ask pardon of every one of the company; a thief they beat severely, and allow him no share of the booty; nay, they even take his own baggage from him, and divide it among themselves. They remain in their head-quarters until the rivers are free of ice; and after the hunting they employ their time in preparing the skins. As soon as the ice is all gone off the rivers, they set out, in those little boats which they came in, on their return home, where they give the sables to the several churches to which they promised them; and then, having paid their tax-furrs, they sell the rest, dividing equally the money, or goods, which they receive for them.

CHAP. VIII.

Of the SEA BEASTS.

UNDER the name of sea beasts are here understood such animals as are called amphibious, which, although they live for the most part in the water, frequently come upon the dry land, and upon, or near it, bring forth their young. Water beasts may be divided into three classes: 1st, Those which live in fresh water lakes, and rivers, as the otter. 2d, Those which live in fresh or salt water, such as seals. 3d, Those which are never found in fresh water, such as sea beavers, sea cats, and others.

Although otters be very common in *Kamtschatka*, yet the price is not low; a very indifferent skin will cost a ruble. They
commonly

commonly hunt them with dogs when the snow comes in drifts, and they wander at too great a distance from the river. They use their skins to make borders round their garments, but principally to preserve the sable-skins, which are observed to be preserved better, when wrapt in otter-skins than any other way.

It is incredible to think what a number of seals there are in the seas and lakes of that country, especially when the fish come up the rivers, which they follow in droves, not only to the mouth, but even far up the stream. So numerous are they that all the islands or sand-banks are quite covered with them, insomuch that small boats are in great danger near these places. When the seals observe any boat approaching they throw themselves in great numbers into the water, which makes such a motion in it as will overset the canoes or small boats, if they go at once into it. No animal has a more disagreeable cry, and their noise is incessant.

There are reckoned to be four sorts of this animal; the very largest of which is catched from 56° to 64° of north latitude. This sort only differs from the others in its bulk, which exceeds that of a large ox. The second species is about the size of a yearling bullock. Their skin is of different colours, something like the skin of a tyger; having several spots of equal largeness on the back, with a white and yellowish belly. Their young ones are as white as snow. The third is yet less than the former. Its skin is yellowish, with large cherry-coloured circles, which take up near the half of its surface. The fourth kind is seen in the large lakes of *Baikaal* and *Oronne*. Its size is like those that are found near *Archangel*; and their colour is whitish.

They are very vivacious: I saw one, that was taken by a hook in the mouth of the Great River, throw itself upon people with great fierceness, even after its skull was broken into pieces. I observed that he was no sooner brought on shore than

than he began to try to run again into the river; and when he found that this was impossible, he began to weep; and when they beat and bruised him, it only made him more fierce and wild.

The seals never go farther from the shore than 30 leagues; and are most commonly to be found near the mouths of great rivers or bays: they will follow the fish 80 versts up a river. They bring forth only one young one, which they nourish with two breasts. The *Tungusi* give the seals' milk to their children for a medicine. The old seals cry like one that strains in vomiting, and the young like people groaning through pain. When the tide goes out they lie upon the dry rocks, and in play push one another into the water; but when they begin to be angry they bite one another very cruelly. They sleep very sound: but, being awakened by the approach of any one, they are in very great fear; and hastening towards the sea, to make the way smoother, as is supposed, they vomit out water.

There are different ways of killing them: In the rivers they shoot them with screwed-barrelled guns; but they must be careful to hit the head, because a hundred bullets will not do them the least hurt in any other place, as they all lodge in the fat that covers their body. They search for them upon shore, and surprising them in their sleep kill them with clubs: or when they sleep, laying their snout upon the ice, they drive a knife quite through the snout, which being fastened to a long thong they drag the animal out.

The seals are not so dear as one would imagine the many uses they put them to should render them; for, besides the use of their fat and flesh, the skins of the larger sort serve for soles of shoes. The *Koreki*, *Olutores*, and the *Tchukotskoi*, also make boats or baidares with them of different sizes, some even so large that they will carry thirty men. These boats have this advantage over those made of timber, in that they are much lighter and go swifter. Of the seals' fat both *Russians* and *Kamtschadales* make candles; and besides the natives esteem it such a delicacy that they can have no feast without it. The flesh they boil or dry in the sun; but if there are great quantities, they smoke or bake it in the following manner: They dig a large pit in proportion to the quantity of flesh or fat, and pave the bottom with stones. Then they fill it with wood and light it below, continuing to add fuel until it be as hot as any oven. After which they take out all the ashes, then lay at the bottom a layer of green poplar wood, upon this another of seals' flesh or fat, each separately; and thus alternately wood and flesh until the pit be quite full. They then cover it with grass and earth, to keep in the heat; and after some hours they uncover it, take out the fat and flesh, and lay it up for the winter. Both flesh and fat thus prepared is much more delicate than what is boiled; besides, it keeps without spoiling for a whole year.

When they have picked all the flesh from the heads of the seals they shew them all the respect that they would to a particular friend that visits them. I saw this ceremony in the year 1740 at the little fort of *Krodakighe*, which stands upon a river of the same name that falls into the Eastern Ocean. It was performed in the following manner: They brought in the skull or head of a seal, bound round with the sweet grass, and placed it upon the floor. Then a *Kamtschadale* entered with a bag filled with the sweet herbs and others, particularly a good deal of birch bark, and placed it near the head; upon which two other *Kamtschadales* rolled in a great stone, and set it opposite to the entry of the hut, about which they laid several stones; and two others tore the sweet herb, and made it into small bunches. The great stone was to signify the sea, the smaller the waves, and the bunches of the sweet herb the seals. This being done, they took three dishes of caviar mixed with kipre, hurtleberries, and seals' fat

fat. This they squeezed into balls, in the middle of which they pressed the sweet herbs which were made to represent the seals: out of the birch bark they made little boats, which they filled with these balls made as above, and covered them with herbs.

After some time they took these boats and balls and tossed them to and fro over the stones as if over waves, that the other seals might see with what respect the *Kamtschadales* treated their friends, and consequently might the more willingly fall into their hands. After this they placed the seals made of the sweet herbs near to the great stone, or sea, and all went out of the hut; but one old man, after he had set upon the threshold a small dish with their broth which he had carried behind them, entered into it again, all the assistants crying aloud four times the word *Lignouleghe*. They could not tell what this term meant; nor could they give any other reason for their so crying out, but that their fathers did so. After this they again rolled the birch boats upon the stones; and going again out of the hut cried, as before, *Kouneoushite aloulaighe*; that is, May the wind blow towards the shore. For while this wind blows a great deal of ice is driven towards the land, which is favourable for their killing the sea animals. Returning into their huts, they rolled their birch boats a third time over the stones. They then put the skulls of the seals into a bag, and every fisher present put in also a little of the sweet grass, with his name and some particular sentence; that the seals might know how they had entertained them, and what valuable presents they had made them.

Having, as they thought, by their entertainment and presents, shewn all respects to their guests, they brought them out to the stair-head, where an old man put still some more of their gruel into the bag, desiring them to carry that to their friends that had been drowned at sea. Then two *Kamtschadales* who had been principally employed in this entertainment, took the bowls that
were

were filled with gruel and the feals made of grafs, and gave one to each fifher. They then went all out of the hut, and cried *Uenic*; a word they ufe in calling to one another when they go to kill the feals or other fea animals. Then taking out the feals made of grafs they threw them into the fire, praying them to make them frequent vifits; after which, returning into the hut, they put out the fire, and eat the gruel that was in the bowls.

The fea horfe is but feldom feen about *Kamtfchatka*, and then only in the moft northernly places. The moft are caught near the cape of *Tchukotfkoi*, being both larger and more numerous there than any where elfe. Their teeth are what we commonly call fifh-bone, the price of which depends upon their largenefs or weight: the deareft are thofe that are about twenty pounds; but thefe are feldom met with, or even fuch as weigh ten or twelve pounds, the common weight being five or fix pounds.

The fea lion * and cat, in their ufual ftructure, differ very little from the fea horfe and fea calf, and are therefore to be reckoned of the fame kind.

Some call the fea lions fea horfes, becaufe they have manes. In their fhape they are like the fea calf; and their necks are bare, excepting a fmall mane of hard curled hairs: the reft of their body is covered with a chefnut-coloured hair. They have a middle-fized head, fhort ears, a fnout fhort and drawn up like a pug dog's, great teeth, and webbed feet. They are found moft frequently about rocky fhores or rocks in the fea, upon which they climb very high, in great numbers. They roar in a ftrange, frightful manner, much louder than the fea calf; and they are thus far of ufe to people at fea, that in foggy weather, by their roaring, they warn them of rocks or iflands being near, as few rocks or iflands in this part of the world are without thefe animals.

* Leo marinus. STELLER.

Although in appearance and size this animal seems to be very dangerous, and marches with such a fierce mien that he looks like a true lion, yet is he such a coward, that at the sight of a man he hurries into the water; and when he is surprised asleep, and awakened either by a loud cry or blows with a club, he is in such fear and confusion, that in running away he falls down, all his joints quaking with terror; but, when he finds no possibility of escaping, he will then attack his enemy with the greatest fierceness, shaking his head and roaring very terribly; and then the boldest must seek to save himself from his rage. For this reason the *Kamtschadales* seldom kill the sea lions at sea, unless when they can surprise them sleeping there, but generally upon land; and when they find them asleep on shore they approach them with great caution, going against the wind. But none dare undertake this game, but such as can trust to their strength or their heels. Stealing upon them, they strike a knife into their breast under their fore paw; the assistants in the mean time tying a cord made of sea calf's skin, which is fastened to the knife, about a stake. Then every one runs off as fast as he can, and endeavours at a distance to wound him with arrows, or knives, which they dart at him; and at last, when his strength is quite wasted, they dispatch him with clubs.

When they find them asleep at sea, they shoot poisoned arrows at them, and get off as fast as possible. The wounded animal, unable to suffer the pain arising from the salt water in the poisoned wound, runs himself ashore, where they kill him outright with darts or arrows; or if the place is not safe for such an attack, they wait until he dies of his first wound, which follows in 24 hours. This game is so honourable among the natives, that the man who has killed most of these beasts is esteemed the greatest hero: for this reason many engage in this dangerous hunting, not only for the flesh, which is looked upon as very delicate, but rather for the honour that attends it. Two or three

three sea lions are a great load for their boats; and, as it is esteemed dishonourable to leave any game which they have caught, they sometimes so overload their boats, that, though they are very expert in the management of them, they and their game go to the bottom together. In these vessels they go to the desert island *Alaide*, which lies out at sea about thirty miles, and are sometimes carried four, five, and even eight days without seeing any land, exposed to the cold of these climates; and without any compass, they return to their habitations by observing the sun or moon.

Of the skins of the sea lion they make cords, shoe-soles, and shoes. The female has two, three, and sometimes four young ones. They couple in the months of *August* or *September*; and are pregnant about ten months, as they generally bring forth their young about the beginning of *July*. The male treats the female with great tenderness, not like the sea cat, but by fondness endeavours to gain her affection. Both male and female seem to take very little care of their young, frequently stifling them under their paws as they suck; nor do they shew any concern at seeing them killed before their eyes. The young are not lively nor full of play, like most other young animals, but are almost continually asleep. Towards the evening the male and female swim out to sea with their brood, but not far from the shore. The young climb upon the mother's back, and rest themselves; the male in the mean time playing about tosses the lazy puppies into the water, to oblige them to learn to swim. Some of them have been thrown into the sea, but instead of swimming away they hasten again to land. They are twice as large as the young of the sea cat.* Although these animals naturally run from a man, yet it has been observed that they are not always so wild; particularly when their young have scarcely learned to swim. Mr. *Steller* lived six days in a high place amongst whole herds of them, and out of his hut saw

several

several of their actions. The animals lay around him, seeming to observe his fire and what he was employed about; and never ran away, although he even went amongst them, and seized some of their young for his dissections, but remained quite at their ease. They went about and quarrelled for their mistress without being disturbed by his presence; and one male fought three days for a female, and was wounded in more than a hundred places. The sea cats never take any part in their quarrels, but endeavour to get out of the way as far as they can, giving place to them; nay, they never hinder the puppies of the sea lion from playing with them, taking all care not to hurt them in the least: but the sea cats shun the company of the sea lions as much as possible.

The old beasts are grey about the head, and certainly live to a great age. They scratch their head and ears with their hinder paw, as the sea cats do; and their manner of standing, going, lying, and swimming, is the same. The great ones low like an ox, and the young bleat like sheep: the old ones send forth a stinking smell, but not so much as the sea cat. In winter and summer they do not always live indifferently upon all places, but seem to have their stations proper for the season. They are never found further north than 56°, although in great plenty about *Kamtschatka*, and the islands of the *American* coast. Their food is fish, seals, sea beavers, or other water or land animals. The old ones eat little in the months of *June* or *July*, when they only lie and sleep, and thence become very lean.

The sea cat is about half the size of the sea lion; in form resembling the seal *, but thicker about the breast, and thinner

---

* *Frederick Marten*, in his voyage to *Greenland*, thus describes the sea dogs, called *Rubbs* or *Seals*: 'Their teeth are 'sharp like dog's teeth; on their toes 'they have black, long, and sharp 'claws; their tail is short; they bark 'like hoarse dogs, but their young mew 'like cats. When they are frightened
by

towards the tail. They have a snout longer than the sea lion's, and larger teeth; with eyes like cows' eyes, short ears, naked and black paws, and black hair mixed with grey, which is short and brittle. Their young are of a bluish black colour.

The sea cats are caught in the spring and in the month of *September*, about the river *Shupanova*; at which times they go from the *Kurilskoy* island to the *American* coast: but the most

' by any noise, they hold up their noses
' very high, and make a long neck like
' our greyhounds, and bark; and when
' thus alarmed we strike them with half
' pikes, or long poles, upon their noses,
' and knock them down half dead; but
' for all that they will recover them-
' selves and rise again. Some of them
' will stand on their defence, bite at,
' and run after us. Sometimes they run
' from the ice to the water, and leave a
' yellow dung behind them which they
' squirt out at their hunters. Their fat
' is about three or four fingers thick,
' and covers the flesh just under the skin.
" They have great livers, lungs, and
' hearts When they couple they are so
' fierce, that we are obliged to kill
' them from our boats, no man daring
' to go near them. One of them near
' eight feet long was not killed, though
" we had cut off most of his fat, and
" notwithstanding all our blows would still
" bite and snap at us I ran another
" several times through the body with
" my sword, which he did not in the
" least regard, he at last got up, and
" ran swifter than I could, and flung him-
" self off from the ice into the sea, and
" went down to the bottom.

From the same author we have also the following account of the sea horse It

' is imagined that these animals, says he,
' feed both on herbs and fish; that they
' eat herbs we conclude from the resem-
' blance between their dung and that of
' the horses', and we suppose they eat
' fish from this circumstance, when we
' threw the skin and fat of a whale into
' the sea, one of these creatures came and
' drew it under water with him. They
' are remarkable for their courage and
' strength, and the resolution with which
' they defend each other is surprising; for
' when any were wounded by my people,
' they made to the long boat, and with
' their great teeth cut holes in it under
' water, whilst others most undauntedly
' erected half their body out of the water
' and endeavoured to get into the boat.
' In one of these engagements a sea horse
' took hold of our harpooneer with his
' long tooth by the waistband of his
' breeches; and had not the waistband
' broke, would certainly have pulled
' him over-board. At *Muff*'s island we
' killed several hundred of them, and
' made a very good voyage. When
" they are killed the sailors only bring
" off the head, as nothing but the two
" great teeth are of any value; these
" also were formerly in greater estimation
" than they are at present.'

are

are catched about the cape of *Kronotzkoy*, as between this and the cape *Shupinskoy* the sea is generally calm, and affords them properer places to retire to. Almost all the females that are caught in the spring are pregnant; and such as are near their time of bringing forth their young are immediately opened, and the young taken out, and skinned. None of them are to be seen from the beginning of *June* to the end of *August*, when they return from the south with their young. The natives were formerly at a loss to conceive where such great herds of pregnant fat animals retired in the spring, and why they returned so weak and lean in the summer: they conjectured, that as they thus regularly swam from the south in the spring, and returned in the summer, their being so lean was owing to their fatigue.

The females bring forth their young there, and being at rest recover their former strength; they nurse their young ones three months, 'till they are able to return with them to their former habitations in the summer. The females suckle their young with two teats, which are placed between their hinder paws; they have seldom more than one; and when they bring forth they gnaw off the navel string like a dog, and greedily eat the after-birth. The young see when they are whelped, their eyes being as large as the eyes of an ox; and have thirty-two teeth, not reckoning their tusks, two of which are on each side, and begin to appear the fourth day after their birth. Their colour at the first is a dark blue; but in four or five days grey hairs begin to appear between their hinder legs, and at the end of one month their belly is black and grey. The male is born larger and blacker, and even continues blacker than the female, which turns almost of a blue colour as she grows up, having only grey spots between her fore legs. The male and female differ so much in the form and strength of their bodies, that one who does not carefully examine them would take them for different species of animals; befides the females are mild and fearful. The male has from eight to fifteen, and even fometimes fifty females, whom he guards with fuch jealoufy that he does not allow any other to come near his miftreffes: and though many thoufands of them lie upon the fame fhore, yet every family keeps apart; that is, the male, with his wives, young ones, and thofe of a year old, which have not yet attached themfelves to any male; fo that fometimes the family confifts of 120. They likewife fwim at fea in fuch droves. Such as are old, or have no miftreffes, live apart; and the firft that our people found upon *Bering*'s ifland were fuch old ones, and all males, extremely fat and ftinking. Thefe fometimes lie afleep a whole month without nourifhment, and are the fierceft of all, attacking all that pafs them; and their pride or obftinacy is fuch that they will rather die than quit their place. When they fee a man coming near them, fome of them rufh upon him, and others lie ready to fuftain the battle. They bite the ftones that are thrown at them, and rufh the more violently upon him who throws them; fo that though you ftrike out their teeth with ftones, or put out their eyes, yet even blind they will not quit their place: nay, they dare not leave it, for every ftep that any one moves off he makes a new enemy, fo that though he could fave himfelf from the attacks of men, his own brethren would deftroy him; and if it happens that any one feems to retire the leaft, then others draw near no prevent his running away; and if any one feems to fufpect the courage of another, or his defign to run away, he falls upon him. This fufpicion of one another is fometimes carried fo far, that for a whole verft one fees nothing but thefe bloody duels; and at fuch a time one may pafs them without any manner of danger. If two fall upon one, then fome others come to fupport the weakeft; for they do not allow of unequal combat. During thefe battles the others that are fwimming in the fea raife their heads, and look at the fuccefs of of the combatants; at length becoming likewife fierce, they come out and increafe the number.

Mr. *Steller* made this experiment :---With his Coffacks he fell upon one of thefe fea cats, and put out his eyes, and irritated four or five more by throwing ftones at them. When thefe purfued him he ran towards the blind one, who hearing the running of his companions, and not knowing whom they purfued, attacked them. Mr. *Steller* retired to a high place, where he obferved the battle for fome hours. The blind one attacked without diftinction all the reft, even thofe who took his part; fo that at laft they all fell upon him, and allowed him no reft either upon the land or in the fea, out of which they dragged him to the fhore, and beat him until he died.

When two of them only fight, the battle lafts frequently for an hour: fometimes they reft awhile, lying by one another; then both rife at once, and renew the engagement. They fight with their heads erect, and turn them afide from one another's ftroke. So long as their ftrength is equal they fight with their fore paws; but when one of them becomes weak the other feizes him with his teeth, and throws him upon the ground. When the lookers on fee this they come to the affiftance of the vanquifhed. The wounds they make with their teeth are as deep as thofe made with a fabre; and in the month of *July* you will hardly fee one of them that has not fome wound upon him. After the end of the battle they throw themfelves into the water to wafh their bodies. The occafions of their quarrels are thefe: ---The firft and moft bloody is about their females, when one endeavours to carry off the miftrefs of another, or the young ones that are females; the females that are prefent follow the conqueror. The fecond is about their places, when one comes too near that of another, which they don't allow, either for want of room, or becaufe they are jealous of their coming too near

their

their mistresses. The third is owing to their endeavouring to do justice, and end the quarrels of others.

The male is very fond of the young ones; on the other hand, the females and young fear him extremely, and he treats them most tyrannically. If you endeavour to catch a young one, the male stands upon the defence, and the female is allowed to save herself and the young one by flight; but if she drops the young one out of her mouth, the male leaves his enemy, and seizing upon her with his teeth beats her against the stones 'till he leaves her for dead. As soon as she recovers, she crawls to his feet, which she licks and washes with her tears that flow in abundance. In the mean time, the male stalks backwards and forwards, gnashing his teeth, and tossing his head like a bear; at last, when he sees they have carried off the young one, he likewise begins to weep; for they shed tears, when they are much wounded or injured, and are not able to revenge the injury.

Another reason of the sea cats going in the spring eastwards to the Desert Islands must be, that resting and sleeping without nourishment for three months, they free themselves from the fat which was troublesome to them, in the same manner as the bears who live the whole winter without nourishment; for in the months of *June*, *July*, and *August*, the old ones do nothing but sleep upon the shore, lying in one place like a stone, now and then looking at one another, and yawning and stretching, without meat or drink; but the young ones begin to walk in the beginning of *July*. When this animal lies upon the shore and diverts himself, his lowing is like that of a cow; when he fights, he growls like a bear; when he has conquered his enemy, he chirps like a cricket; but being vanquished or wounded, he groans or mews like a cat; coming out of the water, he commonly shakes himself, strokes his breast with his hinder paws, and smooths the hair upon it. The male lays his snout to that

of

of the females, as if he was kissing her. When they sleep in the sun, they hold up their paws, wagging them as the dogs do their tails. They lie sometimes upon their backs, at other times like a dog upon their bellies; sometimes contracting, at other times extending themselves. Their sleep is never so sound but that they awake at the approach of any person, how softly soever he goes, and are presently upon their guard; besides their smell and hearing are surprisingly acute.

They swim so fast that they can easily make ten versts in an hour and when they happen to be wounded at sea they seize the boats of the fishers with their teeth, and drag them along with such swiftness that they appear to fly and not to swim upon the water. By this means the boat is frequently overturned and the people drowned, unless he who steers it be very skilful, and observes the course of the animal. As they have a *foramen ovale*, they can keep long under water; but when they grow weak they come to the top to receive fresh air. They often swim upon their back, and so near the surface of the water that their hinder paws are frequently dry. When they go from the shore into the water, or when they dive after having taken breath, they turn themselves like a wheel, as many other large sea animals do. They fasten their fore paws in the rocks, and thus draw up their body, which they can move but slowly in such places, but upon a plain, one is in danger of being overtaken by them. Upon *Bering*'s island there are such numbers of them that they cover the whole shore; so that travellers are frequently obliged for safety to leave the sands and level country, and go over the hills and rocky places. It is remarkable that in this island the sea cats are found only upon the south coast which looks towards *Kamtschatka*. The reason of this may be, that this is the first land they meet with going east from the *Kronotzkoy* Noss.

The manner of catching them in *Bering*'s island was this: They first struck out their eyes with stones, and then killed them by beating out their brains with clubs: but this was a work of so much labour, that three men were hardly able to kill one with 300 strokes; and though sometimes the skull was broken in pieces, and the brains came out, and all their teeth beaten out, yet they would keep their place, standing upon their hinder paws, endeavouring to defend themselves. One of them thus miserably treated was left to see how long it would live, which it did full two weeks without quitting its place. They seldom come ashore about *Kamtschatka*; so that the inhabitants chace them in boats, and throw darts or harpoons at them, which stick in their body; to this harpoon is fixed one end of a rope, and the other is in the vessel; and by this rope they draw them towards the boat; but here they are to be particularly cautious whenever they chace one, if he comes near, not to suffer him to fasten upon the side of the boat with his fore paws, and overturn it; to prevent which some of the fishermen stand ready with axes to cut off his paws. Several of these animals die of old age, but the greatest part of the wounds they receive in the quarrels that happen among them; of which there are sometimes so many, that the shore is covered with bones.

The sea beavers * have not the least resemblance of the other beavers; but the people formerly gave them that name from their downy hair, which resembles that of the beaver. They are as large as the sea cats; their shape resembles the seal, and their head the bear; their fore feet are longer than their hind feet; their teeth small; their tail short and flat, and sharp towards the point; their hair is thick and black as pitch,

---

Lutra marina.

but

but in the old ones it turns grey. The young ones have their hair long, brownish, and very soft. This is the most peaceable of all the sea animals; it never makes any resistance, but endeavours to save itself by flight. The females are very affectionate to their young, and carry such as cannot swim upon their belly between their fore feet; for until the little ones can swim themselves the mother swims upon her back. When the fishermen pursue them, they never quit their young' till the very last extremity; and if they should happen to slip them they presently return to where they hear them cry; so that the fishers endeavour to kill or catch the young, as the most effectual method of taking their dams. They have three different ways of catching them: 1st. By nets placed among the sea cabbage*, whither the beavers retire in the night time, or in storms. 2dly, They chace them in their boats, when the weather is calm, and kill them in the same manner they do sea lions or sea cats. The third method is upon the ice, which in the spring is driven on the coast by the east wind; and this last is so general, that when the ice is driven so strongly upon the shore that the people can pass upon it with snow shoes, they consider it as an acquisition of great treasure, and all the inhabitants upon the coast hunt and kill vast numbers, as they stalk along the ice seeking an opening to get into the water. However, such a drift of ice upon the coast does not happen every year, but when it does, they call it a good year; for the natives, Cossacks, and merchants, find a great advantage from this trade. The *Kuriles* did not esteem the skins of beavers more than those of seals or sea lions before they saw the value that the *Russians* put upon them; and even now they will willingly exchange a dress made of beavers'

* Fucus marinus.

for a good one made of dogs' skins, which they think are warmer, and a better defence against the water.

Besides those already described, there are several other sea animals here, the most remarkable of which is the manati, or sea cow. This animal never comes out upon the shore, but always lives in the water; its skin is black and thick, like the bark of an old oak, and so hard that one can scarcely cut it with an axe; its head in proportion to its body is small, and falls off from the neck to the snout, which is so much bent that the mouth seems to lie below; towards the end the snout is white and rough, with white whiskers about nine inches long; it has no teeth, but only two flat white bones, one above, the other below; its nostrils are near the end of its snout, in length and breadth about an inch and a half; they are double, and within are rough and hairy; its eyes are black, placed almost in the middle, and near in one line with the nostrils, they are no larger than sheep's eyes, which is certainly remarkable in such a monstrous creature; it has no eyebrows nor eyelashes; and its ears are only a small opening; its neck is not easily discovered, the head and body being so nearly joined; however, there are some vertebræ proper for turning the head upon, which it actually does, particularly when it feeds, hanging its head like a cow; its body is round like that of a seal, being thickest about the navel, and growing smaller towards the head and tail; the tail is thick, and bent a little towards the end; it something resembles the beard of the whale, and somewhat the fins of a fish; its paws, which are under its neck, are about 21 inches long, with them he both swims and goes, and by them he takes hold of the rocks, to which he sometimes fastens himself so strongly, that when he is dragged from thence with hooks he will leave the skin of his paws behind: it is observed that these paws are sometimes divided in two, like the hoof of a cow; but this does not seem to be common, only accidental. The females have two teats upon their breasts. The length of the manati is about 28 feet, and its weight about 200 pood. These animals go in droves in calm weather near the mouths of rivers; and though the dams oblige their young always to swim before them, yet the rest of the herd cover them upon all sides, so that they are constantly in the middle of the drove. In the time of flood they come so near the shore, that one may strike them with a club or spear; nay, the author relates that he has even stroked their backs himself with his hand. When they are hurt they swim off to sea, but presently return. They live in families, one near another; and a family consists of a male, female, some half grown, and one small calf: hence it appears that every male has one female. They bring forth their young in the harvest, and never more than one at a time.

They appear to be extremely gluttonous, eating so continually without any regard to their own safety, that they hardly ever lift their heads above the water; so that any one may go among them in boats, and chuse which he pleases to carry off. The half of their body, that is their back and sides, is always above water, upon which flocks of crows settle, and pick the lice out of their skins. They do not feed upon every herb, but, first, upon sea cabbage *, which has a leaf resembling savoys secondly, upon cabbage † resembling a club; thirdly, upon cabbage ‖ resembling thongs; and, fourthly, upon a waved kind of cabbage ‡ : and wherever they have been, though but for one day, heaps of roots and stalks are thrown out upon the shore.

* Fucus Coispus brassicæ sabaudicæ folio cancellatus.   † Fucus clavæ facie.
‖ Fucus scuticæ antiquæ Romanæ facie.   ‡ Fucus longissimus ad nervum undulatus.

When they have eaten their fill, they lie afleep upon their backs As foon as the ebb begins they retire to the fea, fearing to be left upon the fhore. In the winter time they are frequently crufhed by the ice againft the rocks, and thrown out upon the beach. This happens during a ftorm, when the wind is upon the fhore. At this feafon they are fo lean that one may count all their ribs and vertebræ. They are caught with great iron hooks, fomething like the fluke of a fmall anchor. This hook is carried by a ftrong man in a boat with three or four rowers, who when he comes among the herd ftrikes into one of them. Thirty men that are left upon the fhore, and hold one end of a rope which is faftened to the hook, draw the manati towards the land; and in the mean time thofe that are in the boat ftab and cut it 'till it dies. I once faw fome of the fifhers cut off the flefh from the creature, while it was alive, who all the while ftruck the water with its paws with fuch force that the fkin was torn off them; but at laft it expired. It is eafier to catch the old ones than the young: for the laft are more active, and the fkin being fofter the hook frequently loofes its hold. When one of them is ftruck, and ftruggles to clear himfelf of the hook, thofe of the herd that are neareft to him come to his affiftance: fome overturn the boat by getting under it; others lay themfelves upon the rope, as if they could break it; and others endeavour to ftrike out the hook with their tails, which fometimes fucceeds. The love that is between the male and female is extraordinary; for after the male has ufed all methods to affift and refcue the female, he follows her even dead to the very fhore, and has been obferved fometimes even after two or three days to remain by the dead body. This animal cannot be faid to low, but rather brays hard, which is particularly obfervable when it is wounded. It cannot be faid how fharp

their

their fight or hearing is; but both senses appear to be very weak, perhaps from their keeping their heads always under water.

There is such a plenty of manati in *Bering*'s island, that it is sufficient to maintain all the people of *Kamtschatka*. Their flesh, though it takes a long time to boil, tastes well, and is something like beef. The fat of the young resembles pork, and the lean is like veal. This flesh is easily boiled, and swells so much that it takes up double the space when boiled that it did raw. It is impossible to boil the fat about the head and tail; but the ribs and back are very delicate. Some pretend that the flesh of this animal will not keep in salt; but we found the contrary, it appearing to us little inferior to salted beef *.

Besides

---

* That the *Kamtschatka* manati is the same kind of animal with that found by Captain *Dampier* in the rivers of *South America* and at the *Philippine Islands*, is evident from that author's description of it:

' This creature is about the bigness of a horse, and 10 or 12 feet long. The mouth of it is much like the mouth of a cow, having great thick lips. The eyes are no bigger than a small pea, the ears are only two small holes on each side of the head. The neck is short and thick, bigger than the head The biggest part of this creature is at the shoulders, where it hath two large fins, one on each side of its belly. Under each of these fins the female hath a small dug to suckle her young. From the shoulders towards the tail it retains its bigness for about a foot then it groweth smaller and smaller to the very tail which is flat, and about 14 inches broad, and 20 inches long, and in the middle four or five inches thick, but about the edges of it not above two inches thick. From the head to the tail it is round and smooth, without any fin but those two before mentioned. I have heard that some have weighed above 1200lb. but I never saw any so large. The manati delights to live in a brackish water; and they are commonly in creeks or rivers near the sea. 'Tis for this reason, possibly, they are not seen in the South Seas, (that ever I could observe) where the coast is generally a bold shore, that is, high land deep water close home by it, with a high sea or great surges; except in the bay of *Panama*, yet even there is no manati: whereas the *West Indies*, being as it were one great bay composed of many smaller, are mostly low land and shoal water, and afford proper pasture (as I

' may

Besides the above-mentioned animals, Mr. *Steller* saw upon the coast of *America* a new and uncommon sea beast, which he thus describes: Its length is about five feet; its head like a dog's; its ears sharp, and standing up; and its eyes large; upon its upper and under lips it has hairs like a beard; its make is thick and round; thicker towards the head, thin and small towards the tail; the whole body is covered with thick hair, grey upon the back, and red or sorrel towards the belly; the tail fin divides itself into two, the uppermost of which is longest. The author was extremely surprised that he could not discover any feet or paws, as in other sea animals. Its appearance in general was something like the draught of that creature, which *Gesner* gives under the name of sea monkey; and the author thinks that the name of monkey is not improperly applied to this animal for its remarkable activity and many tricks. It sometimes swam after their vessel for two hours, looking first at

' may say) for the manati. Sometimes
' we find them in salt water, sometimes
' in fresh, but never far at sea; and those
' that live in the sea at such places where
' there is no river nor creek fit for them
' to enter, yet do commonly come once
' or twice in 24 hours to the mouth of
' any fresh-water river that is near their
' place of abode. They live on grass
' seven or eight inches long, and of a
' narrow blade, which grows in the sea in
' many places, especially among islands
' near the main. This grass groweth
' likewise in creeks, or in great rivers, near the sides of them, in such
' places where there is but little tide or
' current. They never come ashore, nor
' into shallower water than where they
' can swim. Their flesh is white, both
' the fat and the lean, and extraordinary
' sweet and wholesome meat. The tail
' of a young cow is much esteemed;
' but if old, both head and tail are very
' tough. A calf that sucks is the most
' delicate meat privateers commonly
' roast them; as they do also great pieces
' out of the bellies of the old ones.

' The skin of the manati is of great
' use to privateers; for they cut them
' into straps, which they make fast on
' the side of their canoes, through which
' they put their oars in rowing instead of
' tholes or pegs. The skin of the bull,
' or of the back of the cow, is too thick
' for this use; but of it they make horse-
' whips, cutting them two or three feet
' long at the handle they leave the full
' substance of the skin, and from thence
' cut it away tapering, but very even,
' and square all the four sides. While
' the thongs are green they twist them,
' and hang them to dry, which in a
' week's time become as hard as wood.'

one

one thing and then at another with an appearance of surprize; and would come so near the ship, that he might be touched with a pole; but would retire to a greater distance on observing any on board to stir. He frequently raised one third of his body above the water, standing erect like a man, sometimes for half an hour together; and then darting under the vessel, appeared in the same posture on the other side; and this he would repeat, perhaps thirty times together. At other times he would bring a great *American* sea herb, which is flat and hollow below like the bottom of a bottle, and something sharp above: this he would toss about and catch again with his mouth, playing a thousand apish tricks with it. It has been observed of all sea beasts, that the more they play in fair weather the greater storm is to be expected.

CHAP. IX.

Of FISHES.

THERE are great numbers of whales both in this ocean and in the *Penschinska* sea; they frequently swim within musket-shot of the shore, and sometimes will come close to the very shore, perhaps to rub off the shell-fish that adhere to their bodies and give them no rest; as plainly appears from their lying a long time with their backs above water, to allow the rooks and gulls to pick them off At such time as the fish come out of the sea into the fresh waters, two or three whales are often found together at the time of flood near the mouth of the rivers.

The whales here are from seven to fifteen fathoms long. We can give no account of the different species of whales at *Kamtschatka*, few of them being caught here except in the northern parts by the *Koreki* and *Tchukotskoi*, who feed upon their flesh. In the year 1740 a whale was brought by the flood into the mouth of the *Bolskoi* river; but some Cossacks observing it, went out in boats, and cut it all to pieces; so that next day when I came, to my great disappointment, I neither found flesh nor bones; for these people, who had cut off the flesh, being afraid of punishment for doing it without permission, had buried the bones to conceal their crime. *Steller* observed that more whales were thrown on the eastern than on the western shore, and more in the harvest than in the spring.

The different people have different ways of catching them: the *Kuriles* by throwing their poisoned darts into them: the *Olutores* catch them in nets, made of thongs of the sea horse skin as broad as a man's hand, which they dry in the smoke. These they set in the mouths of the rivers, and the whale pursuing other fish entangles himself in them. With these thongs he is dragged to the shore by the help of numbers who assemble on these occasions, and always perform certain ceremonies. They bring out of their common huts a wooden whale about two feet long; then building a new hut they place this image in it, using several conjurations. After this they light a lamp, and appointing some people to look after it, give orders that it be not allowed to go out from spring to harvest, which is as long as the fishing season lasts. They then cut the whale into different portions, which, looking upon it as their most delicate provision, they prepare in the following manner:---They dry the lean in the sun; and the skin, which they separate from the fat, they beat with hammers, and of it make soles to their shoes, which wears extremely well. They smoke the fat parts, and

and cleaning the guts, they fill them with the oil which runs in cutting the fish, or which they melt from the blubber, having no other vessels to keep it in.

The *Tchukotskoi* kill whales with a harpoon in the same manner as the *Europeans* do, and they catch so many that they never eat those whales that are thrown dead on shore, as some of the neighbouring people do, but only extract their fat for burning. Although the *Tchukotskoi* have large herds of deer, which might be sufficient for their sustenance, yet they are the greatest whale fishers of any people in this part of the globe, and look upon the fat of the whales as the greatest delicacy; besides, having great scarcity of wood, they use it for burning. They make themselves shirts of the intestines of the whales, like the *Americans*; and use them for vessels, like the *Olutores*.

The kasatki, (falsely called the sword-fish) which are numerous in these seas, are very useful to the inhabitants, for these fish frequently either kill or drive the whales on shore. *Steller* had an opportunity of seeing an engagement between the kasatki and whale, both at sea and upon *Bering*'s island. When the kasatki attacks the whale he makes him roar so that he may be heard some miles. If the whale makes off, the kasatki follows him at some distance 'till great numbers of them gather together, and make a general attack. It is never observed that such whales as are thrown on shore have any part eaten out of their bodies; so that this war between the whales and the kasatki must proceed only from a natural enmity. The fishers are so much afraid of these animals that they not only never throw any darts at them, but if possible avoid going near them; nay, they even make offerings to them, begging that they will not hurt them: for if irritated they sometimes overturn their boats.

Mr. *Steller* writes that he was certainly informed, that in the bodies of whales thrown upon the coaſt of *Kamtſchatka*, there have been found harpoons marked with *Latin* letters; but by what means he could be certain of this, I know not; for the natives have no idea of letters; and before our arrival, none of our Coſſacks ever ſaw a *Latin* letter.

Many are the advantages which the *Kamtſchadales* derive from this plenty of whales: of the ſkin they make ſhoe ſoles and ſtraps; they eat the fleſh, as likewiſe the fat which they alſo burn; they ſew their boats with the beard, of which alſo they make nets for foxes and fiſh; out of the lower jaw they form a ſort of ſledge, and make knife-handles, rings, and ſeveral ſmall things of it beſides; the inteſtines ſerve for barrels, and other veſſels; out of the nerves and blood-veſſels they make ropes; and of the vertebræ, ſeats. The moſt delicate pieces of the whale are the tongue and fins. I thought that the whale's fat with grout was not unpleaſant, but I can't ſay, that I was then a proper judge, for hunger makes every thing agreeable.

They never go a fiſhing for the kaſatki, but if this fiſh is thrown on ſhore they uſe its fat like that of the whale. Mr. *Steller* ſays, that, in the year 1742, eight of them were thrown on ſhore at once, near the *Lopatka*; but the diſtance and the bad weather prevented his going to examine them. He was told, that the largeſt never exceed four fathoms in length; that they have ſmall eyes, a wide mouth, and great ſharp teeth, with which they wound the whale; but that they tear up the belly of the whale with a ſharp fin which is upon their backs, is a falſe report; for though this fin is about five feet long, very ſharp, and in the ſea ſtands quite upright, yet it is altogether ſoft, and conſiſts only of fat: nay the animal itſelf is almoſt all fat having hardly any muſcular fleſh.

There is likewise another creature in these seas resembling a whale, but smaller and slenderer: the *Russians* call it a wolf, and the *Kamtschadales*, chethak. Its fat is of such a nature, that, when swallowed, it presently passes insensibly. The natives sometimes use it as a medicine in case of costiveness, but oftener to play tricks with one another. They feed upon the flesh and tongue, which have not the same quality.

Notwithstanding the great plenty of whales upon this coast, the scarcity of food is sometimes so great, that whole villages die of hunger. In the month of *April*, 1739, I saw a melancholy instance of their being obliged, out of necessity, to eat some poisonous whale's fat, at a village upon the river *Berosover*, called *Alaune*, where I observed the people all look pale, as if they had been sick for a long time; when I asked the reason, I was told, that just before my arrival one of the natives was killed by eating of whale's fat; and as all the rest had eat of the same, they dreaded the same fate. In about half an hour, a young healthy man began to groan and complain that his throat burnt; upon which the old women, who are the physicians there, fastened him with ropes to a ladder, and placed themselves on both sides of him with great clubs in their hands, with which they tossed firebrands out of the huts, and the wife of the sick person coming behind him, made several conjurations over his head, begging death to spare him: however he died the next day; but the other inhabitants, as I heard, recovered with difficulty after a long time. This accident did not greatly surprise me; I rather wondered that such things did not happen oftener, especially from those whales which are killed with poisoned darts. However the *Kamtschadales* think so little of the consequences, that they had rather risk their lives than be deprived of the pleasure of eating whale's fat.

After the whales, we must mention the fish * mokoe, which at *Archangel* is called akula. It is about three fathoms long;

---

* Canis Carcharius Autoris.

brings forth its young alive, like the whale; and when its mouth is shut has some resemblance of a sturgeon, but its teeth are very different, being large and terrible. The *Kamtschadales* eat the flesh of this fish, and though it appears to be tough and strong, they say it is exceedingly well tasted. The guts, and particularly the bladder are in high esteem; so that when they catch this fish, they never call it by its name, for fear, as they imagine, they should provoke it to burst its bladder, and render it useless to them. The teeth are sold under the name of serpents teeth.

Several fishes which are common to other seas are found here; as pike, eels, lampreys, cod, and very fine soals in great plenty; but the inhabitants make no account of these fish, and never use them unless in great necessity, or to feed their dogs. Mr. *Steller* observed four different species of flat fish.

There is a fish called * vahnae, which is a species of the cod; is round and thick, with three fins upon its back; and when taken out of the water is of a copper-colour, but presently changes to yellow: its flesh is white, but soft, and of a disagreeable taste; however the inhabitants eat more of it, than of other fish which are much better tasted; the reason indeed is, that they catch this fish in the beginning of the spring, when they can catch no other; a great deal of which they dry in the sun uncleaned, designing it as provision for their dogs.

I saw the fish which they call † terpuk, but it being dry, I could not observe those fine colours which Mr. *Steller* describes. By his description its back is blackish, its sides are reddish, and chequered with fine silver-coloured spots; some of which are square, and others circular: in its shape it resembles the perch.

* Onos vel Asinus Antiquorum.
† Doecogrammos Stelleri.

They angle for this fish near the *Kurilski* islands, and the haven of *Awatscha*, with hooks made of bone or wood.

There are likewise several other kinds of fishes in these seas which are not very common in other places; but as they make no part of their nourishment, and are seldom caught, I shall take no notice of them, my design being only to mention such as serve for food to the inhabitants, in this country which produces no grain. The chief of these are salmon of different kinds, which during the summer come in shoals from the sea up the rivers. Of these they make what they call *eukol*, which they use instead of bread; and they boil up the fat, which serves for butter. They likewise make glue of them.

Before I give a particular description of each species apart, I would communicate some observations which regard the catching of these fish, and which indeed are wonderful proofs of the Divine Providence and the goodness of the Creator, who has blest a place with such abundance of fish where there is neither cattle nor grain.

In *Kamtschatka* the fish come from the sea in such numbers, that they stop the course of the rivers, and cause them to overflow the banks; and when the waters fall there remains a surprising quantity of dead fish upon the shore, which produces an intolerable stink. At this time the bears and dogs catch more fish with their paws than people do at other places with their nets. All the fish that swim up the rivers are of the salmon kind, and are commonly called red fish; but the several sorts are so distinct from each other, that *Kamtschatka* alone is thought to produce as many different species as are to be found in all the world besides. Not one fish remains in *Kamtschatka* longer than six months (except gudgeons); for all that are not caught before the end of *December* die, except in some few deep places where there are warm springs. It is observed of all the different species

of

of salmon in *Kamtschatka*, that they are brought forth and die in the same river, come to their full growth in the sea, and spawn only once during their whole lives: for which purpose they swim up the rivers, and having found a proper place in smooth water, they make a hole with the fins that are under their gills, and there deposit their roes.

In *Siberia* the red fish live in clayey rivers; they remain there several years, and generate every year, having numbers of insects proper for nourishment. They winter in deep pools, and in the spring swim further up for the sake of propagating in the mouths of little rivulets that fall into the great rivers, where they are commonly caught. The young fry swim down to the sea, where they continue 'till they come to their full growth, which Mr. *Steller* thinks is in the third year; and then they return in order to propagate. It is remarkable that those fish which are bred in a great river continue in the sea near to its mouth, feed upon things brought down by the stream, and when the time of spawning approaches they will enter no river but that which produced them. It is also very extraordinary, that those fish which come up the rivers in the month of *August*, though they have time enough to spawn, yet as there remains but little time for their young to return, take a year-old fish of their own kind, which continually follows the male and female; and when the old have covered the roes they continue to ascend, the young one, which is no bigger than a herring, guarding them 'till the month of *November*, at which time it returns with the other fishes. It is very probable that the same thing happens in *Europe*, which may have given occasion, through the difference of their ages, to account them of different species.

Each kind of fish always ascends the rivers at the same time. In the month of *August* sometimes two, three, nay even four species come up at once; but each keeps separate from the other.

The

The different species of those fishes which are here called red fish shall be mentioned in giving an account of the time when they come out of the sea into the rivers; it being remarked that they always observe the same order, the same species which comes out first one year continuing to do so the following. This the *Kamtschadales* find to be so certain, that they call their months by the name of the fish which are then caught.

The largest and best of these fish, and which come first out of the sea, are called chavitsi. It resembles the common salmon, though it is a great deal broader; is about three feet and a half long, and weighs a pood and a half; its breadth is about the fourth part of its length; its nose is sharp, the upper jaw being longer than the lower; its tail is equal; the back is bluish, with some small black spots; its sides are of a silver colour, and its belly white; its gills are long and small; and its flesh is red both raw and boiled.

They swim up the rivers with such force that the water seems to rise like a wall before them; which the *Kamtschadales* observing get into their boats, and throw out their nets. This fish does not come up in such large shoals as the others, nor is such plenty caught as to make *eukol* of it, except upon the river *Kamtschatka*; and even there it is so rare that it is only used on feasts or holydays, and after all it is so fat that it presently turns bitter. The Cossacks, for the most part, salt it, particularly the belly, back, and head. The ribs are dry and hard, but the belly is truly a delicate food, at least no fish there comes up to it; and what they dry in the sun, if not better than the *Jakutski* sturgeon, is at least not worse.

Of all the rivers that run into the Eastern Ocean this fish is only found in the river *Kamtschatka* and the bay of *Awatscha*; and of those that fall into the *Penschinska* sea, only in the *Bolscheretskoi* river: besides, Mr. *Steller* says, that none is to be found further north than 54°, and it is certain that it is not to be found near *Ochotſka*, where it is eſteemed a valuable preſent.

The nets with which this fiſh is caught are made of yarn about the thickneſs of ſugar ropes; and the fiſhing begins about the middle of *May*, and laſts ſix weeks. The *Kamtſchadales* eſteem this fiſh ſo much, that the firſt they catch they bake and eat with great rejoicings. This cuſtom is very diſagreeable to the *Ruſſian* inhabitants who hire the natives to fiſh for them; for however impatient the maſter may be to taſte the new fiſh, the fiſhermen will have the firſt, looking upon it as a great ſin if they do not eat it themſelves, and with all due ceremonies.

The ſecond kind is only called red fiſh, in *Ochotſka*, narka. It is about 21 inches long, and flattiſh; its fleſh is extremely red; its head very ſmall; the ſnout ſhort and ſharp; the tongue bluiſh, with whitiſh ſides; its back bluiſh, with black ſpots; its belly white; and its tail forked. Its breadth is about a fifth part of its length; and it has ſcales large and round, eaſily ſeparating from the ſkin: it weighs about fifteen pounds. It is found in every river that runs either into the *Penſchinſka* or Eaſtern Sea, coming up in great ſhoals; and it is caught about the middle of *June*. The *eukol* that is made of it, though very pleaſant, preſently turns bitter; ſo that for the moſt part they either ſalt this fiſh, or boil it for its fat. There are two things worth notice concerning it: the firſt of which is, that part go before to the heads of the rivers, as if they were ſent out to examine them, where ſome of them are caught before the ſhoals appear at the mouths. The ſecond is, that this fiſh is more plenty in ſuch rivers as run out of lakes than others: nor does it live long in the former, but haſtens directly into the latter; in the depths of which it lies 'till the beginning of *Auguſt*, at which time it comes nearer the ſhore, and tries to get into theſe rivers that communicate with the lakes. Here the inhabitants catch them by nets, dams, or other methods.

The

The third kind of this fish is called keta or kaeko; which is somewhat larger than the narka. The flesh is white; the head flattish and longish; the snout is bent; the teeth, when it has been some time in the river, are like a dog's; its tongue is sharp; its tail a little forked; its back black and green; its sides and belly like other fish; and its skin is without spots. The *eukol* that is made of this fish they call their household bread, being much more plenty than any other; as the season of the fishery, which begins in *July* and ends about the middle of *October*, is drier and more proper for preparing it. This fish is caught in all the rivers both in the *Penschinska* and Eastern seas.

The gorbushe, or crook back, follows or sometimes accompanies the keta. This fish is more plentiful than any other whatever; it is about eighteen inches long, and flattish; its flesh is white; its head small; its snout sharp, and considerably crooked; its teeth small; its back bluish, with round black spots; its sides and belly like the other sorts; and the tail forked. Though this fish is not bad, yet the inhabitants have such plenty of what they esteem better, that they use this only for their dogs.

The last of these kinds that come on shor is called white fish. This fish both in bulk and appearance is very like the keta; they differ in this indeed, that the keta has no spots, and the white fish has long black spots upon its back. It excels in taste all the fishes that have white flesh; and it agrees with the narka in this, that it most frequently haunts those rivers that run out of the lakes, and is caught there in the same manner. The young ones, which accompany the old to take care of the roes and convoy the young fry down, are esteemed by the inhabitants to be a different species, and are called milktchuch. So soon as the old ones have spawned, they take all care to provide for their own safety, retiring immediately to deep places where there are warm springs; and they are chiefly found in the springs near the *Bolscheretskoi* river and the *Opalſkoy* lake: they are caught likewiſe during the whole winter in thoſe ſprings that run into the *Kamtſchatka* from the ſouth; and near to where the old lower fort of *Kamtſchatka* ſtood they alſo abound, which is a great relief to the inhabitants. I myſelf was at this fiſhery in the end of *February*; however I found the fiſh at that time dryer and not ſo well taſted as in the harveſt. This fiſh eats very well, either ſalted, dryed, or ſmoaked. It is caught frequently in the ſame net with the keta and narka; and thoſe which they uſe for this fiſhery are made of yarn about half as thick as that with which they make the nets for the chavitſi, and the meſhes are about an inch and a half wide.

All theſe different ſpecies of fiſh change their colours, turn lean and ugly, their ſnout bends, their teeth grow, and a ſcurf appears upon their ſkins. The chavitſi, narka, and white fiſh, change their ſilver colour to a red; the keta turns likewiſe red, ſtained with black ſtripes. Their fins and tails become reddiſh and blackiſh; in one word, they would never be taken for the ſame fiſh that enter the rivers, if theſe changes were not certain. The gorbuſhe alone preſerves its ſilver colour, and, whenever it loſes that, it dies.

It is incredible with what eargerneſs they go up the rivers, particularly the gorbuſhe. When they come to any place where the ſtream is ſtrong, and thoſe that are weak find it impoſſible by their own ſtrength to get up, they faſten their teeth upon the tail of ſome that are ſtronger, that they may be drawn up by them; ſo that ſeveral of theſe fiſh are found which have their tails bitten.

The true ſalmon may always be reckoned one of thoſe fiſh that come in ſhoals; and are found to go up the rivers *Kompakſve*, *Bircumkin*, and *Etchi*. I never ſaw theſe fiſh indeed, but have heard a great deal of them. Mr. *Steller* writes, that

when

when they return to the sea, it sometimes happens that they are driven by a storm from the mouth of their native river, so that losing their way, the following year they ascend a strange river, which is the occasion of their being found in more plenty in some rivers one year than another.

There are other kinds of red fish which come up the river without any order, and live there the whole winter before they return. Mr. *Steller* says, they stay sometimes four or five years. The first of this species is called, at *Ochotska*, malma, and at *Kamtschatka*, goltsa. When they come out of the sea their colour is clear like silver; the upper part of the snout is blunt, and somewhat bent; the lower sharp, and bent towards the upper. When they are ripped up, and the roes taken out, there appear upon the sides round red spots of different magnitudes, the belly and lower fins become likewise reddish, except the bones which continue white.

The largest fish of this species, which lives sometimes five or six years, comes from the sea into the river *Kamtschatka*, out of which it goes into the rivers that run into it, and by them to the lakes, where it grows almost as big as the chavitsi, though it seldom weighs more than twenty pounds. They are found likewise very large in the *Bistroy* river; there their length is commonly twenty-eight inches, and breadth ten; they are of a dark colour, have large teeth, and the lower jaw is crooked with a knob: it seems indeed of a different species. These of three years old, which have been one year out of the sea, have a long head, are of a silver colour, with small scales, and small red spots; and such as have been two years out of the sea are round and longish, with small heads, and their flesh, which is of a reddish white, is hard and well tasted. With regard to their size; the first year they are long and small; the second, they grow more in breadth than in length; the third, the head grows considerably; and the fourth, fifth, and sixth years, their breadth and thickness increases greatly:

greatly: this obfervation probably holds in all kinds of falmon trouts. In the fourth year alfo, the lower part to the fnout becomes hooked. This fpecies of fifh fwims along with the gorbufhe, and is caught with it in the fame net, which is wove of fmall yarn, the mefhes being about an inch wide. Such as live in the rivers are nourifhed by the roes of other fifh; and in the fummer are found near the heads of fmall rivers, which they leave in the fpring. Such as are caught at the beginning of fummer are falted, but thofe caught later are frozen for the winter.

Another fpecies of fifh is called muikifi, and is about the bignefs of the narka; its fcales are pretty large; its head is of a middling fize; the upper part of its fnout is like that of the goltfa, with the lower part hooked; it has teeth in its jaws and on the fide of the tongue; its back is blackifh, marked with round, or femicircular black fpots; and upon each fide has a large red ftripe, which goes quite from the head to the tail: this diftinguifhes it from all the other fpecies of this fifh: it fwallows all kinds of naftinefs, and often catches the field mice that happen to fwim upon the river; and is fo particularly fond of the nortleberry, that if it fees any growing upon the bank, it throws itfelf out, and feizes either the berry or the leaf of the plant. It is a well tafted fifh, but is not caught in fuch plenty as others are. They do not certainly know the time of its entering the rivers, but imagine it is before the ice is gone.

There is a third kind called kunfha, which is about three feet long; the head makes a feventh part of the length; the fnout is fhort and fharp; its jaws are furnifhed with teeth; its back and fides blackifh, marked with yellow fpots, fome of which are round and others oblong; its belly is white; its lower fins and tail blue; and the flefh white and well tafted. In *Ochotfka* it fwims in fhoals, but at *Kamtfchatka* it is more rare, and confequently more efteemed.

The

The fourth species is the harius, which is well known in *Siberia* and all *Ruſſia*; but thoſe that are here have the back fin longer than the others. Mr. *Steller* writes, that they come up into the rivers upon the firſt going off of the ice; but I never happened to ſee this fiſh in *Kamtſchatka*.

There is another ſpecies of red fiſh which reſembles the golſta, with this difference, that its head is larger, and the upper part of the ſnout a little hooked; its ſides are marked with red ſpots, like the malma: it is ſeldom longer than 20 inches.

Among the ſmall fiſhes which the *Kamtſchadales* feed upon are three ſpecies of ſmelts one of which is called hagatch, the ſecond innaka, and the third uiki. The hagatch is our common ſmelt. The innaka differs from it a little, and is found in great plenty about the lake *Nerpech*. Uiki is thrown ſometimes upon the ſhore in vaſt heaps for 100 verſts together. They are eaſily diſtinguiſhed from the other ſpecies by a rough ſtripe that goes down the ſide. They commonly ſwim three together, and are ſo joined by the afore-mentioned rough ſtripe, that when you catch one the others cannot eaſily diſengage themſelves. The *Kamtſchadales* dry this fiſh as food for their dogs; but in caſe of ſcarcity they uſe it themſelves, although the taſte is very diſagreeable

The laſt kind of fiſh which we ſhall mention is the herring: theſe are found in great plenty in the Eaſtern Sea, but very ſeldom in the bays which lie upon the *Penſchinſka*. In my opinion they don't differ in the leaſt from the herring which we have in Europe; which Mr. *Steller* likewiſe confirms. In the harveſt they are found in large lakes, where they breed and winter: in the ſpring they ſwim towards the ſea. The greateſt fiſhery of them is in the lake *Viliutchin*, which is only about fifty fathom from the ſea, and has communication with it by a ſmall outlet. When theſe herrings enter the lake, this paſſage is ſhut up by the ſand being thrown into it, and remains ſo 'till the month of

March,

March, when it is washed away again by the high water arising from the melting of the snow; which happens regularly every year. The herrings come every day to the mouth of the outlet, as if to inform themselves whether the passage was yet open, and remain there from morning 'till evening, when they return to the deeper part of the lake. The *Kamtschadales* observing this, break holes in the ice near the mouth of the outlet, where they put down their nets, and catch great quantities. This fishery continues so long as the ice remains upon the lake. They catch them likewise with nets in the summer, at the mouths of the rivers; when they boil out the fat, which is as white as butter, and more delicate than that of any other fish; and send it from the lower *Kamtschatkoy* fort (where the greatest quantity is made) as a rare present, to the other forts.

CHAP. X.

Of the BIRDS.

KAMTSCHATKA abounds in birds, but the inhabitants make less use of them than of roots and fishes: the reason of this is, that they don't well know how to catch them; and their fishery is so advantageous to them, that to leave that and go a bird-catching would be as ridiculous as for the husbandman to leave his plough and go a shooting.

I shall here divide the birds into three classes: the first, sea fowls; the second, the fresh-water fowls; and the third, those which frequent the woods and fields.

CLASS I. *Of the* SEA FOWLS.

The sea fowls are found in greater plenty about the coast of the Eastern Ocean, than that of the *Penschinska* sea; for the coast of the Eastern Ocean is more hilly and convenient for breeding.

The ipatka * is well known to all writers of natural history by the name of anas arctica, commonly called in *England* puffins. It is found upon the coast of *Kamtschatka*, and the *Kurilski* islands, and even upon the *Penschinska* bay, almost as far as *Ochotska*. It is about the bigness of, or rather smaller than, a common duck; its head and neck are of a bluish black; the back is black; the belly and all below white; its bill red, and broad towards the root, but somewhat narrower towards the point; upon each side are three furrows; its legs are red, its feet webbed, and its nails small, crooked, and black; its flesh is hard; its eggs are like hen's eggs; it builds its nest with grass on the cliffs of the rocks. The *Kamtschadales* and *Kuriles* wear the bills of these birds about their necks fastened to straps; and, according to their superstition, their shamans, or priests, must put them on with proper ceremony, to procure them good fortune.

Another species of these birds is called meuchagatka †, and in *Ochotska*, igilma: this only differs from the former in being all black, and having two yellowish white tufts upon its head, which lie all along from its ears to its neck like locks of hair. To the best of my remembrance this bird has never yet been described. Mr. *Steller* and I sent some of these species of birds to the Imperial Museum. Among those sent by Mr. *Steller* there was a third kind which is found upon the island *Bondena*, in *Angermannia*, and upon the *Caroline* islands; and is some-

---

* Alca rostri sulcis quatuor, oculorum regione temporibusque albis. LINN. F. suec. v. 42.

† Alca monochroa sulcis tribus, cerro duplici utrinque dependente. Anas arctica cirrata. STELL.

what less than the other two; its colour is like that of the ipatka, except that its bill and legs are black, and that there are two white sprigs upon its forehead, which reach from the eye to the bill.

The aru *, or kara, belongs to this class. It is larger than a duck; the head, neck, and back are black; the bill long, strait, black and sharp; the legs black with a cast of red; it has three black toes, and is web-footed. Great numbers of these are found upon the rocky islands; and the inhabitants kill them for the sake of their flesh, though tough and bad tasted; but more so for their skins, of which, as well as those of other sea fowls, they make themselves garments. Their eggs are reckoned a great delicacy.

There are two kinds of tchaiki, or cormorants, found upon this coast, which are hardly observed any where else. They are about the bigness of a goose, have a strait reddish bill about five inches long, and sharp on the edges, and four nostrils, such as other cormorants have two being near the forehead as are found in other birds which are thought to prognosticate storms, and are thence named Procellaria; their heads are of the middling size; their eyes black; their tails eight inches long; and their legs are covered with hair to the knees, but below them are bare; they have three toes of a bluish colour, and are web-footed; their wings extend more than a fathom; they are sometimes speckled; they appear often near the shore, but can't stand strait upon dry ground, their feet being so near the tail that they are not able to balance their bodies: they fly slow even when hungry, but when full of meat they cannot raise themselves from the ground; and, having eat too much, they ease their stomachs by throwing it up; they have a wide throat, and swallow fish whole; their flesh is very tough and sinewy, therefore the natives seldom eat it, but in great necessity, killing them principally for the sake of their

* Lomvia Hoieri.

bladders,

bladders, which they use instead of corks to their nets. The way of catching them is singular, being angled for as fishes are, in the following manner: they fasten a thick iron, or wooden hook to a long rope or strap, baiting the hook with a whole fish, the point of which comes out near the back fin, and then throw it into the sea; this the cormorants observing gather about it in flocks, and quarrel among themselves who shall have the prize, until the strongest obtains it and swallows it; then being drawn on shore, they take out the hook and bait by putting their hands into its throat. Sometimes they fasten a live cormorant, which they call a decoy, to the rope, and that it may not swallow the bait, tie down its bill with a cord: the others seeing the decoy swim so near the shore, come with greater security to the bait. The *Kamtschadales* make needle cases, and combs to comb their nettles, of the bones of their wings.

Besides the above-mentioned tchaiki, or cormorants, there is another species which haunt the rivers: these are called robbers, because they take the prey from the small birds; their tail is forked like that of the swallow.

The procellaria, or storm birds, are about the bigness of a swallow; their feathers are all black, except the tops of their wings, which are white; their bill and legs black. They haunt about the islands, and before a storm they fly low and skim the sea, and sometimes into the ships, which the sailors look upon as the sign of an approaching violent gale.

The stariki *, or glupisha, belong to this species. The stariki are about the bigness of a pigeon; have bluish bills, and bluish black feathers about the nostrils, which look like bristles; the feathers of the head are of the same colour, interspersed here and there with white ones, which are longer and thinner than the rest; the upper part of the neck is black, but the lower black and

---

* Mergus marinus niger ventre albo, plumis angustis albis auritus. STELL.

white speckled. The belly is white, the wings short, the large feathers of which are black, and the rest blue; the sides and tail are black; the feet are red and webbed; and the nails black and small: it haunts about rocky islands, where it likewise builds its nest: The *Kamtschadales* catch these fowls easier than they do the tchaiki, or cormorants: they put on a fur coat of a particular make, and letting their hands fall down, sit down in a proper place, and wait for the evening; when the birds returning from the sea seek to retire into holes for the night, and in the dark several of them fly into their furs, and are caught.

Among the birds described by Mr. *Steller* are the black starikis*, whose bills are as red as vermillion, the right side of which is crooked; it has a white tuft upon its head. He saw a third species in *America*, which was spotted black and white.

The glupisha are about the largeness of the common river cormorants; and are found upon the rocky islands, in high steep places; their colours are grey, white, and black; and are perhaps called glupisha, that is, foolish, because they frequently fly into the boats. Mr. *Steller* says, that numbers of them are caught in the fourth and fifth *Kurilski* islands, which the inhabitants dry in the sun; they squeeze the fat through the skin, which passes very easily, and use it for burning. He likewise writes that all the rocky islands in the sea between *Kamtschatka* and *America* are covered with them. He has seen some as large as a goose, or an eagle; their bills are crooked and yellowish; their eyes are large like those of an owl; they are black intermixed with white spots over the whole body. He once saw, 200 versts from land, great numbers of them feeding upon a dead whale, which served them also to appearance for lodging; and in his passage through the *Penschinska* sea, he saw many of the glupisha, some of which

---

* Mergulus marinus alter totus niger cristatus, rostro rubro. STELL.

were black, and others white; but none of them came so near the vessel as to be exactly observed.

The * kaiover, or kaior, a bird of this species, is black, with its bill and feet red; builds its nest, which is very curious, upon high rocks in the sea, and whistles very loud, for which reason the Cossacks call it ivoshik, or post-boy. I never saw this bird.

The fowl † urile, of which there is great plenty in *Kamtschatka*, called, by writers, sea ravens, is about the bigness of a common goose, with a long neck and small head; the feathers upon the whole body are of a bluish black, except upon its thighs, where they are white and in tufts; there are also some long white feathers like hairs, here and there upon its neck; it has a red membrane or skin round the eyes, a strait bill, black above and reddish below; and its feet are black and webbed: when it swims it holds up its head, but flying, it stretches it out like a crane; it flies swift, but rises heavily; and feeds upon fish, which it swallows whole: in the night time, these fowls stand in rows upon the edges of the cliffs, from which in their sleep they frequently fall into the water; where they are caught by the stone foxes, who watch for them; they breed in the month of *July*; their eggs are green, about the bigness of a hen's egg, and being boiled thicken a little, but are ill tasted; however the *Kamtschadales* climb the highest rocks in search of them, at the hazard of their lives. They catch them with nets, and in the evening with noofes fastened to a long pole; and these creatures are so void of apprehension, that, though they see the next fowl to themselves taken away, they will sit still and receive the noose, 'till they are all taken off the cliff; their flesh is hard and sinewy; but the natives prepare it in

---

* Columba Groënlandica Batavorum. STELL.

† Corvus aquaticus maximus cristatus periophtalmiis cinnabarinis, postea candidis. STELL

such a manner that, as victuals are there, it is not bad; they roast it in holes dug in the earth, without plucking off the feathers, or taking out the entrails, and when roasted, they skin and eat it.

The natives say that these birds have no tongue; but this is not true, for they cry in the mornings and evenings: Mr. *Steller* compares their noise to the sound of a trumpet.

CLASS II. *Of those Birds which haunt for the most part about the fresh Water.*

The first of this class is the swan, which is so common in *Kamtschatka*, both in summer and winter, that the poorest person can have no entertainment without a swan. When they are moulting they hunt them with dogs, and kill them with clubs: in the winter they catch them in those rivers that do not freeze.

Here are seven kinds of geese, which are distinguished thus: large grey geese, gumenniki, short necks, grey and speckled, white necks, small white geese, and foreign. They all come here in the month of *May*, and depart in the month of *October*, as Mr. *Steller* says; who likewise writes, that they come from *America*, and that he himself saw them pass *Bering*'s island in great flocks, flying east in the harvest and west in the spring. In *Kamtschatka* are principally found the large grey geese, the gumenniki, and the grey and speckled; the small white goose is hardly ever found here. Again, in the North Sea, about *Kolimi* and other rivers, are vast numbers of them; and the best down is brought to *Jakutski* from these places. They catch them at the time they cast their feathers, in the following manner:--- They build huts with two doors, near those places where they most commonly sit at night. The fowler putting a white shirt on, above his cloaths, steals as near the flock as he can; and shewing himself

himself he creeps away upon his hands and feet towards the hut: then going through it, and observing that the geese have followed him, he shuts the door behind him, and running round he comes in at the other door, which shutting likewise, he encloses all the geese.

Mr. *Steller* observed in the month of *July* upon *Bering*'s island an eighth kind of geese, about the bigness of the white speckled. Its back, neck, and belly were white; its wings black; its cheeks white, yet somewhat greenish; its eyes black, with a yellow ring; the bill has a black stripe round it, and is red, with a knob like the *Chinese* or *Muscovy* geese: this knob is bare and yellowish, except that along it there is a small stripe of bluish black feathers. The natives report that this sort of geese is likewise found upon the first *Kurilskoy* island; however they were never observed upon the continent.

The people of *Kamtschatka* have different methods of catching geese when they cast their feathers; sometimes they pursue them in boats; sometimes they hunt them with dogs; but most of them are caught in pits, which they dig near those lakes where the geese haunt, and cover up carefully with grass: these the geese coming upon the shore fall into, and are caught.

There are eleven different species of ducks in *Kamtschatka*; namely, the selesni, sharp tails, tcherneti, plutonosi, svasi, krohali, lutki, gogoli, tchirki, turpani, and stone ducks: of which the selesni, tchirki, krohali, and gogoli, winter among the springs; all the rest come in the spring, and fly away in harvest, as the geese do.

The sharp tails are of that kind which writers call the *anas caudacuta, sive havelda islandica.* They haunt in the bays of the sea, or about the mouths of great rivers: they swim in flocks, and with their cry, which is extraordinary, make no disagreeable musick. Mr. *Steller* writes, that the larynx, or lower part of their throat, has three openings, covered with
thin

thin membranes. The natives call this fowl aangitch, from their manner of crying.

The turpan is called by writers the black duck*. They are not so numerous about *Kamtschatka* as at *Ochotska*, where they are caught in great plenty about the equinox. Fifty or more of the natives here going out in boats surround a whole flock, which in time of the flood they drive into the mouth of the river *Ochotska*; and so soon as it begins to ebb, and the water in the bay turns low, all the inhabitants fall upon them, and kill them with clubs in such numbers, that every one gets 20 or 30 for his share.

The stone ducks † have not hitherto been observed in any other place; they breed in the summer time in the rivers. The drakes are particularly beautiful, their head being like black velvet, and having two white spots upon their nose, which extend beyond the eyes, and end in a clay-coloured stripe behind their head: there is a small white spot near each ear; their bills are broad and flat, like those of other ducks; they are of a bluish colour, and their necks of a bluish black; upon their breasts are black feathers with a white border below; the feathers are smaller and broader above; the fore part of the back and belly are bluish, but more blackish towards the tail; across both wings are broad white stripes with black borders; their sides, under the wings, are of a clay colour; the large feathers of the wings, except six, bluish; these are black and roughish like velvet; the two last are white with black borders, and the second row of the large wing feathers are all black, the third grey, two only of these feathers having white spots upon their ends: their tails are sharp, and their feet pale coloured: they weigh about two pounds. The female is far from being so beautiful: her feathers are black, each

---

* Anas niger. WILLOUGHBY.
† Anas picta capite pulchre fascicato. STELLER.

being somewhat yellowish at the end, with a small white stripe; the head is black, and upon its temples are small white spots: it weighs about a pound and a half.

In the harvest the females are found in the rivers, but none of the drakes: they are very stupid and easily caught where the waters are clear and shallow, for they do not fly away at the sight of a man, but only dive, and therefore may be easily killed with poles, as I myself have frequently done. Mr. *Steller* saw several of this kind of ducks in the *American* islands.

They catch the ducks with nets in the following manner: in a wood that happens to stand between two lakes, or between a lake and a river, they cut a strait passage, through which the ducks fly during the summer; here in the harvest, when the fishery is over, the natives fasten to long poles several nets, which in the evenings they raise as high as the ducks are used to mount: round the nets a string is drawn, by which they can reef them together, as soon as they find the ducks entangled; but they sometimes fly with such force and in such numbers, that they break through. They likewise catch them in small rivers with nets stretched across the stream: but this is a method not peculiar to *Kamtschatka*.

To this class belongs likewise the gagari or columbus, of which there are four species *, three of which are large, and the other small: the first of the largest has a tail; the second a clay coloured spot upon its neck, a little above the crop: the third is called by *Wormius*, the northern lumme; and *Marsilius* calls the fourth the little lumme. The natives pretend to foretel the change of weather by their crying and flying; for they think that the wind must always blow from that point towards which they fly: however they are frequently deceived in their judgment.

* 1. Colymbus maximus. Gesn. Stell. 2. Colymbus arcticus lumme dictus. Worm. 3. Colymbus macula sub mente castanea. Stell. 4. Colymbus five pedicipes cinereus. *Ejusdem.*

Here are also found great numbers of small birds, such as plovers and snipes of different sorts, which they catch with snares and gins.

Class III. *Of the* LAND FOWLS.

The chief of these birds is the eagle, of which there are four species in *Kamtschatka*: the first is the black eagle, with a white head, tail, and feet. These are rare upon the main land of *Kamtschatka*; but, according to Mr. *Steller*, they are found in plenty on the islands between it and *America*. They make their nests (which are near six feet in diameter, and about a foot thick) of shrubs upon high cliffs, and in the beginning of *July*, lay two eggs. The young ones are as white as snow: these he saw upon *Bering*'s island, but not without danger from the old ones, which, even when he did not the least hurt to their young, attacked him with such violence that he could scarce defend himself from them with his stick. The second is the white eagle, which the *Tungusi* call elo: this I saw near *Nertchinski*; however it is not white but grey. Mr. *Steller* says, that this is bred upon the river *Harioufkovoi* which runs into the *Penschinska* sea. The third is the black and white spotted eagle. The fourth, the dark clay-coloured eagle, the extremities of whose wings and tail are spotted: these two last mentioned abound most here. The natives eat the eagles, and esteem them agreeable food.

Here are likewise several other birds of prey, such as vultures, hawks of various kinds, owls, and above all, ravens, crows, and magpies, which are the same with those in *Europe*. Besides, here are great numbers of cuckoos, water sparrows, growse, partridges, thrushes, larks, swallows, and several other small birds, whose appearance in the spring the natives expect with great impatience, and thence begin their new year.

In the conclusion of this chapter we have added a list of some plants, beasts, fishes, and birds, with their names in the *English*, *Russian*, *Kamtschatka*, *Koratski*, and *Kurilski* languages.

A

A LIST of some PLANTS, BEASTS, FISHES, and BIRDS; with their Names in the English, Russian, Kamtschatka, Koratski, and Kurilski Languages.

PLANTS.

English	Russian	Kamtschatka	Koratski	Kurilski
The birch tree	Beresnick	Heby	Lugune	
Poplar	Topslucke	Thispiai	Yakul	
Willow	Vetelnicke	Liumtche	Tekile	
Alder	Olchosnike	Sikite	Nikiliou	Asse
Service tree	Rebenike	Kaihine	Eloene	Koxunoni
Juniper	Moshevelnike	Kahaine	Valvakitche	Pakæpnirumamai
Cherry laurel	Tchelemasnike	Kalhame	Eloene	
Dog brier	Shipovnike	Kavashe	Pitctakachatche	Kopokone
Honeysuckle	Shimslode	Lushinike	Nitchivoy	Enumetam
Barberries	Boiarishnike	Horatenune	Pitkitche	
Brambleberries	Morashka	Shiie	Etiette	Apuumenipe
Wortleberries	Golubitsa	Ningule	Lingule	Enumucuta
Cranberries	Kliukva	Tchikume	Emelkevina	Asitte
Bulberries	Briusnitou	Tchahauhe	Tiunaane	Nipopkipe

BEASTS.

English	Russian	Kamtschatka	Koratski	Kurilski
Sea calves	Tiulenne	Kolha	Memele	Retactore
Sea beaver	Babri	Kaiku	Kalaga	Rahku
Sea cat	Kotti	Tatlatche	Tatatche	Ounepe
A fox	Lifotsa	Tchashiai	Yaivne	Kimutpe
Sables	Cobali	Kemhime	Kitighime	Na
Ermines	Goraoslai	Doitchitche	Imahuhake	Tannerume
A wolf	Volka	Kitaia	Eglinguue	Orgia
Bear	Medved	Kasha	Kainga	
Glutton	Rassamak	Timmi	Haeppi	These beasts are not known in the Kurilski islands
Marmotta	Evrashka	Ciredatche	Gilnak	
Elk	Oleni	Eluahappe	Lugaki	
Stone ram	Kammenoi barenu	Guadinadatche	Kitipe	

FISHES.

English	Russian	Kamtschatka	Koratski	Kurilski
A large kind of salmon	Tchavitche	Tchovnitche	Evotche	Tchivira
Red fish	Krashnoiriha	Kehivishe	Niovoai	Sitchine
The humpback	Gorbushe	Koanautchi	Kalal	Siakipa
Turbot	Kambala	Sigisigh	Alpa	Tantaka
Lampreys	Minoghi	Kanaganshe	Unknown	Unknown
Smelts	Korouchi	Innahu		
Herring	Seldi	Neriner		
Skate	Skata	Kopashu	Kammiahacke	Kapashu
Cod fish	Freska	Battui	Unknown	Unknown
Whales	Kili	Dai	Junghi	Rika

BIRDS.

English	Russian	Kamtschatka	Koratski	Kurilski
Great sea cormorant	Boloshoi tchaika	Atuma	Attume	Pongapiphe
Swan	Lebed	Matame	Kamtchan	
Geese	Goussed	Ksude	Gecloaine	Kuntape
A drake	Celesna	Baine	Gectchogatche	Bakariku
Stone ducks	Kammenia utki	Nikingike	Unknown	Vaiout
Widgeons	Gargari, Ashoai	Yovaiva		Cesse
Eagles	Orli	Selche	Tilmiti	Surgoar
Hawkes	Saholi	Shishi	Tilmitil	
Partridges	Kuropatki	Euihtchitche	Euette	Niepue
Crows	Voronni	Kaka	Tchautchavaola yelle	Paskure
Magpies	Saroki	Nakitchectche	Unkitigin	Kakuk
Ravens	Voronitcherni	Hagulhak	Nimetta yelle	Kuahan
Swallows	Laslotchki	Kaiukutche	Kavalingek	Rikintchire
Larks	Javoronki	Tchelaalai	Geatcheiere	Kahkok
Cuckows	Kokashke	Koakoutchitche	Kaikuke	Etchikumama
Snipes	Kuliki	Soakulutche	Tcheiaa	

CHAP. XI.

Of INSECTS.

AS *Kamtschatka* abounds with lakes and marshes, the swarms of insects in the summer time would make life intolerable there, if it were not for the frequent winds and rains. The maggots are so numerous as to occasion great destruction to their provisions, particularly in the time of preparing their fish, which are sometimes entirely destroyed by them. In the months of *June*, *July*, and *August*, when the weather happens to be fine, the musketoes and small gnats are very troublesome; however the inhabitants do not suffer much from them, as they are at that time, upon account of the fishery, out at sea, where by reason of the cold and wind few of these insects are to be met with.

It is but lately that bugs appeared upon the river *Awatscha*, which were brought thither in chests and cloaths: they are not yet known in *Kamtschatka*. Upon account of the wet weather and storms few of the butterfly kind are found here, except in some woods near the upper *Kamtschatkoi* fort, where they abound. It has been observed that numbers of these insects have settled upon vessels which were 30 versts from the shore: it appears somewhat extraordinary that they should be able to fly to such a distance without resting; most likely the storms so frequent here might drive them out to sea, and by their violence support them.

There are few spiders in *Kamtschatka*; so that the women who are fond of having children, and who have a notion that these insects swallowed render them fruitful and their labour easy, have great trouble to find them. Nothing plagues the natives

natives in their huts so much as the lice and fleas; the women suffer most from the former, by wearing very long, and sometimes false hair. Mr. *Steller* was told, that near the sea is found an insect that resembles a louse, which working itself through the skin into the flesh is never to be cured, unless by cutting the creature intirely out; and that the fishers are very much afraid of them.

It is remarkable that in *Kamtschatka* there are neither frogs, toads, nor serpents. Lizards, indeed, are numerous enough, which the natives look upon as spies sent from the infernal powers for information, and to foretel their death: therefore they are very careful whenever they find them to cut then into small pieces, that they may never carry back news to the power which sent them; and if it happens that the animal escapes alive, it throws them into the greatest grief and despair, as they expect every hour to die, which indeed sometimes happens from their own fear and despondency, and then serves to confirm the superstition to others.

CHAP. XII.

Of the TIDES *in the* Penschinska *Sea and Eastern Ocean.*

IT might perhaps appear sufficient to say, that the tides are agreeable in these seas to what are observed in others; but as I made some observations which appeared to me new, I think it proper to communicate them.

It is a known rule in general, that the ebb and flood happen twice in the natural day, and that the tides are highest about the new and full moon: however, I do no recollect that it has been observed that the ebbs and floods are not equal here, or that they

do

do not happen at fixed times, but according to the age of the moon, as I obferved in the *Penfchinfka* fea; and if this general opinion be true, that the ebbs and floods in other feas are equal, and at fixed hours, then the *Kamtfchatkoi* fea refembles only the White Sea, where I am told that there is one high fpring and one low flood in the fame day. The laft the natives call *maniha*; therefore I thought it proper carefully to relate the difference of the tides here, both with regard to the high water and the maniha: for the better underftanding of which in the original is fubjoined a long journal, which was kept for three months, and likewife the journal of Captain *Elagine*, which was taken at the mouth of the river *Ochotfka*, the *Kurilfki* iflands, and the haven of *Petropaulaufkay*; which we omit, as it would only be a ufelefs burthen to the *Englifh* reader.

Now, in order to be the more intelligible, I muft obferve, that the fea water which flows into the bays does not always run intirely back, but only according to the age of the moon; fo that fometimes in the time of ebb nothing remains but the water of the river which is within its own banks, at other times thefe banks are all overflowed with water. All the fea water runs out about the full and new moon, when the flood follows immediately upon the ebb, and it rifes near eight feet. The flood continues about eight hours, and then it begins to ebb, which continues fix hours; after which it flows again for three hours, the water not rifing quite a foot; at laft the ebb begins, which continues feven hours, and all the fea water runs out In this manner are the floods and ebbs regulated for three days after the full and new moon; at the end of which the time of the flowing and ebbing, and height of the flood and ebb, is lefs, the maniha greater, the fea water which was before faid to run all out now remains in fome part, and as the moon approaches the quadratures, the large tides grow lefs and the maniha greater; fo that after the ebb of the maniha the greater quantity of water remains ftill in the bays, and at laft,

at

at the quarter moons, what were the high tides change into the maniha, and the maniha into them. I reckon the change of the high tide into the maniha, and of the maniha into the high tide, from the time when one tide begins at midday and the other at midnight; or when it begins to flow or ebb at six hours in the morning and six in the afternoon.

I shall likewise communicate the methods that I followed in my observations: In the mouth of a river I placed a stake, divided into feet and inches of the *Paris* measure; the lowest mark was at the height of the river water in the time of the ebb at the new and full moon. This stake I fixed without great trouble, but am obliged to own that I was not able to ascertain exactly the height of the water in the flood, because it always comes in surges, which renders the stake wet somewhat higher than the true depth; nor can I certainly determine whether the water continues at the same height, or not, for any certain time.

OF THE

NATIVES of *Kamtschatka*,

AND THEIR

CUSTOMS *and* MANNERS.

PART III.

CHAP. I.

Of the NATIVES *of* Kamtschatka *in general.*

THE natives of *Kamtschatka* are as wild as the country itself. Some of them have no fixed habitations, but wander from place to place with their herds of rein-deer; others have settled habitations, and reside upon the banks of the rivers and the shore of the *Penschinska* sea, living upon fish and sea animals, and such herbs as grow upon the shore: the former dwell in huts covered with deer-skins, the latter in places dug out of the earth; both in a very barbarous manner: their dispositions and tempers are rough; and they are intirely ignorant of letters or religion.

The natives are divided into three different people, namely, the *Kamtfchadales*, *Koreki*, and *Kuriles*. The *Kamtfchadales* live upon the fouth fide of the promontory of *Kamtfchatka*, from the mouth of the river *Ukoi* to the *Kurilfkaya Lopatka*, and upon the firft *Kurilfkoy* ifland *Schumtfchu*: the *Koreki* inhabit the northern parts on the coaft of the *Penfchinfka* fea as far as the river *Nuktchan*, and round the Eaftern Ocean almoft to *Anadir*: the *Kuriles* inhabit the fecond *Kurilfkoy* ifland, and the other iflands in that fea, reaching as far as thofe of *Japan*.

The *Kamtfchadales* may be divided into the northern and fouthern; the northern people, who live along the river *Kamtfhatka* on the coaft of the Eaftern Ocean as far as the mouth of the river *Ukoi*, and fouthward to the mouth of the river *Nalacheva*, may be efteemed the principal nation; their manners being more civilifed, and their language appearing every where to be the fame; whereas the others fpeak differently on every ifland.

The fouthern nation live along the coaft of the Eaftern Ocean, from the *Nalacheva* to the *Kurilfkaya Lopatka*, and thence along the *Penfchinfka* fea northwards to the river *Harioufkovoy*.

The *Koreki* are commonly divided into two nations; one is called the rein-deer *Koreki*, and the other the fixed *Koreki*. The former wander with their herds from place to place; the latter live near the rivers, like the *Kamtfchadales*. Their languages are fo different that they do not underftand each other, particularly thofe that border upon the *Kamtfchadales*, from whom they have borrowed much of their language.

Some likewife divide the *Kuriles* into two different nations or tribes calling one the diftant and the other the nearer *Kuriles*. By the diftant they underftand the inhabitants of the fecond *Kurilfkoy* ifland and the others that lie near *Japan*; by the nearer *Kuriles*, the inhabitants of *Lopatka* and of the firft ifland. But this divifion is not proper; for though the inhabitants of the firft ifland and the *Lopatka* differ fomewhat from the *Kamtfchadales*

both

both in their language and customs, yet we have reason to believe they are the same people; the difference only arising from their neighbourhood, and intermarriages with the true *Kuriles*.

The *Kamtschadales* have this particular custom, that they endeavour to give every thing a name in their language which may express the property of it; but if they don't understand the thing quite well themselves, then they take a name from some foreign language, which perhaps has no relation to the thing itself: as, for example, they call a priest *Bogbog*, because probably they hear him use the word *Bogbog*, God; bread they call *Brightatin Augsh*, that is, *Russian* root; and thus of several other words to which their language is a stranger.

The names which the *Russians* give these different nations they did not take from the natives, but rather from their neighbours: for example, the name of the *Kamtschadales* was taken from the *Koreki*, who call them *Kontchal*. The derivation of the name *Koreki* is uncertain; however *Steller* thinks that it probably came from the word *Kora*, which in their language signifies a rein-deer; and that the *Russian* Cossacks frequently hearing the word *Kora*, or observing that their whole riches consisted in rein-deer, gave them the name of *Koreki*.

The inhabitants of *Kamtschatka* have three languages, that of the *Kamtschadales*, the *Koreki*, and *Kuriles*; each of which is divided into different dialects. The *Kamtschatka* language has three principal dialects: the first is used by the northern, the second by the southern, which differ so much that one may look upon them as different languages; however, they can understand one another without any interpreter: the third dialect is that which is spoken by those who live upon the *Penschinska* sea, between the rivers *Vorovskaya* and *Teghil*, which is composed of both the above-mentioned dialects and some words taken from the *Koreki*.

The language of the *Koreki* consists of two dialects; one of which is spoken by the rein-deer *Koreki*, and the other by the fixed. We are not, indeed, certain what other dialects may be amongst them, being well acquainted only with those who are subject to the *Russians*; but it is probable that those who are scattered among the islands may have some difference in their way of speaking. The *Kamtschatka* language is spoken half in the throat and half in the mouth: the pronunciation is slow and difficult, and seems to indicate a timorous, slavish, and deceitful people; as in fact they are.

The *Koreki* speak aloud, and in a screaming tone; their words are long, but their sentences short, and their words generally begin with two vowels, and end with one or two more: as for example, uemkai, a rein-deer which has not been driven.

The *Kuriles* speak slow, distinctly, and agreeably: their words are middling, the vowels and consonants being justly mixed: and of all these wild people the *Kuriles* are the best, being honest, constant, civil, and hospitable.

CHAP. II.

Some Conjectures concerning the Names of the Kamtschadales, *and the other Inhabitants of* Kamtschatka.

SOME assert, that the *Kamtschadales* were so named by the *Russians* from the river *Kamtschatka*, but it was called so before the *Russians* had discovered it, and had its name from a chieftain, called *Konchata*.

We cannot find likewise why the *Koreki* call the *Kamtschadales*, *Kontchalo*, nor can they give any reasons for it themselves.

The *Kamtſchadales*, beſides the general name *Itelmen*, diſtinguiſh themſelves by adding the name of the river, or remarkable place where they live, as *Kikſha-ai*, an inhabitant upon the Great River; *Suatchu-ai*, an inhabitant upon the river *Awatſcha*; for the word *ai* being added to any river or remarkable ſituation, denotes inhabitant of that place, as the word *Itelmen* is the general name for inhabitant. Thoſe who think *Konchata* to have been a great captain, ſeem to have applied to him only all the brave actions which ought to be attributed to the ſeveral inhabitants upon the river *Elouki*, who are called *Koatche-ai*, or, in the common way of ſpeaking, *Kontchat*: beſides, this being a received opinion, that the inhabitants of the river *Elouki* are the braveſt of all the *Kamtſchadales*, the *Koreki*, who are their neighbours, might eaſily call the whole nation *Kamtſchadales* from their name *Koatche-ai*; and it is nothing extraordinary to find the word *Koatche-ai* changed into *Kontchala*, and *Kontchala* into *Kamtſchadale*, as we find ſeveral ſimilar examples, not only among theſe barbarous people, but the politeſt nations of *Europe*.

With regard to the place where the *Kamtſchadales* came from, or at what time they firſt ſettled here, we can have no certain account; for all that can be obtained from theſe people is only fabulous tradition; and they pretend that they were created upon this very ſpot, and ſay, their firſt anceſtor was *Kuthu*, who formerly lived in the heavens: however by their manners, cuſtoms, language, dreſs, and other circumſtances, it would appear that the *Kamtſchadales* came over from *Mungalia*. Of the antiquity of theſe people *Steller* gives the following proofs: 1ſt that they have loſt every tradition of their origin. 2d. That before the arrival the *Ruſſians*, they knew little of any other people, except the *Koreki* and *Tchukotſkoi*; and it is but lately that they came to any knowledge of the *Kuriks* and *Japaneſe*, and this was owing to the arrival of the latter among them to trade, from a *Japanese* boat having been cast away upon their coast. 3*d*. That these people are extremely numerous notwithstanding so many are destroyed every year by wild beasts, &c. 4*th*. From their great knowledge of the virtues and uses of the natural produce of the country, which cannot be attained in a short time, not to mention that they have no more than four months in the year left for this enquiry, and great part of those too they must employ in fishing and making provisions for winter. 5*th*. All their instruments and houshold furniture are different from those of other nations, and their necessities seem to have directed the invention of most of them. 6*th*. That their uncultivated state of nature and passions seem to differ very little from that of the brute beasts, pleasures being their only pursuit, having no idea of futurity.

The following reasons incline us to think that they take their origin from the *Mungals*, not from the *Tartars* who live upon the river *Amur*, nor from the *Kuriles* or *Japanese*; for if they had sprung from the *Tartars* it is probable they would have settled about the river *Lena*, where the *Jakutski* and *Tungusi* live at present, these places being formerly uninhabited, and much more fruitful than *Kamtschatka*; nor can we imagine that they were driven thence by the *Jakutski*; the difference of their manners, and make of their bodies from the *Kuriles* is such that we cannot believe they sprung from them; and that their origin should be *Japanese* appears improbable, because their settlement must have been prior to the separation of the *Japanese* from the empire of *China*; and that they were settled there long before the *Japanese* fixed in these islands in the sea of *Kamtschatka* appears from their not knowing the use of iron, or iron ore, though it is above two thousand years since the *Mungals* made their arms and other instruments of iron, and the other *Tartars* knives and daggers of copper; therefore it is probable that the *Kamtschadales* were driven hither by the tyranny

ranny of the Eastern conquerors, as the *Lopari*, *Ostiaks*, and *Samojeds* were driven to the extremities of the North by the encroachments of other *European* nations. If *Kamtschatka* had not been inhabited before the *Tungusi* had got a settlement, it is probable they would have fixed here, as being safer from the dangers of any sudden attacks of their enemies.

Thus it appears likely, that the *Kamtschadales* lived formerly in *Mungalia* beyond the river *Amur*, and made one people with the *Mungals*, which is farther confirmed by the following observations, such as the *Kamtschadales* having several words common to the *Mungal Chinese* language, as their terminations in *ong*, *ing*, *oang*, *chin*, *cha*, *ching*, *ksi*, *ksung*; it would be still a greater proof if we could show several words and sentences the same in both languages: but not to insist only upon the language, the *Kamtschadales* and *Mungals* are both of a small stature, are swarthy, have black hair, a broad face, a sharp nose, with the eyes falling in, eyebrows small and thin, a hanging belly, slender legs and arms; they are both remarkable for cowardice, boasting, and slavishness to people who use them hard, and for their obstinacy and contempt of those who treat them with gentleness.

CHAP. III

Of the ANCIENT STATE *of the Natives of* Kamtschatka.

BEFORE the *Russian* conquest they lived in perfect freedom, having no chief, being subject to no law, nor paying any taxes; the old men, or those who were remarkable for their bravery, bearing the principal authority in their villages, though none had any right to command or inflict punishment.

punishment. Although in outward appearance they resemble the other inhabitants of *Siberia*, yet the *Kamtschadales* differ in this, that their faces are not so long as the other *Siberians*', their cheeks stand more out, their teeth are thick, their mouth large, their stature middling, and their shoulders broad, particularly those people who inhabit the sea coast.

Their manner of living is slovenly to the last degree; they never wash their hands nor face, nor cut their nails; they eat out of the same dish with the dogs, which they never wash; every thing about them stinks of fish; they never comb their heads, but both men and women plait their hair in two locks, binding the ends with small ropes: when any hair starts out, they sow it with threads to make it lie close; by this means they have such a quantity of lice that they can scrape them off by handfuls, and they are nasty enough even to eat them. Those that have not natural hair sufficient wear false locks, sometimes as much as weigh ten pounds, which makes their heads look like a hay-cock.

They have extraordinary notions of God, of sins, and good actions. Their chief happiness consists in idleness and satisfying their natural lusts and appetites; these incline them to singing, dancing, and relating of love stories Their greatest unhappiness or trouble is the want of these amusements: they shun this by all methods, even at the hazard of their lives, for they think it more eligible to die than to lead a life that is disagreeable to them; which opinion frequently leads them to self-murder. This was so common after the conquest, that the *Russians* had great difficulty to put a stop to it. They are chiefly employed in providing what is absolutely necessary for the present, and take no care for the future. They have no notion of riches, fame, or honour; therefore covetousness, ambition, and pride, are unknown among them. On the other hand, they are careless, lustful, and cruel: these vices occasion frequent quarrels and wars among them

sometimes

sometimes with their neighbours, not from a desire of increasing their power, but from some other causes; such as the carrying off their provisions, or rather their girls, which is frequently practised as the most summary method of procuring a wife.

Their trade is likewise not so much calculated for the acquisition of riches as for procuring the necessaries and conveniencies of life. They sell the *Koreki* sables, fox and white dog skins, dried mushroons, or such trifles; and receive in exchange cloaths made of deer-skins and other hides: among themselves they exchange what they abound with for what they want, as dogs, boats, dishes, troughs, nets, hemp, yarn, and provisions. This kind of barter is carried on under a great shew of friendship; for when one wants any thing that another has, he goes freely to visit him, and without any ceremony makes known his wants, although perhaps he never had any acquaintance with that person before: the landlord is obliged to behave according to the custom of the country; and bringing whatever his guest has occasion for, gives it him. He afterwards returns the visit, and must be received in the same manner; so that both parties have their wants supplied.

Their manners are quite rude they never use any civil expression or salutation; never take off their caps, nor bow to one another; and their discourse is stupid, and betrays the most consummate ignorance; and yet they are in some degree curious, and inquisitive upon many occasions.

They have filled almost every place in heaven and earth with different spirits, which they both worship and fear more than God: they offer them sacrifices upon every occasion, and some carry little idols about them, or have them placed in their dwellings; but, with regard to God, they not only neglect to worship him; but, in case of troubles and misfortunes, they curse and blaspheme him.

They keep no account of their age, though they can count as far as one hundred; but this is so troublesome to them that without their fingers they do not tell three. It is very diverting to see them reckon more than ten; for having reckoned the fingers of both hands they clasp them together, which signifies ten; then they begin with their toes, and count to twenty; after which they are quite confounded, and cry, *Matcha?* that is, Where shall I take more. They reckon ten months in the year, some of which are longer and some shorter; for they do not divide them by the changes of the moon, but by the order of particular occurrences that happen in those regions, as may be seen in the following table:

1st. Purifier of sins; for in this month they have a holiday for the purification of all their sins.

2d. Breaker of hatchets, from the great frost.

3d. Beginning of heat.

4th. Time of the long day.

5th. Preparing month.

6th. Red fish month.

7th. White fish month.

8th. Kaiko fish month.

9th. Great white fish month.

10th. Leaf falling month.

This last month continues to the month of *November*, or that of the purification, and it is the length of almost three months; however, these names of the months are not the same every where, but are only proper to the inhabitants upon the river *Kamtschatka*: the inhabitants of the northern parts give them different names, such as,

1st. The month of the rivers' freezing

2d. Hunting month.

3d. Purifier of sins.

4th. Breaker of hatchets, from the great frost.

5th. Time of the long day.

6th. Sea beavers puppying time

7th. Sea calves' puppying time.
8th. Time when the tame deer bring forth their young.
9th. When the wild deer bring forth.
10th. Beginning of the fishery.

Their division of time is pretty singular; they commonly divide our year into two, so that winter is one year, and summer another: the summer year begins in *May*, and the winter in *November*.

They do not distinguish the days by any particular appellation, nor form them into weeks or months, nor yet know how many days are in the month or year. They mark their epochs by some remarkable thing or other, such as the arrival of the *Russians*, the great rebellion, or the first expedition to *Kamtschatka*. They have no writings, nor hieroglyphick figures, to preserve the memory of any thing; so that all their knowledge depends upon tradition, which soon becomes uncertain and fabulous in regard to what is long past.

They are ignorant of the causes of eclipses, but when they happen, they carry fire out of their huts, and pray the luminary eclipsed to shine as formerly. They know only three constellations; the Great Bear, the Pleiades, and the three stars in Orion; and give names only to the principal winds.

Their laws in general tend to give satisfaction to the injured person. If any one kills another, he is to be killed by the relations of the person slain. They burn the hands of people who have been frequently caught in theft, but for the first offence the thief must restore what he hath stolen, and live alone in solitude, without expecting any assistance from others. They think they can punish an undiscovered theft by burning the sinews of the stone-buck in a publick meeting with great ceremonies of conjuration, believing that as these sinews are contracted by the fire so the thief will have all his limbs contracted. They never have any disputes about their land or their huts, every one having land and water more than sufficient for his wants.

Although their manner of living be most nasty, and their actions most stupid, yet they think themselves the happiest people in the world, and look upon the *Russians* who are settled among them with contempt: however this notion begins to change at present; for the old people who are confirmed in their customs, drop off, and the young ones being converted to the Christian religion, adopt the customs of the *Russians*, and despise the barbarity and superstition of their ancestors.

In every *Ostrog*, or large village, by order of her Imperial Majesty, is appointed a chief who is sole judge in all causes, except those of life and death; and not only these chiefs, but even the common people, have their chapels for publick worship. Schools are also erected in almost every village to which the *Kamtschadales* send their children with great pleasure: by this means it is to be hoped, that their barbarity will be in a short time rooted out.

The Inside of a Winter Hut

CHAP. IV.

Of the OSTROGS, *or* HABITATIONS, *of the* Kamtschadales.

UNDER the name of *Oſtrog* we underſtand every habitation confiſting of one or more huts, which are all ſurrounded by an earthen wall or palliſadoe.

The huts are built in the following manner: they dig a hole in the earth about five feet deep, the breadth and length of which is proportioned to the number of people defigned to live in it. In the middle of this hole they plant four thick wooden pillars; over theſe they lay balks, upon which they form their roof or cieling, leaving in the middle a ſquare opening which ſerves them for a window and chimney; this they cover with graſs and earth, ſo that the outward appearance is like a round hillock; but within they are of an oblong ſquare, and the fireplace is in one of the long ſides of the ſquare: between the pillars round the walls of their huts they make benches, upon which each family lies ſeparately; but on that ſide oppoſite to the fire, there are no benches, it being defigned for their kitchen furniture, in which they dreſs their victuals for themſelves and dogs. In theſe huts where there are no benches, there are balks laid upon the floor, and covered with mats. They adorn the walls of their huts with mats made of graſs.

They enter their huts by ladders commonly placed near the fire hearth, ſo that when they are heating their huts the ſteps of the ladder become ſo hot, and the ſmoke ſo thick, as almoſt to suffocate any one who is not inured to bear it: but the natives find no difficulty in going out or in; and though they can only fix their toes on the steps of the ladder, they mount like squirrels; nor do the women hesitate to go through this smoke with their children upon their shoulders; though there is another opening through which the women are allowed to pass; but if any man should pretend to do the same he would be laughed at. The *Kamtschadales* live in these huts all the winter, after which they go out into others which they call balagans: these serve them not only to live in during the summer, but also for magazines. They are made in the following manner: Nine pillars, about two fathom long or more, are fixed in the ground, and bound together with balks laid over them, which they cover with rods, and over all lay grass, fastening spars and a round sharp roof at top, which they cover with bramble, and thatch with grass. They fasten the lower ends of the spars to the balks with ropes and thongs, and have a door on each side one directly opposite to the other.

They have such balagans, not only round their winter habitations, but also in those places where they lay up their food in summer; and they are certainly very convenient in this country on account of the frequent rains, which would surely spoil all their fish if it was not preserved in such places; besides, when they return from fishing and hunting in the harvest, they leave their dry fish here, 'till they can fetch it in the winter; and this without any guard only taking away the ladders. If these buildings were not so high the wild beasts would undoubtedly plunder them; for notwithstanding all their precaution, the bears sometimes climb up and force their way into their magazines, especially in the harvest when the fish and berries begin to grow scarce. In the summer, when they go a hunting, they have, besides their balagans, huts made of grass, in which they dress

their

Summer Huts.

their victuals and clean their fish in bad weather; and the Cossacks boil their salt from sea water in them. The villages, which are well inhabited, having their common huts surrounded with these balagans, make a very agreeable appearance at a distance.

The southern *Kamtschadales* commonly build their villages in thick woods, and other places which are naturally strong, not less than twenty versts from the sea; and their summer habitations are near the mouths of their rivers; but those who live upon the *Penschinska* sea and the Eastern Ocean build their villages very near the shore.

They look upon that river near which their village is situated, as the inheritance of their tribe; and if one or two families at any time desire to live separate from their native village, they build themselves huts upon the same river, or some branch that falls into it; from which it is natural to imagine, that the inhabitants of every village have originally sprung from the same father; and the *Kamtschadales* themselves say, that *Kut*, whom they sometimes call God, and sometimes their first father, lived two years upon each river, and left the children that river, on which they were born, for their proper inheritance; and though formerly the *Kamtschadales* used only to hunt and fish upon their own rivers, they now wander above 200 versts to kill the sea animals upon the *Awatscha*, or the *Kurilskaya Lopatka*.

CHAP. V.

Of their HOUSHOLD FURNITURE, *and other necessary Utensils.*

ALL the *Kamtschatka* houshold furniture consists in dishes, bowls, troughs, and cans made of birch bark. As these people have not the use of metals, we think it is proper to explain, how without the use of instruments of iron, they are able to perform their houshold work, such as building, sawing, making of fire, dressing their victuals; being all the while so ignorant that they can scarcely count ten. How powerfully does necessity work upon the most insensible minds!

Before the arrival of the *Russians* the *Kamtschadales* used stones and bones instead of metals, out of which they made hatchets, spears, arrows, needles, and lances. Their hatchets were made of the bones of whales and rein-deer, and sometimes of agate or flint stones. They were shaped in form of a wedge, and fastened to crooked handles. With these they hollowed out their canoes, bowls, and troughs; but with so much expence of trouble and time, that a canoe would be three years in making, and a large bowl one year. For this reason, a large canoe or trough was in as great esteem among them as a vessel of the most precious metal and finest workmanship is with us; and the village which was in possession of such valued themselves extremely upon it, especially if they were masters of a bowl which would serve for more than one guest. These bowls they dress their victuals in, and heat their broth by throwing red-hot stones into it.

Their knives were made of a greenish mountain chrystal, sharp-pointed, and shaped like a lancet, which was stuck into

Method of producing Fire.

a wooden handle. Of such chryftals were made likewife their arrows fpears, and launcets, with which they continue ftill to let blood. Their fewing needles they made of the bones of fables, with which they not only fewed their cloaths together, but made alfo very curious embroidery.

In order to kindle fire they have a board of dry wood with round holes in the fides of it, and a fmall round ftick; this they rub in a hole 'till it takes fire, and inftead of tinder they ufe dry grafs beat foft. Thefe inftruments are held in fuch efteem by the *Kamtfchadales* that they are never without them, and they value them more than our fteels and flints: but they are excefsively fond of other iron inftruments, fuch as hatchets, knives, or needles; nay, at the firft arrival of the *Ruffians* a piece of broken iron was looked upon as a great prefent, and even yet they receive it with thankfulnefs, knowing how to make ufe of the leaft fragment either to point their arrows or make darts, which they do by hammering it out cold between two ftones. All the favage inhabitants of thefe parts are particularly fond of iron, and know how to manage it very curioufly. As fome of them delight in war, the *Ruffian* merchants are forbid to fell them any warlike inftruments; but they are ingenious enough to make fpears and arrows out of the iron pots and kettles which they buy; and they are fo dextrous when the eye of a needle breaks as to make a new eye, which they will repeat until nothing remains but the point. Even at the time when I was there it was only the better fort and thofe that lived near to the *Ruffians* that made ufe of iron or copper veffels, the reft ftill preferring their wooden difhes.

It is faid, that the *Kamtfchadales* knew the ufe of iron even before the arrival of the *Ruffians*; that they received it from the *Japanefe*, who came to the *Kurilfki* iflands, and once to the mouth of the river *Kamtfchatka*; and that the name which the *Kamtfchadales* give the *Japanefe* of *Shifman* comes from *fhifh*, a needle. The *Japanese* certainly used to come and trade to the *Kurilski* islands, for I found there a *Japanese* sabre, a japanned waiter, and silver ear-rings, which could be brought from no other place.

Of all the curiosities made by these wild people with their stone knives and hatchets, nothing surprised me so much as a chain of whales' bones, found in an empty hut near the *Tchukotskoi* Nofs, made of different links as smooth as if they had been turned, about a foot and a half long, and formed out of one tooth. It is very extraordinary that any of these wild people should with nothing but stone instruments have been capable of making so curious a piece of workmanship, which was worthy of the best artist.

They have two methods of making their boats; one sort of which is called *koaihtahta*, and the other *tahta*. The former do not differ from our fishermens' boats, except that the prow and stern are higher, and the sides lower. The tahta has the prow and stern of an equal height; the middle is not bent out, but rather falls in, which makes it very inconvenient, especially when there is any wind, as being very soon filled with water. They use the koaihtahta only upon the river *Kamtschatka*, but the tahta in most other places. When any planks are sewed upon the tahta they are called baidars, which are used by the inhabitants upon the *Bobrovoi* or Beaver sea in pursuing the sea animals. They split these baidars, and sewing them with whales' beards caulk them with moss or nettles beat soft. The *Kuriles* of the islands and those that live upon the *Lopatka* build the baidars with a keel, to which they sew planks with whales' beard, and caulk them with moss. In *Kamtschatka* they make their boats of poplar wood only; but the *Kuriles*, having no proper wood of their own, are obliged to make use of what is thrown on shore by the sea, and which is supposed to come from the coast of *Japan*, *America*, or *China*. The northern inhabitants of *Kamtschatka*,

the

KAMTSCHATKA, &c.

the settled *Koreki* and *Tchukotskoi*, for want of proper timber and plank, make their baidars of the skins of sea animals.

These boats hold two persons, one of which sits in the prow and the other in the stern. They push them against the stream with poles, which is attended with great trouble: when the current is strong they can scarcely advance two feet in ten minutes; notwithstanding which, they will carry these boats full loaded sometimes 20 versts, and, when the stream is not very strong, even 30 or 40 versts.

In the larger boats they can carry 30 or 40 pood; and when the goods are not very heavy, they lay them upon a float or bridge made between two boats joined together. They use this method in transporting their provisions down with the stream, and also to and from the islands.

CHAP. VI.

Of the LABOUR *appropriated to the* DIFFERENT SEXES.

IN the summer time the men are employed in catching, drying, and transporting fish to their habitations; in preparing bones and sour fish to feed their dogs: the women, in cleaning the fish, and spreading it out to dry; and sometimes they go a fishing with their husbands. After their fishing is over, they gather in the herbs, roots, and berries, both for food and medicine.

In the harvest the men catch the fish that appear at that time, and kill fowl, such as geese, ducks, swans, and the like; they teach their dogs to draw carriages, and prepare wood for their fledges, and other ufes. The women at this time are bufy with their hemp of nettles, in pulling it up, watering, breaking, peeling, and laying it up in their balagans.

The men in the winter hunt for fables and foxes, weave fifhing nets, make fledges, fetch wood, and bring their provifions from feveral places, which they had prepared in the fummer, and could not bring home in the harveft. The women are principally employed in fpinning thread for nets.

In the fpring, when the rivers begin to thaw, the fifh that wintered in them go towards the fea; and the men are bufied in catching them or the fea animals that at this time frequent the bays. The people upon the Eaftern Ocean catch the fea beaver. All the women go into the fields, where they gather wild garlick, and other young tender herbs, which they ufe not only in a fcarcity of other provifion, which often happens at this feafon of the year, but likewife out of luxury; for fo fond are they of every thing that is green, that during the whole fpring they are feldom without having fome of it in their mouths; and though they always bring home a great bundle of greens, they feldom laft them above a day.

Befides the above-mentioned employments the men are obliged to build their huts and balagans, to heat their huts, drefs victuals, feed their dogs, flea the animals, whofe fkins are ufed in cloathing, and provide all houfhold and warlike inftruments: the women are here the only taylors and fhoemakers, for they drefs the fkins, make the cloaths, fhoes, and ftockings: it is even a difgrace for the men to do any thing of that fort; fo that they looked upon the *Ruffians* who came here firft in a very ridiculous light, when they faw them ufe either their needle or awl. The women are likewife employed in dying fkins, in conjuration, and curing of the fick. Their method of preparing and dying fkins, fewing and joining them, is as follows: every fkin which they

ufe

use for cloaths, such as deer-skins, seals, dogs, and beavers, they prepare one way: in the first place, wetting and spreading it out, they scrape off all the pieces of fat or veins that remained after fleaing it, with stones fixed in pieces of wood; then rubbing it over with fresh or sour caviar, they roll it up and tread it with their feet 'till the hide begins to stink; they again scrape and clean it, and continue this 'till the skin is soft and clean. Such skins as they want to prepare without the hair they use at first in the same manner as above; then hang them in the smoke for a week, and afterwards soak them in warm water to make the hair fall off; at last rubbing them with caviar, by frequent treading and scraping them with stones, they make them clean and soft.

They dye the deer and dog skins, which they use for cloathing, with alder bark cut and rubbed very small; but the seal-skins, which they use either for cloathing, shoes, or straps for binding their sledges, they dye in a particular manner: having first cleaned off the hair they make a bag of the skin, and turning the hair side outward they pour into it a strong decoction of alder bark; after it has lain thus sometime, they hang it upon a tree, and beat it with a stick. This operation they repeat 'till the colour is gone quite through the skin; then they rip it open, and stretching it out, dry it in the air; at last they rub it 'till it becomes soft and fit for use. Such skins are not unlike dressed goat-skins: however, *Steller* says that the *Lamushki* have yet a better way of preparing them. These skins they call *mandari*, and they are worth three shillings a-piece. The hair of the seals, with which they ornament their cloaths and shoes, is dyed with the juice of the red wortleberry boiled with alder bark, alum, and lac lunæ; which makes a very bright colour. They used to sew their cloaths and shoes with needles made of bone, and instead of thread they made use of the fibres of the deer, which they split to the size or thickness required.

They make glue of the dried skins of fishes, and particularly of the whale-skin. A piece of this they wrap up in birch bark, and laying it for a little while in warm ashes they take it out; and it is then fit for use, and to me seems as good as the best *Yaick* glue.

CHAP. VII.

Of their DRESS.

THEIR cloaths, for the most part, are made of the skins of deer, dogs, several sea and land animals, and even of the skins of birds, frequently joining those of different animals in the same garment. They make the upper garment in two fashions; sometimes cutting the skirts all of an equal length; and sometimes leaving them long behind in form of a train. They are made of deer-skins, with wide sleeves of a length to come down below the knee: there is a hood or caul behind, which in bad weather they put over their heads below their caps: the opening above is only large enough to let their head pass: they sew the skins of dog's feet round this opening, with which they cover their faces in cold stormy weather, and round their skirts and sleeves they put a border of white dog-skin: upon their backs they sew the small shreds of skins or silk of different colours. They commonly wear two coats; the under coat with the hair-side inwards, the other side being dyed with alder; and the upper with the hair outwards. For the upper garment they choose black, white, or speckled skins, the hair of which is most esteemed for the beauty of its colours.

Men and women, without distinction, use the above-mentioned garments, their dress only differing in their under cloathing, and in the covering of their feet and legs. The women have an undergarment which they commonly wear at home in the houfe, confifting of breeches and waiftcoat fewed together. The breeches are wide, like thofe of the *Dutch* fkippers, and tie below the knee; the waiftcoat is wide above, and drawn round with a ftring. The fummer habits are made of dreffed fkins without hair; their winter garment is made of deer or ftone-ram fkins with the hair on. The undrefs or houfhold habit of the men is a girdle of leather, with a bag before, and likewife a leathern apron to cover them behind: thefe girdles are fewed with hair of different colours. The *Kamtfchadales* ufed formerly to go a hunting and fifhing during the fummer in this drefs; but now this fafhion is changed, and below their girdles they wear linen fhirts, which they buy from the *Ruffians*.

The covering of their feet and legs is made of fkins of different forts; in the fummer time during the rains, they wear the fkins of feals with the hair outwards; but their moft common covering is the fkin of the legs of the rein-deer, and fometimes of the legs of other beafts, the fhaggieft they can find, to preferve them againft the cold. But the fineft bufkins, which both the Coffacks and *Kamtfchadales* ufe in their greateft drefs, are made in the following manner: the fole is of white feal-fkin, the upper part of fine dyed leather, the hind quarters of white dog-skin; what comes round the legs is of dreffed leather or dyed feal-skins: the upper parts are embroidered. Thefe buskins are fo extraordinary, that if a batchelor is obferved to wear them he is immediately concluded to be upon a fcheme of courtfhip.

They wear the fame fort of caps as the people of *Jakutfki*. In the fummer they have a fort of hats of birch bark tied about their head: the *Kuriles* ufe in the fummer time caps made of platted grafs. The women's head-drefs is the perukes that we formerly mentioned; and thefe were fo dear to them, that when they

they came to be Christians they were with difficulty prevailed upon to quit this dress for one more decent: however, at present round the *Russ* settlements all is intirely changed, the women wearing shirts, ruffles, waistcoats, caps and ribbands; which change nobody now complains of, except the very old people. The women do all their work in mittins: they formerly never washed their faces, but now they use both white and red paint; for white paint they make use of a rotten wood, and for red a sea plant*, which they boil in seals' fat, and rubbing their cheeks with it make them very red. They dress most in the winter time, especially when they either receive or pay visits.

The common cloaths for a *Kamtschadale* and his family will not cost him less than an hundred rubles, for the coarsest worsted stockings, which cost in *Russia* 20 kopeeks, cannot be bought here for less than a ruble; and all other things are sold in the same proportion. The *Kuriles* are more able to buy good cloaths than the *Kamtschadales*, for they can purchase for one sea beaver as much as the *Kamtschadales* can for twenty foxes, and one beaver costs the *Kuriles* no more trouble than five foxes do the *Kamtschadales*; for he must be a good hunter who catches more than ten foxes in the winter, and a *Kurili* thinks himself unlucky if he doth not catch three beavers in the season; besides which great numbers are thrown upon the shore by storms.

* Fucus marinus abietis forma. Pinus maritima, seu fucus teres. Dood. Append. 326. Ray Linn.

CHAP. VIII.

Of their DIET *and* LIQUORS, *together with their Method of* COOKING.

HAVING already mentioned that the food of the *Kamtschadales* consists in roots, fish, and sea animals, which are all described in the second part of this book; we shall now relate their method of dressing them. And first, we will begin with the fish, which they use instead of bread. The principal food, called *yokola*, is prepared from every sort of fish, and serves them for household bread. They divide their fish into six parts; the sides and tail are hung up to dry; the back and thinner part of the belly are prepared apart, and generally dried over the fire; the head is laid to sour in pits, and then they eat it like salt fish, and esteem it much, though the stink is such that a stranger cannot bear it; the ribs and the flesh which remain upon them they hang up and dry, and afterwards pound them for use; the larger bones they likewise dry for food for their dogs: in this manner all these different people prepare the *yokola*, and they eat it for the most part dry.

Their second favourite food is caviar, or the roes of fish, which they prepare in three different ways: they dry the roe whole in the air, or take it out of the skin which envelopes it, and, spreading it upon a bed of grass, dry it before the fire; or lastly, make rolls of it with the leaves of grass, which they also dry. They never take a journey or go a hunting without dry caviar; and if a *Kamtschadale* has a pound of this, he can subsist without any other provision a great while; for every birch and alder tree furnishes him with bark, which, with his dried caviar, makes him an agreeable meal; but they cannot eat either separately, for the caviar sticks like glue to the teeth, and the bark, although it should be chewed ever so long by itself, they are hardly ever able to swallow down alone. There is still a fourth method which both the *Kamtschadles* and *Koreki* use in preparing their caviar; having covered the bottom of a pit with grass, they throw the fresh caviar into it, and leave it there to grow sour: the *Koreki* tie their's in bags and leave it to sour; this is esteemed their most delicate dish

There is a third sort of diet, called by the *Kamtschadales tchupriki*, which is prepared in this manner: in their huts over the fire-place they make a bridge of stakes, upon which they lay a heap of fish, which remains there 'till the hut becomes as warm as a bagnio; if there was no great thickness of fish one fire would serve to dress it; but sometimes they are obliged to make two, three, or more fires. Fish dressed in this manner is half roasted, half smoaked, and has a very agreeable taste, and may be reckoned the best of all the *Kamtschatka* cookery; for the whole juice and fat is prepared with a gradual heat, and kept in by the skin, in which it lies as in a bag, and when ready may be easily separated from the fish; as soon as it is thus dressed, they take out the guts, and spread the body upon a mat to dry; this they afterwards break small and put into bags, carrying it along with them for provision; and when dried eat it like the *yokola*.

The *Kamtschadales* have a dish, which they esteem very much, called *huigul*: it is fish laid to grow sour in pits; and though the smell of it is intollerable, yet the *Kamtschadales* esteem it a perfume. This fish sometimes rots so much in the pits that they cannot take it out without ladles; however in that case they use it for feeding their dogs.

Mr. *Steller* says, that the summer *Samojeds* likewise sour their fish; but that the earth being frozen preserves it much
better;

better; the *Jakutſki* alſo dig deep pits, in which they lay their fiſh, ſprinkling it with wood aſhes, and cover it with leaves at top, and over all put a layer of earth: this method is better than any of the former. The *Tunguſi* and Coſſacks of *Ochotſka* preſerve their fiſh in the ſame manner, with this difference only, that inſtead of wood aſhes, they uſe the aſhes of burnt ſea weed. They boil their freſh fiſh in troughs, take it out with boards and letting it cool eat it with a ſoup made of the ſweet graſs.

As for the fleſh of land and ſea animals, they boil it in their troughs, with ſeveral different herbs and roots; the broth they drink out of ladles and bowls, and the meat they take out upon boards, and eat in their hands. The whale and ſea horſe fat they alſo boil with roots.

There is a principal diſh at all their feaſts and entertainments, called *ſelaga*, which they make by pounding all ſorts of different roots and berries, with the addition of caviar, and whale and ſeals' fat.

Before the conqueſt they ſeldom uſed any thing for drink but water: but when they made merry they drank water which had ſtood ſome time upon muſhroons; but of this hereafter. At preſent they drink ſpirits as faſt as the *Ruſſians*: after dinner they drink water; and every one, when he goes to bed at night, ſets a veſſel of water by him, to which he puts ſnow or ice to keep it cold; and always drinks it up before morning. In the winter time they amuſe themſelves frequently by throwing handfuls of ſnow into their mouths; and the bridegrooms who work with the fathers of their future brides find it their hardeſt taſk to provide ſnow for their family in the ſummer time, for they muſt bring it from the higheſt hills be the weather what it will, otherwiſe they would ſo diſoblige as never to be forgiven.

CHAP. IX.

The Method of TRAVELLING *with* DOGS, *and the* FURNITURE *necessary thereto.*

THE Dogs of *Kamtschatka* differ very little from the common house dogs: they are of a middling size, of various colours, though there seem to be more white, black, and grey, than of any other. In travelling they make use of those that are gelded, and generally yoke four to a sledge.

The alaki is made of broad double soft straps, which are put over the dogs' shoulders, the near dog having it over his left, and the off dog over his right. At the end of these alaki's is a small thong, with a hook at the end of it, which is fastened to a ring in the fore part of the sledge.

The pobeshnick is a long strap, and serves instead of a coach pole. It passes through a ring, which is in the middle of the fore part of the sledge; and to it is fastened a chain that keeps the dogs together, that they should not run asunder.

The bridle is a long strap, with a hook and chain, which is fixed to the fore dogs, and is much longer than the pobeshnick, being fastened to a ring in the fore part of the sledge.

The osheiniki, or collars, are broad straps made of bear-skin, and are frequently put upon dogs merely for ornament.

They drive and direct their dogs with a crooked stick about four feet long, which they call the ostal, and sometimes adorn it with different coloured thongs: this is looked upon as a great piece of finery. They drive their sledges sitting upon the right

side

side with their feet hanging down; and it would be looked upon as a disgrace for any one to sit in the sledge, or to make use of any person to drive them, no body doing this but the women.

A set of four good dogs will cost in *Kamtschatka* 15 rubles, and with their harness complete come to near 20.

From the make of their sledges may be seen how difficult it is to travel upon them; for a man is obliged to keep the exactest balance, otherwise he is liable, from the height and narrowness of them, to be overturned. In a rugged road this would be very dangerous, as the dogs never stop 'till they come to some house, or are entangled by something upon the road; for they have this fault, that in going down steep hills they run with all their force, and are scarcely to be kept in: for which reason, in descending any great declivity they unyoke all the dogs except one, and lead them softly down the hill. They likewise walk up hills; for it is as much as the dogs can do to drag up the sledge empty. The narta will carry, besides the provisions for the dogs and the driver, about five poods. With this load, upon a tolerable road, they can travel about 30 versts a day; and without any load, in the spring when the snow is hardened, and upon sliders made of bone, they can travel 150 versts. After a deep snow there is no travelling with dogs 'till a road be made, which is effected by a man going before upon snow-shoes, whom they call *brodovshika*.

The snow-shoes are made of two thin boards, separated in the middle, and bound together at the ends; the fore part is bent a little upwards. They are bound together with thongs, and a place made to slip in the foot, which they likewise tie with thongs. The brodovshika having one of these shoes upon each foot leaves the dogs and sledge, and going on, clears the road for some way; then returning leads forwards the dogs and sledge so far as the road is made; a method which he must continue 'till he comes to some dwelling-house. This is very laborious, but it happens so often, that no guide ever sets out without his snow-shoes.

The greatest danger is when a storm of driven snow surprises them; then they are obliged with all haste to seek the shelter of some wood, where they stay as long as the tempest lasts, which sometimes is a whole week. If a storm at any time surprises a large company of travellers, they dig a place for themselves under the snow, and cover the entry with wood or bramble. The *Kamtschadales* seldom make these temporary huts, but hide themselves commonly in caves or holes of the earth, wrapping themselves in their furrs; and when thus covered, they move or turn themselves with the greatest caution, least they should throw off the snow, for under that they lie as warm as in their common huts: they must only have the convenience of a breathing place; but if their cloaths are tight or hard girt about them, the cold is unsufferable.

If the storms surprise them in an open country where there is no wood, they endeavour to find some hollow place, in which they shelter themselves, but must be careful to prevent being smothered with the snow. The east and south-east winds are generally attended with a moist snow, which wets the travellers; and being followed with the north wind and severe colds, several are then frozen to death.

Another danger attending the traveller is, that in the severest frost several rivers are not quite frozen over; and as the roads for the most part lie close upon the rivers, the banks being very steep, few years pass in which many people are not drowned. A disagreeable circumstance also to those who travel in these parts is their sometimes being obliged to pass through copses, where they run the risk of having their eyes scratched out, or their limbs broken; for the dogs always run most violently in the

the worft roads, and to free themfelves very often overturn their driver.

The beft travelling is in the month of *March* or *April*, when the fnow is turned hard or frozen a little at top; however, there is ftill this inconvenience attending it, that fometimes travellers are obliged to lodge two or three nights in defert places; and it is difficult to prevail upon the *Kamtfchadales* to make fire either for warming themfelves or dreffing victuals, as they and their dogs eat dried fifh, and find themfelves fo warm wrapt in their furrs that they want none; nay, it is furprifing to fee all the people of this climate bearing the cold fo well, that after having flept a whole night very found they awake next morning as refrefhed and alert as if they had lain in the warmeft bed. This feems to be fo natural to all here, that I have feen fome of them lie down with their backs uncovered againft a fire, and notwithftanding the fire has been burnt out long before morning, yet they continued to fleep on very comfortably, and without any inconvenience.

CHAP. X.

Of the Kamtfchadales' *Method of making* WAR.

ALTHOUGH before they were conquered by the *Ruffians*, the *Kamtfchadales* did not feem to have had any ambition of increafing their power, or enlarging their territories, yet they had fuch frequent quarrels among themfelves that feldom a year paffed without one village or other being entiely ruined. The end of their wars was to take prifoners, in order

order to employ them, if males, in their hardest labour or, if females, either for wives or concubines; and sometimes the neighbouring villages went to war for quarrels that happened among the children; or for neglecting to invite each other to their entertainments.

Their wars are carried on more by stratagem than bravery; for they are such cowards that they will not openly attack any one unless forced by necessity: this is the more extraordinary, because no people seem to despise life more than they do, self-murther being here very frequent. Their manner of attacking is this: in the night-time they steal into the enemy's village, and surprise them, which may easily be done as they keep no watch; thus a small party may destroy a large village, as they have nothing more to do than to secure the mouth of a hut, and suffer no body to come out, which only one can do at a time; therefore whoever first attempts to escape is knocked down, or obliged to submit to be bound.

The male prisoners which they take, especially if they are men of any consequence, are treated with all manner of barbarity, such as burning, hewing them to pieces, tearing their entrails out when alive, and hanging them by the feet. This has been the fate of several *Russian* Cossacks during the disturbances of *Kamtschatka*; and these barbarities are exercised with great shew of triumph and rejoicing.

These private differences among themselves were very useful to the Cossacks in their conquest of the whole nation; for when the natives saw the latter attacking one village, so far were they from assisting their countrymen, that they rejoiced at their destruction, not considering that the same was to be their fate next.

In their wars with the Cossacks, they destroyed more by stratagem than by arms; for when the Cossacks came to any village to demand their tribute, they were received with all marks of friendship, and not only the tribute was paid, but likewise great presents were made them. Thus the natives having lulled them into a state of security, they either cut their throats in the night-time, or set fire to their huts, and burnt them with all the Cossacks which were within. By such stratagems 70 people were destroyed in two places, which, considering the small number of Cossacks that were there, was a very considerable loss: nay, it has sometimes happened that when they had no opportunity of destroying the Cossacks at first, they have for two years quietly paid the tribute, waiting 'till they could find an opportunity of doing it.

By this cunning the *Kamtschadales* destroyed at first many Cossacks, but now the latter are more upon their guard, and are particularly afraid of extraordinary caresses, always expecting some bad intention when the women in the night-time retire out of their huts. When the *Kamtschadales* pretend to have dreamed of dead people, or go to visit distant villages, there is reason to dread a general insurrection.

When this happens, they kill all the Cossacks which fall in their way, and even the *Kamtschadales* who will not join in the rebellion. As soon as they hear that troops are coming against them, instead of going to oppose their enemies, they retire to some high place, which they fortify as strongly as they can, and building huts there, wait 'till they are attacked, and then they bravely defend themselves with their bows and arrows, and every other method they can think of; but if they observe, that the enemy is likely to make themselves masters of the fortress, they first cut the throats of their wives and children, and afterwards either throw themselves down the precipice, or with their arms rush in upon their enemies that they may not dye unrevenged: this they call making a bed for themselves. In the year 1740, a girl was brought from *Utkolok* whom the rebels in their hurry neglected to kill; the rest were all murthered, and the rebels threw themselves from the hill, upon which they were fortified, into the sea.

From the time that *Kamtfchatfka* was subdued, there have been only two rebellions which could be properly called so. The first happened in the year 1710, in *Bolfcheretfkoi Oftrog*; and the other in the year 1713 upon the river *Awatfcha*. Both of them were, however, unfortunate for the authors. In the first, great numbers besieged the *Bolcheretfkoi* fort, in which were only 70 Coffacks, 35 of whom making a sally put them all to flight, and in endeavouring to reach their boats which brought them thither, in the hurry such numbers were drowned that the river was almost choaked up by their dead bodies. The rebels upon the *Awatfcha* thought themselves so sure of destroying the *Ruffians* that they brought thongs to bind them; however the rebels were either all killed or taken prisoners.

Their arms are bows and arrows, spears, and a coat of mail: their quivers are made of the wood of the larch-tree, glued round with birch-bark; their bow-strings of the blood vessels of the whale; and their arrows are commonly about four feet long, pointed with flint stones, or bone; and though they are but indifferent, yet they are very dangerous, being all poisoned, so that a person wounded by them generally dies in twenty-four hours, unless the poison be sucked out, which is the only remedy known. Their spears are likewise pointed with flint or bone; and their coats of mail are made of mats, or of the skins of seals and sea horses, which they cut out into thongs, and plait together. They put them on upon the left side, and tie them with thongs upon the right; behind is fixed a high board to defend their head, and another before to guard the breast.

When

When they march on foot it is remarkable that two never go a-breast, but follow one another in the same path, which by use becomes very deep and narrow; so that it is almost impossible for one that is not used to it to walk therein, for these people always set one foot strait before the other in walking.

CHAP. XI.

The Opinions of the Kamtschadales *concerning* God, *the Formation of the World, and other Articles of Religion.*

THE *Kamtschadales*, like other barbarous nations, have no notions of a deity, but what are absurd, ridiculous, and shocking to a humanized mind. They call their god *Kutchu*, but they pay him no religious worship, and the only use they make of his name is to divert themselves with it; they relate such scandalous stories of him as one would be ashamed to repeat. Amongst other things they reproach him with having made so many steep hills, so many small and rapid rivers, so much rain, and so many storms; and in all the troubles that happen to them upbraid and blaspheme him.

They place a pillar upon a large wide plain, which they bind round with rags. Whenever they pass this pillar they throw a piece of fish or some other victuals to it; and near it they never gather any berries, or kill any beasts or birds. This offering they think preserves their lives, which otherwise would be shortened: however, they offer nothing which can be of use to themselves, but only the fins and tails of the fish, or such things as they would be obliged to throw away. In this all these people of *Asia* agree, offering only such things as are useless to themselves.

Besides these pillars several other places are reckoned sacred, such as burning and smoaking mountains, hot springs, and some particular woods, which they imagine are inhabited by devils, whom they fear and reverence more than their gods.

All their opinions concerning both gods and devils are certainly very simple and ridiculous; however, it shews that they endeavour to give an account for the existence of every thing as far as they are able; and some of them try to penetrate into the thoughts of the very birds and fishes; but when once any opinion is established, they never trouble themselves with enquiring whether the thing be possible or not. Hence their religion entirely depends upon ancient tradition, which they believe without examination. They have no notion of a supreme Being that influences their happiness or misery, but hold that every man's good or bad fortune depends upon himself. The world they believe is eternal, the soul immortal, and that it shall be again joined to the body, and live eternally subject to the same fatigues and troubles as in this present life, with this difference only, that they shall have greater plenty of all the necessaries of life: even the very smallest animals they imagine will rise again, and dwell under the earth. They think the earth is flat, and that under it there is a firmament like our's; and under that firmament another earth like our's, in which when we have summer they have winter, and when we have winter they have summer. With regard to future rewards and punishments, they believe that in the other world the rich will be poor and the poor will be rich.

Their notions of vice and virtue are as extraordinary as those they entertain of God. They believe every thing lawful that procures them the satisfaction of their wishes and passions, and think that only to be a sin from which they apprehend danger or ruin; so that they neither reckon murder, self-murder, adultery, oppression, nor the like, any wickedness: on the contrary, they

they look upon it to be a mortal sin to save any one that is drowning, because, according to their notions, whoever saves him will be soon drowned himself. They reckon it likewise a sin to bathe in, or to drink, hot water, or to go up to the burning mountains. They have besides these innumerable absurd customs, such as scraping the snow from their feet with a knife, or whetting their hatchets upon the road. This may, however, be said, that they are not the only people who have ridiculous superstitions.

Besides the above-mentioned gods they pay a religious regard to several animals, from which they apprehend danger. They offer fire at the holes of the sables and foxes; when fishing, they intreat the whales or sea horses not to overturn their boats; and in hunting, beseech the bears and wolves not to hurt them. This was the state of these people the first years of my being amongst them; but now, by the care of the Empress *Elizabeth*, missionaries are appointed to instruct them in the Christian faith. In 1741 a Clergyman was sent by the synod with assistants and every thing necessary for building a church, and instructing this wild people; which has been attended with such success, that not only many of them are baptized, but schools are also erected in several places, to which the *Kamtschadales* very readily send their children: so that in a few years we may hope to see the Christian faith planted in all these northern countries.

CHAP. XII.

Of their SHAMANS, *or Conjurers.*

THE *Kamtſchadales* have none who are profeſſed *Shamans*, or conjurers, as the neighbouring nations have; but every old woman is looked upon as a witch and an interpreter of dreams. In their conjurations they whiſper upon the fins of fiſhes, the ſweet graſs, and ſome other things; by which means they cure diſeaſes, divert misfortunes, and foretel futurity.

They are very great obſervers of dreams, which they relate to one another as ſoon as they awake in the morning, and judge from thence of their future good or bad fortune; and ſome of theſe dreams have their interpretation fixed and ſettled. Beſides this conjuration they pretend to chiromancy, and to foretel a man's good or bad fortune by the lines of his hand; but the rules which they follow are kept a great ſecret.

CHAP. XIII.

Of their CEREMONIES.

THE *Kamtſchadales* always celebrated three days in the month of *November*, which is hence called the month of Purification. *Steller* imagines, that this was firſt inſtituted by their anceſtors to return thanks to God for all his bleſſings; but that afterwards, through the ſtupidity of theſe people,

people, it has been perverted by foolish and ridiculous ceremonies; and this appears the more probable, because that, after their summer or harvest labour is over, they look upon it as a sin to do any work, or make any visits, before this holiday, which if any one neglects he is obliged to expiate it at that time, if not before. From hence we may see that the ancestors of this people were accustomed to offer up the first fruits of their summer labours to God, and to make merry with one another. The northern and southern *Kamtschadales* have different ceremonies in the celebration of their holidays, which are extremely silly, and conunt of many ridiculous anticks. I shall give a slight sketch one of these assemblies in the southern *Kamtschatka*.

After many strange ceremonies they introduce a little bird and a fish, which they roast upon the coals, and divide amongst them, when every one throws his share into the fire as a sacrifice, or an offering, to those spirits which come to their feasts; then they boil dried fish, the broth of which they pour out before their image, and eat the fish themselves; and then take the birch-tree out of the hut, and carrying it to their magazines, lay it up there to be kept for the whole year. Thus ends the festival.

CHAP. XIV.

Of their FEASTS *and* DIVERSIONS.

THEY make feasts when one village entertains another, either upon the account of a wedding, or having had a plentiful fishing or hunting. The landlords entertain their guests with great bowls of opanga, 'till they are all set a vomiting;

ing; sometimes they use a liquor made of a large mushroon, with which the *Russians* kill flies. This they prepare with the juice of epilobium, or *French* willow.

The first symptom of a man's being affected with this liquor is a trembling in all his joints, and in half an hour he begins to rave as if in a fever; and is either merry or melancholy mad, according to his peculiar constitution. Some jump, dance, and sing; others weep, and are in terrible agonies, a small hole appearing to them as a great pit, and a spoonful of water as a lake: but this is to be understood of those who use it to excess; for taken in a small quantity it raises their spirits, and makes them brisk, courageous, and chearful.

It is observed, whenever they have eaten of this plant, they maintain that, whatever foolish things they did, they only obeyed the commands of the mushroon: however, the use of it is certainly so dangerous, that unless they were well looked after it would be the destruction of numbers of them. The *Kamtschadales* do not much care to relate these drunken frolicks, and perhaps the continual use of it renders it less dangerous to them. One of our Cossacks resolved to eat of this mushroon in order to surprise his comrades; and this he actually did, but it was with great difficulty they preserved his life. Another of the inhabitants of *Kamtschatka*, by the use of this mushroon, imagined that he was upon the brink of hell ready to be thrown in, and that the mushroon ordered him to fall upon his knees, and make a full confession of all the sins he could remember, which he did before a great number of his comrades, to their no small diversion. It is related, that a soldier of the garrison having eaten a little of this mushroon, walked a great way without any fatigue, but at last, having taken too great a quantity, he died. My interpreter drank some of this juice without knowing of it, and became so mad, that it was with difficulty that we kept him from ripping open his

his belly, being, as he said, ordered to do it by the mushroon.

The *Kamtschadales* and the *Koreki* eat of it when they resolve to murder any body; and it is in such esteem among the *Koreki*, that they do not allow any one that is drunk with it to make water upon the ground, but they give him a vessel to save his urine in, which they drink, and it has the same effect as the mushroon itself. None of this mushroon grows in their country, so that they are obliged to purchase it of the *Kamtschadales*. Three or four of them are a moderate dose, but when they want to get drunk they take ten.

The women never use it; so that all their merriment consists in jesting, dancing, and singing. Their dance is in this manner: The two women that are to dance spread a mat in the middle of the room, and kneel down upon it opposite to one another, having a little tow in each hand. At first they begin to sing very low, moving a little their hands and shoulders; by degrees they raise their voice, and encrease the motions of their bodies, 'till they are quite out of breath and fatigued. This strange, uncouth entertainment, as it appeared to me, seemed greatly to delight the *Kamtschadales*: so strongly is every nation prejudiced in favour of its own customs.

In their love-songs they declare their passion to their lovers, their grief, hope, and other affections. The women generally compose them, and have clear, agreeable voices. Though they do not want an inclination for musick, yet they have no musical instrument, except a simple flute, and upon that they cannot play any tune.

Another of their amusements is mimicking other people in their speaking, walking, and all other actions. Whenever a stranger comes to *Kamtschatka* they give him a new name, and observe every thing about him very carefully, which they mimick for their diversion in all their entertainments. They sometimes smoke tobacco, and tell stories; all which merriments are generally in the night time. They have also professed buffoons or jesters; but their wit is intolerably indecent and obscene.

CHAP. XV.

Of their FRIENDSHIP, and HOSPITALITY.

WHEN any one of this country seeks the friendship of another he invites him to his hut, and for his entertainment dresses as much of his best victuals as might serve ten people. As soon as the stranger comes into the hut, which is made very hot for his reception, both he and the landlord strip themselves naked: then the latter sets before his guest great plenty of victuals; and while he is eating it the host throws water upon red-hot stones, 'till he makes the hut insupportably hot. The stranger endeavours all he can to bear this excessive heat, and to eat up all the victuals that were dressed; and the landlord endeavours to oblige his friend to complain of the heat, and to beg to be excused from eating all up. It is reckoned a dishonour to the landlord, and a mark of niggardliness, if he should be able to accomplish this. He himself eats nothing during the whole time, and is allowed to go out of the hut; but the stranger is not suffered to stir 'till he acknowledges himself overcome. At these feasts they over-eat themselves so much, that for three days they cannot bear the sight of victuals, and are scarce able to move, from repletion.

When the stranger is gorged, and can no longer endure the heat, he purchases his dismission with presents of dogs, cloaths, or whatever is agreeable to his landlord; in return for which he receives old rags, and useless lame curs. This, however, is reckoned no injury, but a proof of friendship; and he expects, in turn, to use his friend in the same manner. And if that man, who has thus plundered his friend, returns not his visit in proper time, he does not thereby save his presents, for the guest pays him a second visit, at which time he is obliged to make him what presents he is able; but if, either out of poverty or avarice, he makes him none, it is looked upon as the greatest affront, and he must expect this man always to be his enemy: besides, it is so dishonourable that no body else will ever live in friendship with him afterwards.

In their banquets they treat their friends in the same manner, only they do not torment them with heat, nor expect any presents. When they entertain with the fat of seals or whales, they cut it out into slices; and the landlord kneeling before his company, with one of these slices in one hand and a knife in the other, thrusts the fat into their mouths, crying in a surly tone, *Ta na,* and with his knife he cuts off all that hangs out of their mouths, after they are crammed as full as they can hold. Whoever wants any thing from another may generally obtain it upon these occasions; for it is reckoned dishonourable for the guest to refuse his generous landlord any thing. An instance of this happened, between a *Kamtschadale* and a newly christened Cossack, just before I arrived, and was then the common subject of conversation. The Cossack, according to the custom of that country, had a *Kamtschadale* to his friend, who he heard was possessed of a very fine fox-skin, which he greatly desired, but which the *Kamtschadale* would by no means part with. The Cossack invited him to his hut, where he entertained him with vast plenty of victuals, and by throwing water upon burning-hot stones made the heat of the hut intolerable to his friend the *Kamtschadale,* 'till at last he was obliged to beg for mercy.

This the Coſſack would not grant 'till he had obtained a promiſe of the fine fox-ſkin. It ſhould ſeem, that this entertainment could not be agreeable to the *Kamtſchadale*: however, he ſeemed to be pleaſed with it, and to ſwear that he never thought it poſſible to make ſuch a heat, or that the Coſſacks could entertain their friends with ſo much reſpect; and declared, that though he looked upon his fox-ſkin as an ineſtimable rarity, yet he parted from it with pleaſure on that occaſion, and ſhould always remember the noble entertainment of his friend.

CHAP. XVI.

Of their COURTSHIP, MARRIAGES, &c.

WHEN a *Kamtſchadale* reſolves to marry, he looks about for a bride in ſome of the neighbouring villages, ſeldom in his own; and when he finds one to his mind, he diſcovers his inclination to the parents, deſiring that he may have the liberty of ſerving them for ſome time: this permiſſion he eaſily obtains, and, during his ſervice, he ſhews an uncommon zeal in order to ſatisfy them of what he can do. After having thus ſerved, he deſires liberty to ſeize his bride; and if he has happened to pleaſe the parents, his bride, and her relations, this is preſently granted; but, if they diſapprove of it, they give him ſome ſmall reward for his ſervices, and he departs. It ſometimes happens that theſe bridegrooms, without diſcovering any thing of their intention, engage themſelves in ſervice in ſome ſtrange village; and though every one ſuſpects their deſign, yet no notice is taken of it, 'till either he or his friend declares it.

When

When a bridegroom obtains the liberty of seizing his bride, he seeks every opportunity of finding her alone, or in the company of a few people; for during this time all the women in the village are obliged to protect her; besides she has two or three different coats, and is swaddled round with fish nets and straps, so that she has little more motion that a statue. If the bridegroom happens to find her alone, or in company but with a few, he throws himself upon her, and begins to tear off her cloaths, nets, and straps; for to strip the bride naked constitutes the ceremony of marriage. This is not always an easy task; for though she herself makes small resistance, (and indeed she can make but little) yet, if there happen to be many women near, they all fall upon the bridegroom without any mercy, beating him, dragging him by the hair, scratching his face, and using every other method they can think of to prevent him from accomplishing his design. If the bridegroom is so happy as to obtain his wish, he immediately runs from her, and the bride as a proof of her being conquered, calls him back with a soft and tender voice: thus the marriage is concluded. This victory is seldom obtained at once, but sometimes the contest lasts a whole year; and after every attempt the bridegroom is obliged to take some time to recover strength, and to cure the wounds he has received. There is an instance of one, who, after having persevered for seven years, instead of obtaining a bride, was rendered quite a cripple, the women having used him so barbarously.

As soon as the above ceremony is over, he has liberty next night to go to her bed, and the day following, without any ceremony, carries her off to his own village. After some time, the bride and bridegroom return to the bride's relations, where the marriage feast is celebrated in the following manner; of which I was an eye-witness in 1739.

The bridegroom, his friends, and his wife, vifited the father-in-law in three boats. All the women were in the boats, and the men being naked pufhed them along with poles. About one hundred paces from the village to which they were going, they landed, began to fing, and ufed conjurations with tow faftened upon a rod, muttering fomething over a dried fifh's head, which they wrapped in the tow, and gave to an old woman to hold. The conjuration being over, they put upon the bride a coat of fheep's fkin, and tied four images about her: thus loaded fhe had difficulty to move. They went again into their boats, and came up to the village, where they landed a fecond time; at this landing-place, a boy of the village met them, and taking the bride by the hand led her, all the women following.

When the bride came to the hut, they tied a ftrap round her, by which fhe was let down the ftairs, the old woman who carried the fifh's head going before her. The head fhe laid down at the foot of the ftairs, where it was trodden upon by the bride and bridegroom and all the people prefent, and then thrown into the fire.

All the ftrangers took their places, having firft ftripped the bride of fuperfluous ornaments. The bridegroom heated the hut and dreffed the victuals which they had brought with them, and entertained the inhabitants of the village. The next day the landlord, entertained the ftrangers with great fuperfluity, who on the third day departed; the bride and bridegroom only remained to work fome time with their father. The fuperfluous drefs which was taken from the bride was diftributed among the relations, who were obliged to return them prefents of far greater value.

The former ceremonies only relate to a firft marriage; for in the marriage of widows, the man and woman's agreement is fufficient; but he muft not take her to himfelf before her fins are taken away. This can only be done by some stranger's first lying with her for once; but as this taking off of sin is looked upon by the *Kamtschadales* as very dishonourable for the man, it was formerly difficult to find one to undertake it; so that the poor widows were at a great loss before our Cossacks came amongst them; since which they have been in no want of strangers to take away their sins. Marriage is forbidden only between father and daughter, mother and son; a son-in-law may marry his mother-in-law, and a father-in-law his daughter-in-law; and first cousins marry frequently. Their divorce is very easy, consisting only in a man's separating beds from his wife: in such cases the man immediately marries another wife, and the woman accepts of another husband, without any further ceremony.

A *Kamtschadale* hath two or three wives, with whom he lies by turns. Sometimes he keeps them all in one hut, and sometimes they live in different huts. With every maid that he marries he is obliged to go through the above-mentioned ceremonies. Though these people are fond of women, yet they are not so jealous as the *Koreki*. In their marriages they do not seem to regard the marks of virginity. Nor are the women more jealous; for two or three wives live with one husband in all harmony: even though he also keeps several concubines. When the women go out they cover their faces with a sort of veil; and if they meet any man upon the road, and cannot go out of the way, they turn their backs to him, and stand 'till he is passed. In their huts they sit behind a mat or a curtain made of nettles; but if they have no curtain, and a stranger comes into the hut, they turn their face to the wall, and continue their work. This is to be understood of those that retain their ancient barbarity; for several of them now begin to be civilized to a certain degree, though all of them still preserve a rude harshness in their manner of speaking.

CHAP.

CHAP. XVII.

Of the BIRTH *of their* CHILDREN.

IN general thefe people are not fruitful, for I could never learn that any one man had ten children by the fame woman. Their women, as they fay, have commonly very eafy births: *Steller* was prefent at the delivery of one of thefe women, who went out of the hut about her ordinary bufinefs, and in a quarter of an hour afterwards was carrying her child in her arms, without any change in her countenance. He likewife relates, that he faw another woman who was in labour three days, and to his great furprife was at laft happily delivered of a child, which came double, prefenting the hips firft. The conjurers attributed the occafion of this unnatural pofture to the father, who in the time that the child ought to have been born was employed in making fledges, and bending the wood over his knee. Such ridiculous caufes do they affign for every uncommon effect. The women are delivered upon their knees, in prefence of as many people as are in the village, without diftinction of age or fex. They wipe the new-born child with tow, and tie the navel-ftring with thread made of nettles, and then cut it with a knife of flint: they throw the placenta to the dogs. They put chewed epilobium upon the navel, and wrap the infant in tow inftead of fwaddling cloaths: then every one careffes it, taking it in their arms, kiffing it, and rejoicing with the parents. This is the only ceremony which they ufe. They can hardly be faid to have profeffed midwives, and for the moft part the mother or neareft relation performs the office.

The women, as was mentioned above, who defire to have children, for this purpofe eat fpiders. Some child-bed women, that they may the fooner conceive again, eat the navel-ftring of the child. There are others who have as great averfion to having children, and procure abortions by different poifonous medicines, in which they are affifted by fome knowing old women; but this can never be done, as it is well known, but at the hazard of their own lives. There are others, who are fuch unnatural wretches as to deftroy their children when they are born, or throw them alive to the dogs. They ufe likewife feveral herbs and different conjurations to prevent conception. Their fuperftition, alfo, is fometimes the occafion of great barbarity; for when a woman bears twins, one of them at leaft muft be deftroyed, and fo muft a child born in very ftormy weather; though the laft can be averted by fome conjurations. After the birth, the women, to recover their ftrength, make ufe of fifh broth, made with an herb which they call *hale*; and then in a few days return to their ordinary diet.

CHAP. XVIII.

Of their DISEASES *and* REMEDIES.

THE principal difeafes in *Kamtfchatka* are the fcurvy, boils, palfy, cancer, jaundice, and the venereal diftemper. Thefe difeafes they think are inflicted upon them by the fpirits that inhabit fome particular groves, if ignorantly they happen to cut any of them down. Their principal medicines confift in charms and conjurations, but at the fame time they do not neglect the ufe of herbs and roots. For the fcurvy they ufe a certain herb which they rub upon their gums, as also the leaves of the cranberry * and blackberry †. The Cossacks cure themselves with decoctions of the tops of cedar, and by eating wild garlick. The good effects of this medicine were felt by all the people that were in the *Kamtschatka* expedition.

Boils are a most dangerous disease in *Kamtschatka*, causing the death of numbers. They are very large, being often two and sometimes three inches over; and when they break they open in about forty or fifty little holes. It is looked upon to be a very dangerous case, when no matter comes from these openings; and those that recover are confined to their beds, sometimes six and sometimes ten weeks. The *Kamtschadales* use raw hare-skins to bring the matter to a suppuration. The palsy, cancer, and *French* disease, are supposed to be incurable; the last, they say, was not heard of before the arrival of the *Russians*. There is likewise another distemper which they call *jushutch*, which is a sort of scab, that surrounds the whole body under the ribs like a girdle. When this does not come to suppurate and fall off, then it is mortal, and, they say, every one must have this once in his lifetime, as we have the small-pox. Mr *Steller* gives a more ample account of their diseases and remedies. He relates, that they use with success the spunge for drawing out the matter in these boils. The Cossacks apply to their boils the remains of the sweet-grass ‖ after they have extracted their brandy, and this often successfully resolves them.

The women use sea rasberries ‡ to hasten their delivery; and also a sort of coral, which they make into powder like crab-eyes, in a gonorrhea. Against costiveness they use the fat of the sea wolf; in gripes, pains of the bowels, and colds, they use a

---

* Vaccinium ramis filiformibus repentibus, foliis ovatis perennantibus.
† Impetrum.   ‖ Spondylium foliolis pinnatifidis.   ‡ Species fuci.

decoction of the pentaphylladis fruticosus, and that not without success. To wounds they apply the bark of the cedar, and with this they pretend they can even extract arrows.

In costiveness they likewise drink the broth of their stinking fish, and in fluxes they eat lac lunæ, which is very common in this country. For the same distemper they likewise use meadow-sweet and tormentilla root.

Those who have sore throats use a decoction of the epilobium, which is also used by women in hard labours. When they are bit by a dog, or wolf, they lay the bruised leaves of the ulmaria upon the wound, drinking at the same time a decoction of them: this decoction they also admininister in the belly-ach and scurvy. The leaves and stalks bruised they use in burns. The decoction of this herb mixed with fish they use also in the tooth-ach; they hold it warm in their mouths, and lay a piece of the root upon the affected tooth. They use a species of gentian in the scurvy, and almost against every disorder. In the *French* disease they apply the chamaenchododendros, but seldom to any advantage: in fluxes they use the quercus marina: in swellings of the legs and scurvy, they drink a decoction of the dryas; and procure sleep by eating the seed of the ephedra. They foment their eyes with a decoction of feramus.

The inhabitants of the *Lopatka* use clysters, which probably they learned from the *Kuriles*: they prepare them from a decoction of different herbs, sometimes with fat and sometimes without: this they put into a seal's bladder, fastening to it any pipe which they can procure, and apply it in the common way: this medicine is in high esteem among them, and used in most distempers.

In the jaundice, they have a medicine, which they look upon as infallible. They take the roots of the iris sylvestris, and after cleaning them, beat them in warm water, and apply the juice, which they squeeze out, as a clyster, continuing it for two days three times a day: this produces a purging, and generally gives great relief. After some time, if the cure is not completed, they repeat it again. They neither use lancets nor cupping glasses, but with a pair of wooden pincers draw up the skin, and pierce it with an instrument of chrystal made on purpose, letting out as much blood as they want.

In pains of the back they rub the part affected before a fire with a root of the cicuta, being careful not to touch the loins, which they say would produce spasms. In pains of the joints they place upon the part a little pyramid, made of a fungus which grows upon the birch-trees, and set the top of it on fire, letting it burn 'till it comes to the skin, which then cracks, and leaves a wound behind that yields a great quantity of matter. The wound they cure with ashes of the fungus, but some give themselves no trouble about it at all. The root of the anemonides, or ranunculus, they use to hurt or poison their enemies; and they likewise poison their arrows with it.

CHAP. XIX.

Of the BURIAL *of the* DEAD.

THE burial of the dead, if one can call throwing them to the dogs a burial, is different here from what it is in any other part of the world; for instead of burning or laying the dead bodies in some hole, the *Kamtschadales* bind a strap round the neck of the corps, draw it out of the hut, and deliver it for food to their dogs: for which they give the following reasons; that those who are eaten by dogs will drive with fine dogs in the other world; and that they throw them round near the hut, that evil spirits, whom they imagine to be the occasion of their death, seeing the dead body, may be satisfied with the mischief they have done. However, they frequently remove to some other place, when any one has died in the hut, without dragging the corps along with them.

They throw away all the cloaths of the deceased, not because they imagine they shall have occasion for them in the other world, but because they believe that whoever wears the cloaths of one that is dead will certainly come to an untimely end. This superstition prevails particularly among the *Kuriles* of the *Lopatka*, who would not touch any thing which they thought had belonged to a dead person, although they should have the greatest inclination for it. The Cossacks make use of this superstition to prevent one another sometimes from selling readymade cloaths, by assuring the buyer that they belonged to a dead person.

After the burial of the dead they use the following purification: Going to the wood they cut some rods, of which they make a ring; and creeping through it twice, they carry it to the wood, and throw it towards the west. Those who dragged out the body are obliged to catch two birds of one sort or other; one of which they burn, and eat the other with the whole family. The purification is performed on the same day; for before that they dare not enter any other hut, nor will any body else enter their's. In commemoration of the dead, the whole family dine upon a fish, the fins of which they burn in the fire.

CHAP. XX.

THIS chapter in the original contains an account of three different dialects of the *Kamtschadales*; which, as they are very unintelligible to an *English* reader, we thought proper to omit.

CHAP. XXI.

Of the NATION *of the* KOREKI.

AS the *Koreki* and *Kuriles* agree in most of their customs and habits with the *Kamtschadales*, we shall only take notice of those things wherein they differ from them or from one another. The *Koreki*, as is above related, are divided into the rein-deer or wandering *Koreki*; and those that are fixed in one place who live in huts in the earth like the *Kamtschadales*, and in every other respect indeed resemble them; so that whatever remarks we make are to be understood of the wandering *Koreki*, unless otherwise expressed.

The fixed *Koreki* live along the coast of the Eastern Ocean, from the river *Ukoi* as far as the *Anadir*, and along the coast of the sea of *Penschina* round the *Penschina* bay to the ridge *Nuktchatmnin*; out of which the river *Nuktchan* rises. From these rivers they take different appellations, by which they are distinguished one from another. The wandering *Koreki* sojourn with their herds of deer, and extend from the Eastern Ocean west to the head of the rivers *Pens-china* and *Omolona*, north to the *Anadir*, and south to the rivers *Lesnaya* and *Karaga*. Sometimes they come even over these bounds, approaching very near to *Kamtschatka*; but this indeed happens very seldom, and only when they are afraid of the *Tchukotskoi*, who are their most dangerous neighbours. The people that they border upon are the *Kamtschadales*, the *Tchukotskoi*, *Ukageri*, and the *Tungusi* or *Lamuti*.

The *Tcukotskoi* should be accounted a race of the *Koreki*, which in truth they are; if so, then it may be said that the country of the *Koreki* is of far greater extent, for the *Tchukotskoi* possess northward from the river *Anadir* as far as the *Tchukotskoi* promontory. Indeed, those *Tchukotskoi* that live north of the river *Anadir* are not subject to the empire of *Russia*, but frequently make incursions upon those that are, both *Koreki* and *Tchukotskoi*, killing and making them prisoners, and driving off their herds of deer. In the summer time they fish not only in the seas near the mouth of the *Anadir*, but even come up the river a great way, when those people who are subjects to *Russia* frequently fall into their hands.

The *Koreki* differ not only in their manners from one another, but also in the form of their bodies. The wandering *Koreki*, as far as I could observe, are of small stature, and very lean; they have small heads, and black hair, which they shave every day; their face is oval, their eyes small, eyebrows hanging, nose short, mouth large, and their beard black and pointed, which they frequently pluck. The fixed *Koreki*, though not of a very large stature, are however taller than the former, and thicker and stronger made; especially those that live towards the north, who resemble a good deal the *Kamtschadales* and *Tchukotskoi*.

There is besides a very great difference in their customs and habits. The wandering *Koreki* are extremely jealous, and sometimes kill their wives upon suspicion only; but when

any

any are caught in adultery, both parties are certainly condemned to death. For this reason the women seem to take pains to make themselves disagreeable; for they never wash their faces or hands, nor comb their hair, and their upper garments are dirty, ragged, and torn, the best being worn underneath. This they are obliged to do on account of the jealousy of their husbands; who say, that a woman has no occasion to adorn herself unless to gain the affections of a stranger, for her husband loves her without that. On the contrary, the fixed *Koreki*, and *Tchukotskoi*, look upon it as the truest mark of friendship, when they entertain a friend, to put him to bed with their wife or daughter; and a refusal of this civility they consider as the greatest affront; and are even capable of murdering a man for such a contempt. This happened to several *Russian* Cossacks before they were acquainted with the customs of the people. The wives of the fixed *Koreki* endeavour to adorn themselves as much as possible, painting their faces, wearing fine cloaths, and using various means to set off their persons. In their huts they sit quite naked, even in the company of strangers.

The whole nation is rude, passionate, revengeful, and cruel; and the wandering *Koreki* are also proud and vain: they imagine that no people in the world are so happy as themselves, regarding all the accounts that strangers give of the advantages of other countries, as so many lies and fables; for, say they, " If you could enjoy these advantages at home, what made you take so much trouble to come to us? You seem to want several things which we have; we, on the contrary, are satisfied with what we possess, and never come to you to seek any thing". One great reason of their pride and haughtiness may be owing to the settled or fixed *Koreki*, who shew the greatest fear and awe of them; so that if one of their deer-herds should come to a hut of the latter, they all run out to meet him, treat him with the greatest

greatest ceremony, and bear every affront. It was never heard that the settled *Koreki* did the least injury to any of the wanderers; and this is so firmly believed, that our tax-gatherers think themselves entirely safe, when they converse with those who live in huts, if they are guarded by one of the reindeer *Koreki*: which may appear very strange, considering that the settled *Koreki* are much their superiors in strength; and it can only be attributed to that general respect which poor people pay to the rich: for the poverty of the settled *Koreki* is so great, that they depend upon the others in a great measure for their cloathing. The rein-deer *Koreki* call the others their slaves, and treat them accordingly; but they behave very differently to the *Tchukotskoi*, who are so terrible to them, that fifty of the rein-deer *Koreki* dare not stand against twenty of these; and if it was not for the protection of the Cossacks of *Anadir*, the *Tchukotskoi* would have rooted them out by this time. As every nation has something commendable, so the *Koreki* are more honest and industrious than the *Kamtschadales*, and seem to have a greater sense of shame.

It is difficult to form an exact account of the numbers and different families of the *Koreki*, but it is thought that all together they are more numerous than the *Kamtschadales*. They live in such places as abound with moss for their rein-deer, without regarding the scarcity of wood or water: in the winter time they can use snow for water, and for firing moss or grass, of which they have plenty every where. Their manner of living, especially in the winter time, is still more disagreeable than that of the *Kamtschadales*: for being frequently obliged to change their habitations, the huts which they come into are all frozen; and when they begin to thaw them by the fires, which are usually made of green shrubs or grass, there arises a smoke, so pernicious to the eyes, that it is enough to blind a person entirely in one day.

Their huts are made much in the same manner as those of other wandering people, but less than those of the *Calmucks*. In the winter they cover them with raw deer-skins, and in the summer with tanned. They have no flooring or separation within their huts; in the middle only are four little stakes driven, between which is their hearth. To these stakes they commonly tie their dogs, which frequently drag the victuals out of the kettles while it is dressing; and notwithstanding their masters beat them very severely, they generally come in for a share of every piece. A man must be very hungry to be able to eat with these people. Instead of washing their kettles or platters they give them to the dogs to lick, and the very flesh which they tear from the mouths of the dogs they throw again into the kettles without washing it.

The *Tchukotskoi* winter huts are much preferable to those of the *Koreki*, being much warmer and more roomy. Several families live in the same hut, all having their proper benches, upon which deer-skins are spread, whereon they sit or sleep. Upon each bench a lamp burns day and night, for which they use fish-oil and a wick of moss. They have an opening in the top, which serves for a chimney; however they are almost as smoaky as those of the *Koreki*, but so warm, that in the coldest places the women sit naked. The cloaths which they wear are made of rein-deer skins, not differing in the least from those of the *Kamtschadales*, who purchase them from the *Koreki*. They feed upon the flesh of the rein-deer, in which they very much abound, some of the rich having ten or twenty thousand; nay, one of the chiefs was said to have one hundred thousand: but yet they are so penurious, that they are sorry to kill any for their own use, satisfying themselves with such as die naturally, or are killed by the wolves. Of this carrion, indeed, they have plenty; and they are not ashamed to excuse themselves from entertaining travellers by telling them that none of their

deer

deer are killed or have died lately. For particular guests, indeed, they will kill some of their stock, and at such times only they have a hearty meal. They never milk the rein-deer, nor know any use of milk. They eat their flesh for the most part boiled, and what they do not consume immediately they dry with the smoke in their huts. One of their principal dishes is called *yamgaya*, which is made thus; they put the blood of the beast mixed with some fat into its stomach or paunch, which they hang up and smoke. Our Cossacks reckon this a great delicacy. Besides, the *Koreki* eat every other animal except dogs and foxes. They use, in general, neither herbs, roots, nor barks of trees; but the poor feed on them in time of great scarcity; nor will any catch fish, except the deer-herds, and that very seldom. They make no provision of berries for the winter, but only eat them fresh in the summer. They think nothing can be sweeter than cranberries beat up with the root saran and deer's fat. I had an opportunity of seeing one of their chieftains exceedingly surprised upon the first sight of sugar, which he took for salt; but tasting it was so pleased with its sweetness, that he begged some pieces to carry to his wives: but, as he was not able to resist the temptation of so delicious a rarity, he ate it all up on the road; and when he came home to his house, although he swore to the women that he had tasted salt sweeter than any thing he had ever tasted before, yet they would not believe him, insisting that nothing could be sweeter than cranberries with deer's fat and lilly-roots.

They ride only in the winter time on sledges drawn by rein-deer, but never mount upon their backs in the summer, as they say the *Tungusi* do. Their sledges are made about a fathom long: the sides are about four inches thick, but rather thinner at the fore part, where they are bent upwards: the two side-pieces are joined together by small pieces of wood. They yoke two deer before every sledge. The harness is somewhat like that they use for reins of the dogs; the harness of that deer which is on the right side being fastened to the left side of the sledge, and that of the deer on the left side to the right side of the sledge. Their bridles and reins are something like the collars of horses. Upon the deer's forehead they have four little bones, made like teeth, but very sharp, which are used as bits to pull them in when they run too fast; for these sharp bones piercing the skin stop them at once. The right hand deer only has these bones; for if that is stopped, the deer upon the left has not strength to run away. The drivers sit near the fore part of the sledge; and if they want to turn to the right they only draw the rein, but when they would turn to the left they beat the right side of the deer. They drive them with a goad, which is about four feet long, having a sharp piece of bone at one end, and at the other a hook: with the bone they prick the deer to go forwards, and with the hook they lift up the harness when it happens to fall down.

Travelling with rein-deer is much swifter than with dogs: good cattle will go 150 versts a day; but you must take care to feed them frequently, and to stop often to allow them to stale; for you may kill them in one day, or at least make them good for nothing. Deer that are used for draught are bred to it, as horses. The male they geld, which is done by piercing the spermatick vessels, and tying them tight with thongs. The rein-deer which the *Koreki* use for draught feed along with the others; and when they want to part them, they drive them all home; then crying aloud in a particular manner, the draught cattle separate themselves from the rest; and if any of them should remain, they are beat most unmercifully.

The settled *Koreki* have likewise some rein-deer, but very few, and those such as they only use for drawing. The *Tchukotskoi*

kotskoi have great herds, and yet feed for the most part upon sea animals. The *Koreki* would be miserable if they wanted the rein-deer: for they know no way of keeping themselves alive, as they do not understand how to catch fish; and if they did, could not soon provide themselves with boats, nets, or dogs: so that the poorer sort are employed by the richer in feeding their deer, for which they receive meat and cloaths; and if they have any small stock of their own, they are allowed to feed them with their master's cattle.

The rein-deer *Koreki* exchange their deer and deer-skins with the neighbouring people for the very finest furrs, of which they have always a large stock by them.

The religion of the *Koreki* is more absurd than that of the *Kamtschadales*, at least that little chief, of whom I had my information, seemed to have scarce any idea of a God; they seem more to respect evil spirits, which, according to their opinion, inhabit the rivers and woods: this respect seems to be owing to their fear. The settled *Koreki* acknowledge for their God, the *Kuta* of the *Kamtschadales*. They have no fixt time of worship or offering sacrifices; but, whenever they please, they kill either a rein-deer or a dog, which they fix upon a stake, turning its face towards the east, leaving only the deer's head and tongue upon the stake. They themselves do not know to whom they make these sacrifices, and only use these words, *Vio coing yack ne la lu, han he vau*; that is, This to you, and may you send us something that is good. The time of sacrificing is when they are going to pass any river or waste, which they think the devils inhabit; then they kill one of their deer, and eating the flesh, they fasten the bones of the head upon a pole, which they fix opposite to the habitation of the spirits. When the *Koreki* are afraid of any infectious distemper, they kill a dog, and winding the guts upon two poles, they pass between them.

During their sacrifices their *shamans* or sorcerers beat a little drum like that used by the *Jakutski*, and the neighbouring nations. Some of the *Shamans* are reckoned physicians, and are thought, by beating upon the drum, to drive away distempers. In the year 1739 I had an opportunity of seeing, at the lower *Kamtschatkoi* fort, the most famous *Shaman Carimlacha*, who was not only of great reputation among these wild people, but was also respected by our Cossacks, for the many extraordinary feats that he performed; particularly that of stabbing his belly with a knife, and letting a great quantity of blood run out, which he drank: however this he performed in such an awkward manner, that any one, who was not blinded by superstition, might easily discover the trick. At first, sitting upon his knees, and beating some time upon his drum, he struck his knife into his belly, and then, from below his furred coat, he drew out a handful of blood, which he eat, licking his fingers. I could not help laughing at the simplicity of the trick, which the poorest player of legerdemain would have been ashamed of. One might see him slip the knife down below his furr, and that he squeezed the blood out of a bladder which he had in his bosom. After all this conjuration he thought still to surprise us more by shewing us his belly all bloody, pretending to have cured the wound which he had not made. He told us, that the evil spirits appeared to him in different forms, and came from different places; some came from the sea, others out of the burning mountains; some of them were very large, and some very small; some had no hands, and some were half burned; the spirits of the sea were much finer dressed than the others, and appeared to him as it were in a dream, and at such a time they tormented him so much, that he was almost out of his senses.

When the sorcerers pretend to cure any distemper by their conjurations, sometimes they order a dog to be killed, at other times

times to set little rods round their huts. When they kill a dog, one person holds it by the head, another by the tail, and a third stabs it in the side; when it is dead they stick it upon a stake, turning its face towards the nearest burning mountain.

Their civil policy is as rude as their religious; they know nothing of dividing the year into months; they have names indeed for the four seasons. They have only names for the four cardinal winds. Of the constellations they know the Great Bear, which they call, in their language, the wild rein-deer; the Pleiades they name the duck's nest; and the Milky Way the scattered river.

The distance of places they reckon by their day's journey, which is between 30 and 50 versts.

Before they were subject to the Empire of *Russia* they never had any government or chief magistrate among them, only those that were rich had some sort of authority over the poor; nor before that did they know any thing of an oath. At present, instead of swearing upon the cross or gospel, our Cossacks oblige them to hold a musquet by the barrel, threatening, that whoever does not observe this oath will certainly be shot by a ball. This they are so much afraid of, that rather than clear themselves by this oath, if guilty, they will confess their crime.

They are quite ignorant of all good manners, not only in common compliments, but in receiving strangers, whom they treat with an air of superiority. When they entertain their guests they don't oblige them to over-eat themselves, as the *Kamtschadales* do, but give them what they have in sufficient plenty; their best victuals is fat meat, and all these barbarous nations are excessively fond of fat. The *Jakutski* would lose an eye for a piece of fat horse flesh, and the *Tchukotskoi* for a fat dog. The *Jakutski* know that the stealing of any cattle is punished with the loss of all their goods; yet, if they have an opportunity, they can't restrain themselves from stealing a fat horse, comforting themselves amidſt all their misfortunes, with the pleaſure of having once in their life made a delicious meal.

Amongſt all theſe barbarous nations, excepting the *Kamtſchadales*, theft is reputable, provided they do not ſteal in their own tribe, or if done with ſuch art as to prevent diſcovery; on the other hand, it is puniſhed very ſeverely if diſcovered, not for the theft, but for want of addreſs in the art of ſtealing. A *Tchukotſkoi* girl cannot be married before ſhe has ſhewn her dexterity in this way.

Murder is not looked upon as a great crime unleſs it be in their own tribe, and then the relations of the murdered generally revenge it, but no one elſe takes any notice of it.

In their marriages the rich match with the rich, and the poor with the poor, with little regard either to beauty or any other accompliſhment. They marry for the moſt part into their own family, ſuch as with a firſt couſin, an aunt, or mother-in-law; and, in ſhort, with any relation except their own mother or daughter. The ceremonies of courtſhip are the ſame as among the *Kamtſchadales*. Although the bridegroom ſhould be very rich, yet he is obliged to ſerve three or five years for his bride; during which time they allow them to ſleep together, though the form of catching the bride ſhould not be performed, which they leave 'till the marriage be celebrated, and that is done without any great ceremony. They have ſometimes two, and ſometimes three wives, whom they keep at different places, giving them a herd of deer and a keeper. Their greateſt pleaſure is to go from place to place and examine their cattle; and it is ſurpriſing that the *Koreki*, notwithſtanding their herds are ſo numerous, and they are quite ignorant of arithmetick, can immediately diſcover the leaſt loſs, and even deſcribe all the marks of the deer that is miſſing.

They have a great fondneſs for their children, and breed them up from their infancy to labour and oeconomy. Thoſe that are rich, as soon as the child is born, set apart for him a certain number of rein-deer, which however he cannot claim 'till he comes to maturity. The old women give names to the children, with the following ceremonies :---They set up two little rods, which they tie together with threads, to the middle of which they hang a stone wrapped in a piece of sheep-skin; then they ask of the stone in a muttering voice the name they shall give, and running over those of several of their relations, whatever name the stone shakes at they give to the child. The child-bed woman does not shew herself nor come out of the hut for ten days; if they are obliged to remove their habitations during that time, she is carried in a covered sledge. They give their children the breast till they are three years old and upwards; but they use neither cradle nor swaddling cloaths.

They carefully attend those who are sick, and their *Shamans*, or conjurers, treat them in the manner above related; but they know nothing of the virtues of drugs or plants.

They burn their dead in the following manner :---Having first dressed them in their finest apparel, they draw them with those deer which they think were their favourites to the place where they are to be burned. Here they erect a great pile of wood, into which are thrown the arms of the deceased and some houshold furniture, such as their spear, quiver and arrows, knives, hatchets, kettles, &c. Then they set fire to the pile; and while it is burning, kill the deer that drew the corps, upon which they feast, and throw the fragments into the fire.

They celebrate the memory of the dead only once, and that a year after their death. All the relations then assemble; and taking two young rein-deers that have never been in the draught, and a great many deers' horns, which they have been collecting through the whole year for that purpose, they go to the place where the body was burned, if near, or if at a distance, to some other high place, where they kill the deer;

and the *Shaman,* driving the horns into the earth, pretends that he fends a herd of deer to the dead. After this they return home, and in order to purify themselves, they pass between two rods which are fixed in the ground; the *Shaman,* at the same time beating them with another, conjures the dead not to take them away.

In all other customs and ceremonies they agree with the *Kamtschadales*; as in making war, which is generally by surprising their enemies. Their arms consist in bows, arrows, and spears, formerly pointed with bones or flint. Their women are employed in dressing their furrs, making cloaths and shoes. The *Koreki* women, indeed, are employed in cookery, which those of *Kamtschatka* are not.

CHAP. XXII.

ACCOUNT *of the Nation of the* KURILES.

THE manners of the *Kuriles* resemble those of the *Kamtschadales* so much, that we should have taken no notice of them separately if their external appearance and language were not very different. We can give no account of their origin more than of the other inhabitants of *Kamtschatka*.

These people are of a small stature, black haired, round visaged, somewhat swarthy, and withal more well-favoured than any of their neighbours. Their beards are thick, and their whole body is covered with hair, in which they particularly differ from all the other *Kamtschadales*. The men shave their heads as far back as the crown, allowing the other hair to grow to its full length. This custom they have probably taken from the *Japanese*, with whom they have some commerce. The women only cut the fore part of their hair, that it may not fall into their eyes. The lips of the men are blackened about the middle; the women's are entirely black, and stained round; their arms are likewise stained with different figures as far as the elbows. This custom they have in common with the *Tchukotskoi* and *Tungusi*. Both men and women wear silver rings in their ears, which they get from the *Japanese*.

Their cloaths are made of the skins of sea fowls, foxes, sea beavers, and other sea animals; and are generally composed of the skins of very different creatures, so that it is rare to see a whole suit made of the same sort of skins. The fashion resembles more that of the *Tungufi*, than the *Kamtfchadales*. Though they are fo little regardful of uniformity in their own country cloathing, they are very proud to acquire fuch as are made of cloth, ferge, or filk, particularly thofe of a fcarlet colour; but fo little care do they take of them when they have got them, that they will wear them when employed about the dirtieft work.

Their huts are much the fame as thofe of the *Kamtfchadales*, only they keep them a little cleaner, covering generally the floor and walls with mats made of grafs. They feed for the moft part upon fea animals, and very little upon fifh.

They are as ignorant of a deity as the *Kamtfchadales*. In their huts they have idols made of chips or fhavings curioufly curled. Thefe idols they call *Ingool*, and are faid to venerate them in fome degree, but whether as good or evil fpirits I never could learn. They facrifice to them the firft animal which they catch, eating the flefh themfelves, they hang up the fkin before the image; and when they change their huts they leave the fkin and the idol there. If they make any dangerous voyage they take their idol along with them; which, in cafe of imminent danger, they throw into the fea, expecting by this method to pacify the ftorm; and with this protector they think themfelves fafe in all their excurfions.

They travel in the fummer time in boats, in the winter in fnow fhoes. The men are employed in catching of fea animals, the women in fewing, during the winter; but in the fummer they go out with their hufbands to hunt.

They are more civilized than the neighbouring people, being fteady honeft, and peaceable; their way of fpeaking is foft and modeft; they have a refpect for old people, and an affection for each other, particularly their relations. It is a pleafure to fee with what hofpitality they receive fuch as come to vifit them from other iflands: thofe that come in boats,

boats, and those that receive them from the huts, march in great ceremony, dressed in all their warlike accoutrements, shaking their swords and spears, and bending their bows, as if they were going into an engagement, and dancing up to each other 'till they meet, shewing the greatest signs of delight, embracing and hugging one another, and shedding tears of joy. The people of the huts then carry the visitants into their habitation, where they entertain them in the best manner, standing and hearing them relate all the adventures that have happened to them in their voyage. The honour of this relation is reserved for the oldest, who is always the orator; he informs them of every thing that has happened since the last meeting, how they have been employed, how they lived, where they travelled, whom they saw, what good fortune or misfortune has happened to them, who have been sick, or who are dead. This relation sometimes continues for three hours. When the stranger has ended, the oldest of the people who are visited gives him an equal information of every thing that has happened to them. Before this the rest must not speak to one another; then, according as circumstances are, they either condole with, or congratulate, each other, and finish the entertainment with eating, dancing, singing, and telling of stories.

In their courtships, marriages, and the education of children, they differ very little from the other *Kamtschadales*. They have two or three wives, with whom they never publickly sleep, but steal to them privately in the night time. They have an extraordinary way of punishing adultery: the husband of the adulteress challenges the adulterer to a combat, which is performed in the follo ing manner: both the combatants are stripped quite naked, and the challenger gives the challenged a club about three feet long, and near as thick as one's arm; then the challenger is obliged to receive three strokes upon his back from the challenged, who then returns him the club, and is treated in the same manner;

ner; this they perform three times, and the result is generally the death of both the combatants: but it is reckoned as great dishonour to refuse this combat, as to refuse an invitation to a duel among the people of *Europe*. If any one prefers his life or safety to his honour, the adulterer then is obliged to pay to the husband of the adulteress whatever he demands, either in skins, cloaths, provisions, or other things.

The women have a harder time in child-bearing than the *Kamtschadales*, for they say, the *Kuriles* women do not recover after child-bearing for three months. The midwives give names to the children when they are born, which they always keep. If they have twins they destroy one.

Such as die in the winter they bury in the snow; but in the summer they are buried in the earth. Self-murder is as frequent here as among the *Kamtschadales*.

of the

CONQUEST of *Kamtſchatka*.

PART IV.

CHAP. I.

Of the firſt DISCOVERIES *made of* Kamtſchatka, *and the Planting of* Ruſſian *Colonies there.*

THO' the *Ruſſian* territories upon the Frozen Ocean, from the river *Lena* eaſt to the river *Anadir*, were of prodigious extent, yet it was judged proper to give orders to every commiſſary to inform himſelf of the countries beyond the *Anadir*, and to endeavour to bring the inhabitants under ſubjection. By this means a knowledge of *Kamtſchatka*, and of the different people who inhabit it, was long ago obtained; eſpecially ſince the *Koreki*, which live

upon

upon the *Penschinska* and *Olutorskoy* seas, came from *Anadir*, and had communication with the inhabitants of *Kamtschatka*, to whose country they frequently travelled. But we have still no authentick account who was the first *Russian* that discovered these places: there is, it seems, a tradition of one *Theodot*, who for the sake of trade went into *Kamtschatka* as far as the river *Nicula*, which river is now called after him, *Theodotoshine*. They pretend, that he went out of the river *Bova* into the Frozen Ocean with seven boats; that, being separated from the rest by a storm, he was driven to *Kamtschatka*, where he passed the winter; that the next summer, going round the *Kurilskaya Lopatka* through the *Penschinska* sea, he arrived at the river *Teghil*, where he and all his company were murdered by the *Koreki*, which disaster was occasioned by their having seen one of the *Russians* kill another with fire arms; for the *Koreki* upon observing the effect of these weapons at first esteemed the *Russians* as some superior beings; but perceiving them to be mortal, they were glad to free themselves from such dangerous neighbours. This tradition is confirmed by the account of one *Simeon Deshnef*; who relates, that their voyage was very troublesome, and that they were driven at last upon that promontory to the east of the river *Anadir*: however, all this seems to be very uncertain. There is likewise an account, that in the year 1660 they recovered a woman who had been carried away from *Jakutski* by the *Koreki*, and who related, that *Theodot*, with one of his companions died there of the scurvy; that others of them were murdered; and that the remainder, who escaped in boats, were never heard of. The *Kamtschadales* acknowledge that some winter huts upon the river *Nicula* were built by *Russians*.

All these different reports may easily be reconciled, if we suppose that *Theodot* and his companions were lost between *Anadir* and *Olutorskoy*. They had wintered in *Kamtschatka*, upon the river *Teghil*; whence in returning to *Anadirsk* over land,

land, he died upon the road, and his companions were either murdered or loft. However, at any rate, this difcovery was of no great confequence to the intereft of the empire, as no information of the country was thereby obtained; fo that the firft difcovery of *Kamtfchatka* may be attributed to the Coffack *Atlafof*.

This *Atlafof* was fent from *Jakutfki* to the fort *Anadirfk* in the year 697. He was ordered to fee if he could difcover new countries, and bring them in fubjection to the empire of *Ruffia*, by the affiftance of the *Koreki Yukageri*, who lay near *Anadirfk*. In the year 1698 he fent out one *Luke Morofkoi*, with fixteen *Koreki*, in order to gather in the taxes at the moft diftant places; who at their return reported, that they had not only been among the *Koreki*, but even within four days' journey of *Kamtfchatka*; that they had taken one of their little forts, and had got a letter written in a language which no body could underftand. Upon this, *Atlafof*, with fixty Coffacks and as many *Yukageri*, marched into the country of *Kamtfchatka*, in order to make difcoveries, and to prevail upon them to pay tribute, which he by fair methods obtained from the *Acklanfki*, but the fort *Talofki* he reduced by force. After this, as they relate, he divided his company into two corps; the one of which he fent to the Eaftern Ocean, under the command of *Luke Morofkoi*, and with the other he in perfon went towards the *Penfchinfka* fea. Upon the *Pallana* his allies, the *Yukageri*, rebelled againft him, killed three of his Coffacks, and wounded *Atlafof* himfelf and fifteen others; however he overcame the *Yukageri*, and killed them all. Notwithftanding this misfortune he purfued his journey fouthwards. Upon the river *Teghil* he joined the party under *Morofkoi*, and exacted tribute from the people that lived upon the *Napan*, *Kigil*, *Itche*, *Sintche*, and *Harufof*, and refcued a *Japanefe* prifoner that he found among the *Kamtfchadales*.

Returning from the river *Itche* he went to the river *Kamtfchatka*, where he built the upper *Kamtfchatkoi* fort, and left in it *Potap Sirukof*, with fifteen Coſſacks. *Atlaſof* returned from this journey to *Jakutſki* the 2d of *July* 1700, and brought along with him the *Japaneſe* he had reſcued, and the *Kamtſchatka* tribute, which confiſted of 3200 ſables, ten ſea beavers, ſeven pieces of beavers' ſkins, four otter ſkins, ten grey foxes, and 191 red foxes; and 440 ſables on his own account. With this tribute he was difpatched to *Moſcow*, where, for his ſervices, he was made Chief of the Coſſacks at *Jakutſki*, and was ordered to return again to *Kamtſchatka*, and to take along with him from *Tobolſka*, *Jeniſei*, and *Jakutſki*, 100 Coſſacks. Orders were ſent to *Tobolſka* to furniſh them with ſome ſmall cannon, colours, a drummer, arms, and ammunition. However *Atlaſof* was prevented from this expedition before the year 1706; for in the year 1701, upon the river *Tunguſi*, he plundered a boat with *Chineſe* goods, belonging to *Logan Dobrini*, whoſe ſervant petitioned againſt him, at the Chancery of *Jakutſki*, for which he and ten of the principal robbers were put in priſon; and in the year 1702 *Michael Zinoveef*, who had been there formerly, was ſent chief of this expedition.

All this time the Coſſack *Potap Sirukof* lived quietly in the fort of *Kamtſchatka*, and for three years received no injury from the inhabitants: for he did not demand any tribute, but only traded with them like a merchant. At laſt they determined to leave the fort; but on their return to *Anadirſk*, he and all his companions were ſet upon and killed by the *Koreki*. His ſucceſſor appears to have been *Timothy Cobelof*, who is reckoned the firſt governor of *Kamtſchatka*. In his time a fort was built upon the river *Karakeef*, about half a verſt diſtant from the firſt. He built winter huts upon the river *Yelofka*, and gathered voluntary tribute upon the river *Kamtſchatka*, and upon the *Penſchinſka* and Beaver ſea coaſt; with which he returned, in the year 1704, to *Jakutſki*. At the ſame time a party of the *Anadirſki* Coſſacks, under the command of *Andrew Kutin*, built ſeven winter huts upon the river *Yaka*, which

falls

falls into the Eastern Ocean, and began to gather taxes from the neighbouring *Koreki*.

Michael Zinoveef, sent in place of *Atlasof* from *Jakutski*, succeeded *Cobelof*; which place he held 'till he was relieved by *Kolesof*, in the year 1704. In his time he made books of tribute, in which the names of the *Kamtschadales* were inserted; he transported the winter huts to a more convenient place, built a little fort upon the great river, and having brought things into tolerable order, he returned to *Jakutski* with his tribute. *Kolesof* arrived there in the harvest 1704, and continued to the year 1706; for the *Outori* killed two persons on their journey that ere appointed to relieve him, viz. *Vasili Protopopof* in 1704, and *Visili Shelcocosnicof* in 1705. In his time was the first expedition undertaken against the *Kuriles*, about twenty of whom they brought back with them, and drove all the rest away. He carried all his tribute safe to *Jakutski*, notwithstanding he was way-laid at the fort *Kasuki*, upon the river *Pingin*, by the *Koreki*, but he retired to another little fort called *Aklanski*, where he lived about fifteen weeks, 'till the winter way became passable. During this time the *Koreki* of *Kasuki* tried several times to surprise him, but he was defended by the inhabitants of *Acklanski*. Here *Kolesof* met seven people that were sent with presents and ammunition to the fort of *Kamtschatka*; as he was in great want of the latter, for their security he added to them thirteen of his own party, and gave the command to *Simon Lomgaf*, whom he ordered likewise to gather tribute round the three *Kamtschatka* forts.

At the departure of *Visili Kolesof* all the tributary *Kamtschadales* were tolerably quiet; but afterwards, when *Theodore Anqudenof* was commissary in the upper fort, *Theodore Yaregin* in the lower fort, and *Demetrie Yaregin* upon the Great River, the inhabitants of the Great River rebelled, burned the fort, and murdered all the inhabitants: at the same time five tax-gatherers were killed upon the Beaver Sea. The reason of their rebellion perhaps might be, that the taxes were gathered with feverity, which was the more intolerable, as formerly they had never been accuftomed to pay any, and therefore endeavoured, by the murder of their oppreffors, to recover their ancient liberty: befides, they imagined that thefe *Ruffians* might be themfelves fome runaways, as they had never obferved any new faces among them; they hoped too, that the *Koreki* and *Olutores* would prevent the arrival of new recruits from the *Anadirfk*, as they heard that they had murdered two commiffaries, with the Coffacks under their command; however they were deceived in their hopes, for a great many of them were killed by their future conquerors, and their numbers very much reduced.

All this while the Coffacks were obliged to be very much upon their guard, and keep themfelves clofe in their forts. In the year 1705 *Atlafof* was freed from prifon, and fent commiffary to *Kamtfchatka*, with full authority, the fame as he was invefted with in the year 1701. The abfolute power of punifhing with rods, or even the knout, was no otherwife circumfcribed than by a recommendation to do ftrict juftice, and to treat the *Kamtfchadales* in particular with lenity and tendernefs. He went from *Jakutfki* accompanied by a great number of Coffacks, furnifhed with warlike ftores, and two pieces of brafs cannon; but fo far did he forget the favour of the pardon he had obtained for his former robbery, and difregard his new inftructions, that before he arrived at *Anadirfk* he began to exercife his cruelty upon thofe that were under his command, and became fo intolerable that they fent a petition thence againft him to *Jakutfki*. Notwithftanding this he arrived fafely at *Kamtfchatka* in the month of *July* 1707, and took the chief command over all the commiffaries that were there.

In the month of *Auguft* he ordered one *John Taretin*, with feventy Coffacks, to march againft the rebels who had killed the tax-gatherers upon the Beaver Sea. He met with no oppofition

before

before the 27th of *November*, in his whole march from the upper fort to *Awatſcha*, but coming near the bay of *Awachinſkay*, which is called at preſent the haven of *Peter* and *Paul*, they were met in the evening by 800 *Kamtſchadales*, who thought themſelves ſo certain of overcoming the Coſſacks, that they reſolved not to kill but take them all priſoners, every one being furniſhed with a rope to bind them.

The next day *Taretin* went to the bay of *Awatchinſkay*, where he found all the boats and veſſels of the rebels; but they had hidden themſelves in the woods on each ſide of the road; and allowing the headmoſt to paſs they ruſhed out upon the middle from both ſides. The Coſſacks defended themſelves ſo well, and fought ſo obſtinately, that great numbers of the rebels were killed, and the reſt ſaved themſelves by flight; ſix of the Coſſacks were ſlain, and ſeveral wounded. There were only three *Kamtſchadales* taken priſoners. After this action the inhabitants continued in a ſtate of rebellion till the year 1731. From this expedition the Coſſacks returned to the upper fort with what tribute they had gathered, and ſome hoſtages. Hitherto the government of *Kamtſchatka* had been in tolerable order, and the Coſſacks preſerved a regard for their commanders; but afterwards they began to commit great irregularities, plundering the inhabitants, ſeizing their perſons, and murdering others, in defiance of the governor.

CHAP. II.

Of the MUTINY *of the* COSSACKS, *and their Discovery of the Islands lying between* Kamtschatka *and* Japan.

THE Cossacks were dissatisfied with *Atlasof*. This discontent, encreasing by his continued ill conduct and their own licentiousness, made them resolve to deprive him of the command, which they did in *December* 1707; and they wrote to *Jakutski*, in their own vindication, that he gave them none of those provisions which were gathered from the *Kamtschadales*, for their sustenance; for they being otherwise employed in the fishing time, than in catching fish, must starve, unless the governor would supply them from the publick stores, which they charged him with embezzling for his own private advantage. They also accused him of having taken bribes to let the hostages go, which rendered the natives so insolent, that the tax-gatherers upon the *Penschinska* sea were obliged to save themselves by flight. To this they added his cruel treatment of *Daniel Belaiof*; and that, when the other Cossacks begged of him that he would not cut and slash any of them in his passion, but punish them as his orders directed in case they were found guilty, he replied, that if he was to kill them all he should not be punished for it: they besides represented, that he endeavoured even to irritate the natives against the Cossacks; for having called some of the principal people of the former, he told them, he had wounded that Cossack because he and others would have forced him to take the bread and provisions from them, their wives, and children; upon which the *Kamtschadales* in that neighbourhood left the place, and killed three Cossacks; that he had taken to his own use most of the goods that were sent from *Jakutski* to make presents of to the natives; and that he had compelled one of the *Kamtschadales* to give him a black fox-skin for his own use, which the said native had designed to pay in as a tribute.

This accusation of their's, though it may be a proof of their former mutinous disposition, yet gives us room to believe that a great deal of what they alledged was true, he being a man of a very bad character and conduct, and exceedingly avaricious, as appeared by the great riches he had amassed in so short a time: but it is scarce credible that he should endeavour to irritate the natives against his own people, on whose protection the safety of his own life depended; for the intended murder of the tax-gatherers upon the *Penschinska* sea was more to be attributed to their own oppression of the natives than to any misrepresentation of *Atlasof*, as it appeared they threatened to kill some *Kamtschadales*, who insisted on paying but one sable instead of two.

They conferred the command on *Simeon Lomyof*, imprisoned *Atlasof*, and confiscated all his effects to the treasury, which consisted of 1234 sables, 400 red foxes, 14 grey foxes, and 75 sea beavers, besides a great number of other furrs. *Atlasof* escaped, and fled to the lower fort, of which he endeavoured to obtain the command, but was prevented by the commissary *Theodore Yaregin*. During these confusions, the petition that was sent against *Atlasof* reached *Jakutski*. The governor, fearing that the dissentions and differences between *Atlasof* and the Cossacks might occasion the loss of *Kamtschatka*, sent to court for farther directions; and in the interim dispatched *Peter Tcherekof*, with fifty-five Cossacks, two pieces of cannon, and ammunition. While *Tcherekof* was upon the road, advice was brought from *Kamtschatka* that the Cossacks had taken the command from *Atlasof*: upon which orders were sent after *Tcherekof*, to examine strictly

into

into all this affair, and tranfmit his report to the *Jakutſki* Chancery, by the commiſſary *Simeon Lamyof* for their reſolution, and that by the ſame hand he ſhould likewiſe ſend all the taxes which were gathered. But *Tcherekof* had left *Anadirſk* before this order arrived, and, as the road from thence to *Kamtſchatka* was dangerous, the meſſenger durſt not go any farther, for the travelling along the *Olotorſki* and *Penſchinſka* ſeas was ſo very unſafe that on the 20th of *July* 1709, notwithſtanding *Tcherekof*'s force, they were fallen upon in the day-time, their ſtores and baggage were plundered, ten of them killed, and the reſt ſurrounded 'till the 24th, when they made a bold puſh, and fought their way through with the loſs of two more of their company.

During the government of *Tcherekof* two things happened that deſerve notice: 1ſt, The unfortunate expedition of the Coſſack Lieutenant *John Haritonof* with forty men againſt the rebels upon the North-Eaſt River, who fell upon him in great numbers, killed ten of his people, and wounded moſt of the reſt, whom they likewiſe kept beſieged four weeks. 2d, A bark from *Japan* being caſt away on the Beaver ſea coaſt, *Tcherekof* went with fifty men and reſcued four of the *Japaneſe* from the natives, whom on that occaſion he reduced to obedience, as alſo the inhabitants round the rivers *Jupinof* and *Oſtrova*, and obliged them to pay their tribute.

In the month of *Auguſt*, when *Tcherekof* returned to the upper *Kamtſchatka* fort, he found the Lieutenant *Myeronof*, who was ſent to relieve him; ſo that at this time there were three chiefs at *Kamtſchatka*, namely, *Atlaſof*, *Tcherekof*, and *Mieronof*.

When *Tcherekof* had delivered up to *Mieronof* the command, he left the upper *Kamtſchatkoi* fort in the month of *October*, and taking with him the tribute he had gathered, with a proper convoy, marched to the lower fort, where he reſolved to winter, and in the

the summer to sail through the *Penschinska* sea. *Joseph Mieronof* came likewise to the lower fort upon the 6th of *December*, to give orders concerning the building boats for carrying off the tribute; and having left proper directions for this purpose with *Alexi Alexander*, he set out with *Tcherekof* to the upper fort, on the 23d of *January* 1711: but he was murdered on the road by the twenty Cossacks who were his convoy. In the mean time thirty-one of the others went to the lower fort, where they killed *Atlasof*. The heads of this mutiny were *Daniel Anfiforof* and *John Kosorofki*, who shared the goods of those they put to death; and inviting all the rest to join with them, their number increased to seventy-five. All *Atlasof*'s furrs and goods which were carried to *Teghil* they brought back, seized on all the stores which were got ready for *Tcherekof*'s voyage, and destroying the sails and cordage returned to the upper fort on the 20th of *March*.

On the 17th of *April* in the same year, these mutineers sent a petition to *Jakutski*, confessing the murder of *Tcherekof* and *Mieronof*, without mentioning that of *Atlasof*. In this petition they endeavoured to excuse their conduct, by accusing these commissaries of tyranny and avarice, and charging them with having embezzled the effects of the government, and purchasing goods upon their own account, from which they received incredible profits; and that they had treated both the natives and Cossacks with great severity, to avoid which they were obliged to give them up their best effects, and to receive their salary in what goods they thought fit to allow them, and those taxed at what price they pleased; which oppression they exercised in confidence that no petitions against them would ever reach *Jakutski*. To this petition they joined a list of the effects of *Tcherekof* and *Mieronof*, which they had found: *Tcherekof*'s consisted of 500 red foxes, and 20 sea beavers; *Mieronof*'s, of 800 sables, 400 brown foxes, and 30 sea beavers.

This year in the spring, the seventy-five persons before mentioned marched against the rebels, and built a fort upon the Great River, thinking to merit their pardon by so essential a piece of service as the reduction of that district. On the 1st of *April* they destroyed a fort of the *Kamtschadales*, which lay between the rivers *Bistroy* and *Goltsofka*, where now the *Russian* fort *Bolscheretskoi* stands. There they remained without any disturbance from the *Kamtschadales* 'till *May*; on the 22d the *Kamtschadales* and *Koreki* came in boats down the Great River in such numbers that they threatened to smother them with their caps without using any other arms. On the 23d of *May*, the Cossacks, after having performed divine service, for they had a priest along with them, made a sally with one half of their party, and firing upon the *Kamtschadales* several times, killed great numbers of them: however they continued the fight 'till the evening, when at last the Cossacks obtained the victory. Such numbers of the rebels were killed and drowned in this engagement, that the river was full of dead bodies; but the *Russians* had only three men killed, and some few wounded. This success was followed by the subjection of all the villages and forts upon the Great River, who consented to pay their tribute as before. They went into the country of the *Kuriles*, and even unto the first island; all the inhabitants of which they likewise made tributary. This was the first time that any *Russian* had been upon either of these islands.

In the year 1711, *Vasili Savastianof* was sent to succeed *Mieronof*; for they had no account yet of his having been murdered, nor had they any knowledge at *Jakutski* of the fate of the other commissaries. *Savastianof* gathered the taxes about the upper and lower forts: *Ansiforof*, the head of the mutineers, had done the same upon the Great River, and came to the lower fort pretending to have returned again to his duty; however he came accompanied with such a strong party that he was in no danger of being called to account for his mutiny, but was sent as tax-gatherer to the Great River. As he returned towards the *Penschinska* sea, he reduced to obedience the rebels upon the rivers *Konpackova* and *Worofski*, and obliged them to pay the tribute, which they had refused for some time. He was surprised by the rebels upon the river *Awatscha* in the month of *February* 1712: When he with 25 Cossacks came among them, they received him in a large hut, built on purpose, with a private entry under it. They made him very rich presents, promised to pay the full tribute, and gave hostages as an earnest of their sincerity: but the following night they set fire to the hut, and burned both the *Russians* and their own hostages together; who were so irritated against the *Russians*, that when the people called to them to come out of the hut, they begged that they would have no regard to them, but burn the Cossacks by any means.

The punishment of the murderers of *Ansiforof* deterred the natives from the like attempts, and procured a lasting security to the tax-gatherers. A party was sent out to catch the murderers where they could find them: at this time there was one man taken, who being put to the torture confessed not only the murder of the three commissaries, but likewise a great many other dangerous designs, as that they resolved to destroy the upper and lower forts of *Kamtschatka*, murder the governor *Shepetkof*, plunder the fort of all the goods, and fly to the islands; but they were prevented in this by the great number of Cossacks which they found.

Shepetkof, giving the command to *Constantine Koserof*, left *Kamtschatka* on the 8th of *June* 1712, and sailed with the tribute which he had gathered over the *Olutorskoy* sea, and up the river of the same name as far as it was navigable for boats. Then he was obliged to fortify himself against the attacks of the *Olutores*, who on the road had several times fallen upon him.

him. He continued in this little fort 'till the 9th of *January* 1713, with 84 Coffacks. In the mean time he fent to *Anadirfk* for a reinforcement, and carriages to tranfport the tribute. There were fent him 60 Coffacks, and a great number of reindeer; with which he fet out, and arrived fafe at *Jakutfki* in the month of *January* 1714. This was the only tribute which had arrived fafe, upon account of the confufions, fince the year 1707. It amounted in all to 13,280 fables, 3282 red, 7 black, and 41 blue foxes, and 259 fea beavers.

After the departure of *Shepetkof*, *Kregezof*, who was commiffary in the upper *Kamtfchatkoi* fort, went with feveral under his command to the lower fort, feized upon *Yaregin* who was commiffary there, put him to all kind of torture, plundered the fort, and obliging *Yaregin* to turn monk gave the command of the fort to *Bogdan Kanafhof*; who continued there 'till the arrival of *Vafili Kolefof*, formerly a lieutenant of the Coffacks; and *Kregezof* with 18 of the mutineers returned to the upper *Kamtfchatkoi* fort, where he was very troublefome to the lower fort for a long time.

Kolefof was fent from *Jakutfki* in the year 1711, with orders to enquire into the conduct of the mutineers, and arrived at *Kamtfchatka* on the 10th of *September* 1712; where he condemned two of the rebels to death, and branded feveral others. The lieutenant *Koferof*, who was head of the mutiny after the death of *Anfiforof*, and feveral others, were punifhed; but *Kregezof*, who was ring-leader in the laft mutiny, not only refufed to fubmit to his jurifdiction, but threatened even to attack him, and to deftroy the lower fort. In confequence of which he marched againft him with cannon and 30 men of his party, and was joined in his march by other Coffacks from the Great River: however he did not accomplifh his defign, but was obliged to return to the upper fort, where in

KAMTSCHATKA. 253

a very short time his own people took the command from him, and put him in prison; for finding that the other Cossacks did not join him, they imagined it would be impossible for them to pass the lower fort in their way to the sea. Whereupon they divided themselves into two parties; one of which stood by *Koserof*, and the other joined *Kolesof*. By this means *Kolesof* made himself master of the upper fort in the year 1713. *Kregezof* was punished with death, with some others of the ring-leaders, and the rest were fined: those Cossacks and tax-gatherers, who continued in their duty, were rewarded. Thus an end was put to the rebellion.

After this *Kolesof* sent *Koserofki* with 55 Cossacks, 11 *Kamtschadales*, and some cannon, ordering them to build small vessels upon the Great River, and to make discoveries upon the islands that belong to *Japan*. In this expedition they reduced to obedience several of the *Kuriles* who dwelt upon the *Lopatka*, and the first and second *Kurilski* islands. They also procured some account of the islands that were more distant, which traded with the inhabitants of the city *Matma*, and who brought to them iron kettles, varnished cups and platters, sables, and different sorts of stuffs made of cotton and silk. *Koserofki* brought a sortment of these merchandises along with him.

CHAP.

CHAP. III.

Of the COMMISSARIES *who succeeded* Vasili Kolesof *until the great Insurrection at* Kamtschatka; *with the Discovery of a Passage through the* Penschinska Sea *from* Ochotska *to* Kamtschatka.

IN *August*, 1713, *John Inesiski* was sent to relieve *Vasili Kolesof.* In the time of his government he built a church at a place called the Springs, whither he designed to remove the lower fort, which was afterwards executed; the former situation being on a marsh, which was sometimes overflowed by the high water. This fort continued until the year 1731. In the time of the great rebellion, it was burned down by the rebels. He likewise marched against those who rebelled upon the river *Awatscha*, who had murdered *Ansiforof* with his 25 Cossacks. His strength consisted of 120 Cossacks and 150 *Kamtschadales.* The rebels had fortified themselves so strongly, that they held out two weeks; but at last they set their fort on fire, which was burned with all the people that were in it: the rest submitted, and promised to pay their tribute. They likewise took and burned the fort *Paratoon.* After this time the *Kamtschadales* upon *Awatscha* began regularly to pay their tribute; for before this they generally gave but just what they pleased, being almost always in a state of rebellion.

In 1714 *Yanisioski*, and the former commissary *Vasili Kolesof*, who had not been able to undertake the journey to *Jakutski* for want of hands in the year 1713, passed in boats over the *Olutorskoy* sea, and arrived the latter end of *August* upon the river *Olutora*, where they found *Athanasius Petrof*; who being joined by a great many Cossacks from *Anadir*, together with the *Yukageri*, defeated the *Olutores*, destroyed their strongest places, and in place thereof built a *Russian* fort. Here they remained until the winter. The taxes which both these commissaries brought along with them were 5640 sables, 751 red foxes, 10 blue, 137 sea beavers, 4 ounces of gold in bits, which were taken from the *Japanese*, whose vessels had been wrecked upon the coast of *Kamtschatka*. Upon the departure of these commissaries a garrison of 100 men, a lieutenant, and two priests, were left in the new fort upon the *Olutora*.

On the 2d of *December* 1714, the *Yukageri* who were with *Petrof* fell upon him near to *Acklanskey* fort, and having murdered him, the people that were with him seized upon the tribute. The commissaries *Kolesof* and *Yanisioski*, with sixteen others, escaped into the *Acklanskey* fort, but were not able to save their lives; for the *Yukageri* surrounding the fort prevailed upon the *Koreki* to murder these people, who had trusted themselves to their protection. The occasion of this misfortune was owing to the tyranny and oppression of *Petrof*. All pains were taken to recover the plundered goods, but to very little effect, as they were divided among so many different nations and people; so that some of the richest furrs fell into the hands of those who knew so little of their value, that for one or two pipefuls of tobacco they would sell a fine sable or fox skin. This disturbance of the *Yukageri* and *Koreki* continued more or less 'till the year 1720, when they were reduced to obedience by *Stephen Trifonof*, a gentleman of *Jakutski*, who went against them with a great number of Cossacks. So far had they carried their designs, that they endeavoured to prevail upon the *Tchukotski* to join in their rebellion, and to destroy the fort of *Anadir*.

After the murder of the commissaries the tribute of *Kamtschatka* was no more carried through *Anadir*, but sent directly by sea to *Ochotska*, which is by far a more convenient and less dangerous passage; so that now the road to *Anadir* is entirely neglected. This passage by sea was discovered in the year 1715, by one *Cosmus Socolof*, who was under the command of Colonel *Ylchin* sent to describe the islands that lie upon that sea. At this time *Alexi Petriloski* was commissary at *Kamtschatka*, against whom the Cossacks began again to mutiny; and by the consent of *Socolof*, they took the command from *Petriloski*, put him under arrest, and confiscated his goods. He was the occasion of his own misfortunes, by extortion, an unbounded avarice, and tyrannically oppressing to the last degree every man under his command. By these means he had acquired such riches in a very short time, that they far exceeded two whole year's tribute of *Kamtschatka*.

The natives were tolerably quiet all this while, excepting some small differences between the *Kuriles* of the *Lopatka* and another tribe, which was the cause of the destruction of several tributary *Kuriles*. The tribe, who was the first beginner of this confusion, was so much afraid of being punished by the *Russians*, that they would never come to any terms of accommodation. However, at last, they were reduced with no great trouble. The conduct of the *Russian* commissaries and tax-gatherers was so irregular, and so disagreeable to the natives, that the most fatal consequences were to be feared.

To *Petroloski* succeeded as commissary *Cosmus Vaichelashof*, to whom succeeded *Gregory Kamkin*. In the year 1718, at once three commissaries were sent from *Jakutski*; *John Uvarofski* to the lower *Kamtschatkoi* fort, *John Porotof* to the upper, and *Basil Kochanof* to the fort upon the Great River. According to custom, the Cossacks very soon deprived them all of their authority, and put them into prison, where they continued half a year, and at last escaped. However, the authors of this mutiny were brought to *Tobolski*, and punished with death.

While

KAMTSCHATKA. 257

While the Coffacks perfevered in this mutiny, feveral of the taxgatherers were murdered by the natives.

John Charetonof, who had been appointed commiffary, in 1719 marched againft the rebellious *Koreki*; but being furprifed by them he and feveral of his company were killed, which was done in this manner: The rebels pretending to fubmit, gave them hoftages and prefents; but afterwards fell upon *Charetonof*, and killed him and feveral others. However, they paid very dear for this treachery; for fome of the Coffacks, recovering from their furprife, drove them into their fort, where they burned or killed every man of them. In the following years, until the great rebellion of *Kamtfchatka*, nothing remarkable happened, if we except thofe confiderable expeditions that were fent out in the years 1727, 1728, 1729, to make difcoveries among the iflands of the *Kuriles*. The firft was conducted by two mariners, *John Evrinof* and *Theodore Lufin*, who returned in 1727. In 1728 was fent out the firft great fea expedition, to difcover and defcribe all the coaft towards the north. Having proceeded as far as the latitude 67° 17', they returned to *Peterfbourg* in the year 1730. In 1729 a party arrived there under the command of Captain *Paulutfkoy*, and a chief of the Coffacks called *Sheftocof*. They were ordered to go along the coaft towards the fouth to make proper difcoveries, and to bring all the inhabitants of thefe places, either by fair means or force, to pay a regular tribute; and for that purpofe, to build forts, and endeavour to eftablifh fome commerce. They built fome forts, and defcribed the coaft as far as the river *Udan* upon the *Chinefe* frontiers. *Sheftocof* was killed in the year 1730 by the *Tchukotfkoi*, who had fallen upon the tributary *Koreki*; and Captain *Paulutfkoy* was ordered to join Colonel *Merlin*, in quelling the rebellion of *Kamtfchatka*. He was indeed fo far more fuccefsful than *Sheftocof*, that he feveral times defeated the *Tchukotfkoi*, and for fome time rendered the *Koreki* and *Anadirfkoi* fafe from their inroads.

In the summer of the year 1729, a *Japanese* vessel was wrecked upon the coast of *Kamtschatka*: there were seventeen men on board, all of whom, except two, were murdered by Lieutenant *Stimicof*, who happened to be there at that time. The two survivors were sent to *Petersbourg*, where they had the satisfaction of seeing the murderer of their countrymen publickly executed. In 1730 *John Novogorodof*, and in 1731 *Meyer Shedfordin*, were tax-gatherers in *Kamtschatka*. We only mention them as being the occasion of the great rebellion, which we are now to describe.

CHAP. IV.

Of the REBELLION *of* Kamtschatka, *the Burning of the Lower Fort, the Subjection of the Rebels, and their Punishment.*

THE natives had resolved for a great while to destroy all the *Russians* who were in *Kamtschatka*; but since the discovery of the passage over the *Penschinska* sea, and the arrival of vessels with new people, it appeared to them too dangerous: but when Captain *Bering* with his fleet sailed on the expedition of *Kamtschatka*, and most of the Cossacks who were settled in *Kamtschatka* were ordered to join Captain *Paulutskoy* at *Anadir*, to suppress the rebellious *Tchukotskoi*, very few Cossacks were left in *Kamtschatka*. This the natives looked upon to be the wished-for opportunity; and during the whole winter the *Nishnashaltalski, Klutchefski,* and *Yalofski Kamtschadales*, under pretence of visiting one another, travelled through all *Kamtschatka*, and instigated the other inhabitants to join in their designs,

under

under pain of being intirely deftroyed. By thefe means all *Kamtfchatka* entered into a ftate of open rebellion; and hearing that *Shefticof* was killed by the *Tchukotſkoi*, they reported that thefe people were marching againſt *Kamtſchatka*, with a view either to have a pretence for collecting themſelves together, or that the *Ruſſian* Coſſacks, out of fear of theſe people, might defire the *Kamtſchadales* to guard them. Their meaſures were ſo well concerted, that it was a fingular inftance of Providence that any of the *Ruſſians* were preferved; for if they had once been driven intirely out of the country, it would have been difficult for them to have re-eftabliſhed themſelves. The counſels of the *Kamtſchadales* were far from being fuch as one would expect from favages; they endeavoured to prevent any correſpondence with *Anadirſk*, and kept a ftrong guard upon the fea-coafts, where they might feize upon any of the *Ruſſians* that arrived. The chief authors of this rebellion were one *Yaloſski Toyon*, or chieftain called *Fetka Harchin*, who had frequently ſerved the *Ruſſians* as an interpreter, and a chieftain of the *Klutchefski*, called *Chugotche*.

While this conſpiracy was in agitation, the commiſſary *Shacurdin* was on his departure from *Kamtſchatka*, with a confiderable party to guard the tribute. They had failed from the mouth of the river *Kamtſchatka* towards *Anadir*, but ſoon after contrary winds obliged them to return. The *Kamtſchadales*, informed of their departure, and ready for the revolt, gathered together, and failing up the river *Kamtſchatka* killed every *Ruſſian* Coſſack they could find, burned their ſummer huts, and carried off their wives and children into flavery. Their chief ftrength was directed againſt the fort; where arriving in the night, they fet fire to the prieſt's houfe, concluding that the fire would bring out all the inhabitants. In this they fucceeded too well, murdering almoft every perſon, without ſparing either fex or age. They burned all the houſes, except the fortifications and church, where the goods both of the public lick and private people were kept. Those who escaped this massacre fled to the mouth of the river, and carried the news to their countrymen, who had not yet left the coast. When the *Klutchefski* chief, *Chugotche*, heard of the taking the lower *Kamtschatka* fort he marched thither, killing or taking prisoners all the *Russians* he met with; and joining *Harchin*, he informed him that the *Russian* vessels were yet upon the coast, for which reason he judged it proper to strengthen themselves in the fort; and sending accounts of their success to all their countrymen, ordered them to join him. The next day they divided all the plunder, and dressed themselves in the *Russian* habits; and some of them, putting on the priest's robes, celebrated their own religious ceremonies and conjurations. *Harchin* ordered a new-baptised *Kamtschadale*, who had learned to read *Russ*, to say mass in the *Russian* manner, and dressed in the priest's robes; for which he made him a present of 30 red fox-skins.

The 3d day after the taking of the fort arrived a *Russian* skipper, *Yacob Hens*, with 60 Cossacks, who was sent with a design to recover the fort from the rebels. He endeavoured by all methods to persuade them to return to their duty, assuring them of a general pardon; but they would not give ear to him: nay, *Harchin*, their chief, told him that he had no business there, and that he was commissary of *Kamtschatka*, and would himself gather the taxes, so that they did not want any Cossacks among them. Upon which *Hens* sent to his vessels for some cannon, and began on the 26th of *July* to fire upon the fort, where he made a very large breach, which caused great confusion amongst the besieged, and gave an opportunity for the women that were prisoners to escape. *Harchin*, finding it impossible to defend the fort, made his escape disguised in women's cloaths; and although he
was

was pursued by several, yet he made such expedition that they could not overtake him. After this 30 of the besieged who remained surrendered themselves; but a *Klutchefski* chieftain, *Chugotche*, with a few people that joined him, held out to the last man. During their defence the powder magazine was set on fire, which reduced the fort and all the riches in it to ashes. In this siege the Cossacks had four men killed, and a great many wounded. How many of the *Kamtschadales* were killed was not known, their bodies being consumed in the fire; not one escaped alive, for those who surrendered were killed by the Cossacks, in revenge for the loss of their wives and children.

The sudden return of the *Russian* party was the occasion that this revolt was so easily quelled; for it prevented their assembling in such numbers, as they otherwise would have done. However, it was not yet intirely over, for *Harchin*, with some other chieftains, collected a good number of people together, and resolved to march to the sea side, and attack the *Russian* vessels which were there. But, in the very beginning of his march, he was met by a party of *Russians*, which obliged him to fortify himself upon the left side of the river *Kluchefka*; the Cossacks encamping upon the right, several skirmishes ensued between them. When *Harchin* saw that he could not accomplish his design, he proposed to treat with the Cossacks, and offered to come to their camp, if they would send one Cossack as an hostage for him; which they granted. He demanded, That they should not intirely ruin the *Kamtschadales*, and promised that for the future they would all live peaceably, only desiring that they would allow him to go and prevail upon his friends and relations to consent to this agreement; which being granted, he sent word, that he could not prevail with them to make peace; and that even his own brother, and a chieftain, *Javatche*, who had accompanied them, had refused to return.

The

The next day *Harchin* came to the bank of the river with some other chiefs, and desired, that the Cossacks would send a boat to bring him over, and give him two Cossacks in hostage; which they agreed to: but no sooner was he come over than they made him prisoner, and ordered the hostages to throw themselves into the river, and swim over, while they fired upon the *Kamtschadales* on the opposite bank, who, when their chief was made prisoner, presently separated; but, being pursued by different parties, most of them were destroyed. The chieftain *Teghil*, having defended himself a great while, at last murdered his wife and children, and killed himself; the chieftain *Chugotche*, in vain solliciting the inhabitants upon the river *Koseretsha Shapina* to join him, was in the end murdered by them. After this rebellion, which appeared at first very dangerous, and threatened the intire destruction of the Cossacks, was quieted by the arrival of succours, things continued in pretty good order at *Kamtschatka* until the year 1740, when the *Russians* had seven people killed by the natives.

When this rebellion was over, orders were sent as soon as possible to Major *Merlin*, with another officer and some regulars, together with Major *Paulutskoy*, to inquire into the cause of this rebellion, and the murder of the *Japanese*, and to send the report thereof to *Jakutski*; he was at the same time to build a new fort, which he did a little lower than the mouth of the river *Ratuga*: this was called the lower fort of *Kamtschatka*. Having examined into the cause of the rebellion, three of the *Russians* were found guilty of death and executed; and two of the chief rebels, with some others, both Cossacks and *Kamtschadales*, were punished. All the natives, whom they had either taken prisoners, or had made slaves of, were restored to their liberty. Those *Kamtschadales* who were put to death, seemed to go to execution without the least concern, and under the torture they were scarcely heard to moan; nor could they force them to confess

fess any thing more than what they had done voluntarily before.

Since this time all things are intirely quiet there; and it is hoped they will continue so, affairs being brought into such order, that the natives themselves could not wish for more, being only obliged to pay their taxes, without the least oppression, which consist only in one skin for every man of such creatures as he is used to hunt, such as sables, foxes, or sea beavers. Justice, except in criminal cases, is administered by their own chieftains. The Cossacks are forbidden to demand former debts, which they pretended were due from the natives. Their principal happiness consists in the conversion of several of them to Christianity; to which end her Majesty has been graciously pleased to appoint missionaries and schoolmasters, who keep schools in the principal villages for the instruction of the youth, both natives and Cossacks; and they begin now to be so much improved, that they even laugh at their former barbarity.

CHAP. V.

The present STATE *of the* FORTS *and* VILLAGES *of* Kamtschatka, *with a particular Account of each.*

THERE are five *Russian* forts in *Kamtschatka*: the 1st called the *Bolscheretskoi*, the 2d upper *Kamtschatka*, 3d the lower *Shaltolski*, 4th the haven of *Petropaulauskay*, and 5th on the river *Teghil*. The *Bolscheretskoi* fort stands upon the northen bank of the *Bolschaia-reka*, or Great River, between the mouths of the rivers *Beestra* and *Golsoftka*, 33 versts from the *Penschinska* sea. The fort is 70 feet square; the east and north sides are fortified with palisades, the south and west with

different

different buildings; the entrance into the fort is by a small gate on the west side. Beyond the fort was a chapel, now converted into a church consecrated to St. Nicholas, with a belfry upon pillars. There are about 30 houses of inhabitants, one publick house for selling brandy, and a distillery. There are about 45 Cossacks; and though their children pay the common head tax, yet 14 of them do duty with the other Cossacks. This fort is the weakest of all; but they seem to be very secure, as the neighbouring *Kamtschadales* were almost the first that submitted, and have always been faithful, and lived peaceably. With regard to its situation it has great advantages: first, all vessels that come by sea can come into the Great river, from which they receive their goods at the first hand: secondly, they receive great profits from the persons that arrive there, whom they furnish with lodging and board: thirdly, they are great gainers by the transporting goods from thence to the other forts: fourthly, they have a better opportunity than the others of getting *Kamtschatka* beavers, which is now reckoned a principal commodity: fifthly, in the summer they have the greatest plenty of fish, which they catch with little trouble and expence; for this reason the commander in chief of all the *Kamtschatka* forts generally lives here, sending out deputies to the others. The only disadvantage they have is, that in the summer, during the time of fishing, they are very subject to rainy weather, which spoils a great many of their fish, and thereby reduces them to great difficulties for food. If this river was furnished with wood sufficient the difficulty might be removed, as instead of drying them in the sun they might smoke them, as the inhabitants of *Ochotska* do. But this is impracticable because of the distance of the wood, and the trouble of bringing it down. It is so scarce here, that what they absolutely must have for the boiling of salt and train oil, they are forced to provide at the distance of three days' journey, and can bring no more than will serve to make 40 pounds of salt.

The

The upper fort of *Kamtschatka* was the first built, and for some years reckoned the principal, as the chief commissary lived there. It stands upon the left bank of the *Kamtschatka*, near the mouth of the little *Kaly*, about 69 versts from the rise of the *Kamtschatka*, 242 versts in the straight road from the *Bolscheretskoi* fort. It is 17 fathom square; the gate fronts the river, and over it is a warehouse. Within the fort is the office for receiving the taxes, a room for keeping the hostages, and two magazines. Without the fort is a church consecrated to St. *Nicholas*, the commissary's house, a publick house, distillery, and 22 private houses for the accommodation of the garrison, which consists of 56 Cossacks. This fort has the advantage of the *Bolscheretskoi*, the weather being here generally pretty good, and the wood, though only poplar, can be procured with little trouble, and is so large and substantial that it is very useful for building: besides the soil is better here, being much fitter for agriculture than any of the other parts. The fishery is indeed very poor, being at such a distance from the sea. The fish come up in small numbers, and so very late, that the inhabitants of the *Nishnashaltalski* fort make all their winter provision before they begin to fish in the upper fort; so that almost every spring there is a scarcity of provisions. Their salt and train oil they either buy from the inhabitants of the lower fort, or, notwithstanding the great distance, they go themselves and boil it at the mouth of the river *Kamtschatka*, which is 400 versts from the upper fort. Formerly they used to have great plenty of sea beavers in the Beaver Sea, but at present very few of them are caught; so that the inhabitants have their only hope of support from agriculture, to which if they apply themselves, they may expect more profit than from any commerce with the natives; and, if they neglect it, it will be impossible for them to live there.

The lower *Kamtschatka* fort is 397 versts distant from the upper fort, and stands upon the same side of the river, about 30 versts from its mouth. The fort is a parallelogram made with palisades; its breadth is 40, and its length 42 fathoms. In the fort is a church dedicated to the Virgin *Mary*, the office and magazine for the taxes, stores, and the commissary's house. These are all built of larch wood, and much neater than in any other fort. Without the fort are 39 private houses, besides the publick house and distillery. The male inhabitants are 92, of all ranks.

This fort, with regard to the necessaries of life, may be reckoned preferable to any other. Here the inhabitants catch plenty of fish, which they dry and salt in sufficient quantities for provision through the whole year: here they have wood enough, not only for building their houses, but also for building ships, to which the river serves as an harbour; and by its proximity to the sea they boil so much train oil and salt as to supply the other forts. Game is here so plenty, that the poorest Cossack seldom dines without a swan, goose, or duck; and through the whole winter, in the springs, they catch fresh fish. Wild berries of all sorts are here in great abundance, which the inhabitants lay up in store for the winter, and which next to fish is the greatest part of their sustenance; and the best *Kamtschatka* sables are caught near the river *Teghil*. All the goods which they get from the *Koreki*, such as deer-skins, and even the flesh of the deer itself, are cheaper here than any where else: besides, this is a most fruitful soil, where they may cultivate corn of all sorts. The only inconvenience that they have is, that both *Russian* and *Chinese* goods are dearer here than at any other fort, which is owing to their land-carriage from the *Bolscheretskoi Ostrog* hither, which costs four rubles a pood.

The fourth fort was built upon the bay of *Awatscha*, in the year 1740; and inhabitants were brought hither from the upper and lower *Kamtschatka* forts. The houses are tolerably good, particularly those which were built for the people of the *Kamtschatka*

chatka expedition upon the haven of *Petropaulauſkay*. Its great beauty is its church, which is finely ſituated, and very well built. This fort has almoſt the ſame advantages and diſadvantages as the *Bolſcheretſkoi* fort, with this difference, that here the hunting of the beaver is more convenient; but the water is bad and unwholſome, ſo that they ſend frequently from this bay to the river *Awatſcha* for their freſh water.

We can give no account of the fifth fort, which was built upon the river *Teghil* after my departure from *Kamtſchatka*. It was garriſoned with 37 male inhabitants. Mr. *Steller* tells us, that this fort was built with a view to reſtrain the ſettled *Koreki*, and for a ſtage to thoſe who travel round the *Penſchinſka* ſea to *Ochotſka*; and, in caſe of neceſſity, to protect the rein-deer or wandering *Koreki* againſt the *Tchukotſkoi*. The inhabitants of this fort can deprive thoſe of the lower *Kamtſchatka* fort of ſeveral advantages, becauſe they lie more convenient for hunting the ſable upon the river *Teghil*, and the *Koreki* rather chuſe to bring their goods to them than to the two other forts, as being nearer.

CHAP. VI.

Of the Manner in which the Coſſacks live there; of their DISTILLERY, PROVISIONS, *&c.*

THE Coſſacks of *Kamtſchatka* live almoſt in the ſame manner as the natives, feeding like them upon roots and fiſhes; and their occupations are nearly the ſame. In the ſummer they catch fiſh for their winter proviſion, and gather nettles, of which they make nets. Their difference only ſeems to confist in this, that the Coffacks live in houses, and the natives in huts under ground; the Coffacks usually eat their fish boiled, and the natives mostly dry; besides, the Coffacks dress their's several ways different from the natives. As it is impossible for people to live there without the help of women, who are so necessary in many parts of their work, such as cleaning their fish, drying their roots, spinning and making their shirts and cloaths, and as the Coffacks first settled in *Kamtschatka* without their wives, whom upon account of the difficulty of the journey they could not transport thither, I shall now relate what methods they used to make up for this deficiency.

One may easily imagine, that the Coffacks did not reduce these people without using force; and in these wars they took prisoners many women and children as well as men, and obliged them to perform all the labour. The care of overlooking these servants was entrusted to such as they made their concubines, whom they frequently married if they had any children by them; and sometimes the natives offered them their daughters, whom they promised to marry as soon as the priest arrived: so that it sometimes happened that the Coffacks had a marriage and christening at the same time; for then there was but one priest in all *Kamtschatka*, who lived in the lower fort, and once in a year, or once in two years, visited the other settlements.

The Coffacks, a people rude enough themselves, seemed to be pretty well pleased with the manner of living here, using the natives as their slaves, who furnished them with sables and other furrs in abundance, and passing the greatest part of their time in playing at cards: their only want seemed to be that of brandy. Before there were any brandy shops they used to meet in the office where the tax was received: here the gamesters brought their furrs, and, when they had no furrs, even their slaves;

and

and sometimes they played 'till both parties had pawned their cloaths for brandy. Such way of living, one may easily believe, was attended with great confusion; but what the poor slaves suffered is almost incredible, being obliged sometimes to change their masters twenty times a day.

The invention of making spirits happened accidentally. The Cossacks, after the manner of the natives, made a great provision of all kinds of berries for the winter. It happened sometimes that they began to ferment in the spring, and could be used no other way than in drink. This drink was observed to cause drunkenness when taken in great quantities; upon which they began to distil it, and, to their great surprise and pleasure, found that it produced a good spirit. They have since discovered that they could make brandy from an infusion of the sweet grass, and now they have spirits in plenty. Their method of preparing this herb for distillery we have already explained.

Those that are curious to know whence the Cossacks settled here obtained their riches, must be informed that they owe them to the following circumstances: first, when they conquered the natives they made all the plunder they could: secondly, every party of Cossacks, that was employed in gathering the taxes, obliged each tributary native, besides the crown tax, to give them four fox-skins and one sable, which they divided among themselves: thirdly, by their commerce with the natives, whom they obliged to pay a very high price for every trifle they furnished them with. Although, at present, the Cossacks are forbidden to take any thing more than the crown tax, yet they are still allowed to set what price they please upon their goods; and indeed they sell them, or change them for furrs, at very great profits, and sometimes for provisions, nets, and boats. Without this they would not be able to live upon their small pay, which is no more than what they used to receive at *Jakutski*, and, both in money and provisions, does not amount to above 14 rubles

rubles a year; and here they cannot maintain and cloath themselves for less than 40.

CHAP. VII.

Of their TRADE.

ALTHOUGH from the very beginning some people went along with the tax-gatherers, who carried little trifles to dispose of among the natives, these people could not be called merchants, because they did duty in the same manner as the Cossacks. By degrees many of them got themselves enrolled under that name, on paying the poll-tax, and as such settled with their families in these places; but the true merchants began to bring considerable quantities of goods first to *Ochotska*, and then to *Kamtschatka*, at the time when the second expedition to *Kamtschatka* took place. The number of the people increasing made the demand greater; and their profits were so considerable, that several, who came out of *Russia* as common labourers, in six or seven years began to trade for 15000 rubles or more: but, on the other hand, some were ruined from their extraordinary gains, which led them into various sorts of luxury and extravagance: and those merchants particularly who sent factors thither run the greatest risk; however, the principals had the satisfaction to find that the government took care to see justice done them.

After the expedition to *Kamtschatka* the trade began to be upon another footing, the officers and servants in this expedition buying their goods of the merchants for ready money; whereas they were obliged to give the inhabitants credit 'till they returned from their travelling among the *Kamtschadales*, when they were paid in furrs of different forts. In fine, the exchange of goods with the *Kamtfchadales* and *Chinefe* is fo profitable, that, notwithftanding all expences occafioned by the diftance, dearnefs of tranfport, and other difficulties, we may reckon that a 1000 rubles will produce 4000, provided they remain but one year in *Kamtfchatka*; but if they remain longer, there is a confiderable lofs. The reafons of this are, firft, that upon their arrival, being flattered with the high prices of things, they fell every thing, even their own cloaths and provifions, hoping foon to leave the country, in which if difappointed, they are obliged to buy them back again at double price: fecondly, that the furrs by lying, lofe their colour and value: thirdly, that the place is exceffively expenfive in regard to lodging, warehoufe-room, victuals, and feveral other particulars.

Goods demanded in *Kamtfchatka*, befides the natural produce of *Ruffia*, are *European* goods, from *Siberia*, *Boharia*, and the *Calmuks*. From *Europe* they receive coarfe cloaths of various colours, linen, ferges, knives, filk and cotton handkerchiefs, red wine, a little fugar, tobacco, and feveral toys. From *Siberia*, iron, feveral iron and copper veffels, and inftruments, fuch as knives, hatchets, faws, and fire-fteels; alfo wax, hemp, yarn for nets, tanned deer-fkins, coarfe *Ruffian* linen and cloth. From *Boharia*, and the country of the *Calmuks*, they bring feveral different forts of cotton goods. From *China*, feveral filk and cotton ftuffs, tobacco, coral, and needles, which are much preferred to thofe from *Ruffia*. From the *Koreki* they receive great quantities of rein-deer-fkins, both dreffed and undreffed, which they may fell in what quantities they pleafe at any time. Merchants muft take care not to have too great a ftock of any other goods; for the inhabitants of this place, *Ruffians* as well as natives, never buy any thing before they are in abfolute want of it, even if they could buy it at half price.

The

The goods sold at *Kamtſchatka* at prime-coſt ſcarcely exceed 10 or 12,000 rubles, but the ſales amount to 30 or 40,000 rubles; and if a merchant carries theſe *Kamtſchatka* goods to the fair upon the frontiers of *China*, he may receive double the price he buys them at; ſo that this commerce may eaſily appear to be very advantageous.

The goods that are brought out of *Kamtſchatka* conſiſt of furrs, ſuch as ſea beavers', ſables', foxes', and a few otters' ſkins. As there was formerly no money in this country, the way of trading was in exchange for furrs; and now they have money, they fix the price by the ſkins, reckoning a good fox-ſkin at a ruble.

All goods brought out of *Kamtſchatka* pay 10 per cent. duty, but the ſables 12.

CHAP. VIII.

The Different ROADS *between* Jakutſki *and* Kamtſchatka.

THOUGH it may at firſt appear needleſs to mention all the different roads to *Kamtſchatka*, eſpecially as ſeveral of them are now no more uſed, yet, upon due conſideration it will be found to ſerve for an illuſtration of the different ſettlements of the *Ruſſian* colonies, and to ſhew what people are ſubject and pay taxes to each of theſe ſettlements. It will alſo explain the manner of reducing theſe people and making them tributary, and deſcribe the difficulties of this journey, although there had been no danger from an enemy, in which the tax-gatherers were continually expoſed to hunger and cold in an unknown country, whereby many of them loſt their lives. The Coſſacks were only able to make this journey

journey during the winter, and had no other provisions or stores than what they dragged after them upon small sledges: and as they were obliged to go through great wastes, where sometimes by reason of the drifts of snow they were forced to stay several days in the same place, their provisions were entirely consumed; so that they were obliged to eat their leathern belts, straps, and shoe-soles. It is a thing incredible that a man upon the road could live 10 or 12 days without victuals, and yet in *Kamtschatka* they pretend that this has frequently happened to several.

From *Jakutski* the road to *Kamtschatka* was down the river *Lena* to its entrance into the Frozen Ocean, and thence by sea to the mouth of the river *Indigirka* and *Cova*, from whence they proceed over land to the *Penschinska* or *Olutorskoy* sea, and coast it round by the shore in boats. However this road was attended with great inconveniences; for in the best season, when the sea was free from ice and the wind favourable, they could not perform it in less than one year; but if the one happened to be contrary, or the other frozen, their boats were frequently broken to pieces, and the voyage cost them sometimes two, and sometimes three years. From *Jakutski* to the mouth of the river *Yani* is 1960 versts. However this road is now entirely disused.

Another passage was all by land: from *Jakutski* they went to the stage of *Aldanski*, from thence to upper *Yanski*; thence through *Zachiversk*, *Uyandski*, *Alaseski*, upper and lower *Covimski*, to the fort of *Anadir*; thence to the lower *Kamtschatka*, and thence to the upper fort upon the *Bolscheretskoi*.

The *Alazinska* stage stands at a good distance from the mouth of the *Alassa* river, which falls into the Frozen Ocean. It is about 509 versts distant from *Uyandinska*.

The *Anadirska* fort lies on the left of the river *Anadir*, about 963 versts from the lower *Kovinska*. From the fort *Anadirska* to the lower *Kamtschatka* is 1144 versts. This is at present

present the common road as far as *Anadirska*, but seldom to *Kamtschatka*, unless it be necessary to visit the different posts.

A third passage is mostly by water. They sail down the *Lena* from *Jakutski* to the conflux of the river *Aldan*, up the *Aldan* to the mouth of the river *Mai*, up the *Mai* to the entrance of the river *Judoma*, and up the *Judoma* as far as the place called the cross of *Judoma*; from thence over land to *Ochotska*, whence they go in boats to the *Bolschaia-reka* or Great River, or by land along the coast of the *Penschinska* bay: but the last is not quite safe upon account of the *Koreki*, who are frequently in rebellion. However, this passage up the rivers to the cross of *Judoma* is very tedious; and it is reckoned a piece of good fortune to make the passage in one summer: there are likewise several troublesome water-falls in this passage.

The fourth, and most convenient road in the summer-time, lies over the hills; and as I travelled this myself, I shall give my own journal, which perhaps may be of some use in laying down the geography, the common maps wanting most of the rivers in this part.

From *Jakutski* they go down the river *Lena* to *Yarmunka*, where they prepare themselves for their journey. The next place to this is *Kumatki*; we then passed some villages, and the following day crossed the river *Sola*. This river rises about 100 versts from the ridge, and falls into the *Lena* about six versts below where we passed it. We fed our horses by the lake *Kutchugna*, about 11 versts beyond the *Sola*; and lodged upon the lake *Oryoncamus*, 13 versts from the last place. The 3d day, passing the lake *Hatila*, we fed our horses upon the lake *Arelaka*; and lodged that evening upon the lake *Talba*. In about 14 versts from *Talba* we began to ascend the ridge; passing which, we went through the deserts *Quubalag*, *Keindu*, and fed our horses by the lake *Satagg*, 20 versts distant from *Talba*. We came next to the lake *Ala-atbaga*, where we lay that night.

In a few verſts from *Ala-athaga* we came to the little river *Kocora*, which, 22 verſts below the place where we paſſed it, falls into the river *Tata*: we went down to its very mouth. There are ſeveral lakes near it; and a verſt before we came to the laſt is a ſtation where generally the horſes are changed, and where cattle are bought for ſuſtenance in paſſing the deſerts. Every traveller buys ſome in his turn, which are divided equally among all the company. They endeavour to purchaſe them as ſmall as they can, that every one may only have ſuch a portion as he can conſume; for even though roaſted or baked it is preſently filled with maggots. This ſtation is kept by Coſſacks ſent from *Jakutſki*: it lies 15 verſts from the place where we paſſed the river *Kocora*. Having lodged here one night, we ſet out next morning, and paſſed the lakes *Emiti* and *Talbachan*, about one verſt and a half from the mouth of the *Kocora*. Then we travelled through the deſerts of *Karakoi* and *Tetaca*, and lodged that night by a little lake. Our road was near the ſide of the river *Tata*: this day we travelled about 15 verſts. The places that we remarked beyond this were, the deſerts of *Choraita*, *Menay*, *Koratoi*, *Tavalac*, and *Suſun*, and the little river *Tula*, which falls into the *Tata* about four verſts below where we paſſed it, and 13 diſtant from where we lodged the night before. Thirteen verſts from *Tula* the river *Namgare*, after a courſe of about 60 verſts, falls into the *Tata*. Between theſe two rivers are lake *Cungi*, and the deſerts *Sadochta* and *Betegeti*. Beyond the *Namgara* lies the lake *Neerga*, and the waſte places *Kalachku*, *Boorgunechtec*, and *Taalgeram*. Two verſts from the *Tata*, and 14 from *Namgara*, is the ſtation *Jockſovanſka*, kept by Coſſacks from *Jakutſki*: here we lodged. Travelling about four verſts and a half we paſſed the river *Tata*, which, as we were told by the people, riſes there about 150 verſts above our paſſage, and about as much below it falls into the river *Aldan*. Four verſts beyond the *Tata* we paſſed the little river *Lebagana*, which runs into the *Tata*. Between these rivers lies the lake *Yeleyegnok*. Half a verst from the river *Lebagana* we passed the river *Besurac*, which a little below falls into the *Lebagana* upon the right hand. Five versts farther is the river *Badaranac*, which falls into the *Besurac*. Passing a ridge we came to the spring of the river *Tuguta*, which, after a course of 30 versts falls from the left into the river *Kamgal*. The passage over the ridge is three versts. Going down the left side of the river *Taguta* we saw the lake *Utal*, and passed the river *Kirtak*, which falls into the *Taguta* five versts from its spring. Two versts and a half from *Kirtak* we lodged upon the lake *Besictaki*: from this lake to the ford of the river *Amga* is 18 versts. We crossed the river *Besurac*, which falls into the *Taguta* upon the left, and passed by the lakes *Mycharelac* and *Taguta*, near which are other lakes, *Taraga*, *Maralac*, and *Melca*. Half a verst from *Melca* is the passage over the river *Amga*, which is about 40 or 50 fathoms broad, and falls into the *Aldan* about a verst and a quarter below the passage. Between the mouth of the river *Amga* and *Tama* is about 119 versts. This river is remarkable, by having several people settled here for agriculture: however they have made very little progress; nay, they have even forgot their native language, and have acquired the language and customs of the *Jakutski*; so that they can be distinguished in nothing but by their being Christians. Here we were obliged to wait all night for the ferry. The next morning we went up the other side of the *Amga*, and about two versts from the ferry we came to the little river *Ulbuta*, which loses itself in the *Amga*. We ascended this river to its spring, and then going over to the spring of the *Chuoptchunu*, went down that rivulet to its entrance into the river *Nocha*. The river *Chuoptchunu* runs through the lake *Darka*; and the *Nocha* falls into the river *Aldan* about 120 versts from its rise. From the *Nocha* we went 12 versts over a ridge and came to the river *Voroni*, which falls into the *Nocha*

Two

Two versts further is the little river *Yilga*, which after a course of 20 versts falls into the *Nocha*: here we lodged. One verst beyond our quarters is the river *Atctachhatch*, which we ascended eight versts; then leaving it, four versts further we came to the *Chipanda*, along which we went 16 versts to where it falls into the river *Aldan*. The river *Chipanda* runs through the lakes *Bileor*, *Druk*, and *Chipanda*. The *Aldan* is a large navigable river, which falls into the river *Lena* upon the right side, 200 versts below *Jakutski*. We passed this river in boats: the ferry lies eight versts above the mouth of the *Chipanda*. From *Yalmanca* to this place the country was full of woods; though the greater part was larch and birch, yet upon the river *Amga* we now and then met with some fir-trees, but rarely a poplar. From the *Aldan* we travelled to the river *Bela*, which is 20 versts. Upon the road we saw several lakes, and the river *Keriatma*, which falls into the river *Aldan*. Here we lodged. The next day our road lay up the river *Bela*, upon which we passed the rivers *Sacil*, *Ulac*, and *Lebvena*, where we lay: this day we travelled 20 versts. The following day we passed the river *Argadchika*; and nine versts further lies the hill *Telahi*, a little beyond which begins the black forest: three versts further we took up our quarters. The next day, upon account of the rain, we did not move before four o'clock in the afternoon. Five versts beyond the black forest runs the river *Hagolla*, and 20 versts further the *Chagdolla*; both which run into the same *Bela*. During this journey we passed the river *Bela* three times. As the summer had been pretty dry, our passage was very favourable, being able to ford it; but in a wet season it frequently is attended with great danger. They are obliged to pass it upon floats, which, by the strength of the current, are frequently driven upon rocks or the trunks of trees. There is great plenty of wood upon the river *Bela*. Our road lay up the *Chagdolla*; in the space of 16 versts we crossed it seven times. About 15 versts

verſts from the laſt paſſage we came to the river *Unacam*, which is about 30 fathoms broad, and falls into the *Aldan*. Our road lay along this river to its very riſe. Ten verſts beyond the place where we paſſed it is a little river whoſe name we could not learn; upon which, half a verſt from its mouth, is a lake which they call *Buſkeol*, that is, Icy lake, as the ice in it does not thaw during the greateſt heats in ſummer. It lies between high rocky hills; its length is about 150 fathoms, and breadth 80; The thickneſs of the ice is about two feet, and it appears like the ſpring ice, bluiſh and full of holes. Here it is always cold in the hotteſt day. We now travelled 20 verſts over the hills, and came again to the river *Bela*, which we paſſed. Next day we travelled eight verſts further, and came to the head of the *Akera*, which falls into the *Yuna*: Our road lay ſeven verſts along this river. Then we aſcended the river *Yuna*, and paſſed it about 18 verſts from the *Akera*: this river falls into the *Aldan*. Next day we paſſed the river *Antcher*, and lay this night by the *Terrena*, or the little ice magazine, about 200 fathoms long and 50 broad. Five verſts from *Terrene* is another ice magazine, which is ſeven fathoms long and three broad; and ten verſts further, all upon the ſame river, is yet a third; five verſts from which laſt is the riſe of the river *Akachon*, which falls into the *Yuna*.

From *Yalmanka* we departed the 9th of *July*, 1737, and arrived at *Ochotſka* the 19th of *Auguſt*. We reſted ſeven days upon the road, and travelled thirty-four. It may be ſaid, in general, from *Jakutſki* to the ford of the river *Bela* the road is tolerable; but from thence to *Ochotſka* as troubleſome as one can eaſily imagine, lying always upon the ſteep banks of rivers, or through thick woods: The banks of the rivers are full of looſe round ſtones, ſo difficult to paſs, that it is ſurpriſing how the horſes can travel over them. The higher the hills, the more miry they are; and on the very tops of them are ſuch bogs and ſloughs, that if a horſe breaks the ſurface he ſinks without any poſſibility of recovering

covering him: it is terrible to see the earth bending like waves for ten fathoms round one. The best time of travelling from *Jakutski* is from the beginning of summer until the month of *July*; for if they wait 'till *August* they are in danger of being surprised by the snow, which falls very early on the mountains.

We took our departure from *Ochotska* on the 4th of *October*, in the Fortuna packet-boat, which had sailed thither from *Kamtschatka*. At night there was such a leak in our vessel, that the people below were up to their knees in water; and though we worked with two pumps, and baled it with kettles and pans, and whatever fell in our way, yet the water decreased very little: besides our vessel was so heavily laden that it came over the gunnel. We had therefore no other means of saving our lives than by lightening the vessel, for at this time there was a dead calm; so that all upon deck, or about the sides of the ship, was immediately thrown overboard: but as this produced very little advantage, about 400 pood was cast out of the hold, which relieved us; the water in the vessel began to decrease, and at last was intirely cleared, However, the pumps were still kept going, and no body except the sick were excused: in this manner we sailed 'till the 14th of *October*. Besides the continual fatigue of pumping we were exposed to violent cold and continual sleet. This day at nine in the morning we arrived at the mouth of the *Bolschaia-reka*; but, as if all our voyage was to be unfortunate, our sailors, not knowing whether the tide was ebbing or flowing, mistook the ebb for the flood, and ran into the mouth of the river. They were no sooner come to the broken water, which is very great at the beginning of the ebb or flood even in the calmest weather, and was at present much increased by a strong north wind, than we lost all hopes of advancing up the stream. It was therefore the opinion of several, that we should go out again to sea, and wait the time of the flood: but lucky was it for us that we did not pursue this resolution; for during the whole week following there was such a strong north wind we should in that case have been driven so far out to sea that we must all have perished: but the majority insisted on running the vessel on shore, which we did about 100 fathoms south of the mouth of the river. In the evening, at the next high water, we took out the mast, and the following day several planks; the rest was stove to pieces, and carried away by the sea. Now we could observe in what danger we had been, for we found all the planks of the vessel quite black and rotten.

We lived upon the coast 'till the 21st; and during our stay there happened an earthquake, but so inconsiderable that we hardly knew of it, but imputed the motion we observed to our having been tossed so long at sea: however, some *Kuriles* who came down informed us, that in the place of their habitations it had been very violent, and that the water rose exceeding high. On the 21st of *October* we entered the *Bolschaia-reka* in boats that were sent to us from the fort, and on the 22d in the evening we arrived at the fort.

Notwithstanding that the journey from *Jakutski* to *Kamtschatka* is very troublesome, yet the return is tolerably agreeable; for the vessels that winter at *Kamtschatka* depart early in the summer, when the weather is generally fair and the days long; and at that time one can go by water even to the ferry of the river *Bela* or the *Aldan*, and from thence on horseback to *Jakutski*. The only trouble that they have is before they come to the cross of *Judoma*.

In my return I came from *Ochotska* to *Judoma* in seven days, and from thence to the mouth of the *Mai* in five days, and from thence to *Jakutski* in five days more; so all together make 17: however, upon account of the rapidity of the stream, the passage up the *Uda*, which I have made in five days, sometimes costs five or six weeks.

The END.

INDEX.

A

Acklanskoy fort, two commissaries murdered there 23
Adultery, not sinful 204
    punished with death by the Koreki 224
    how punished by the Kuriles 237
America, accounts of that part, which lies directly east from Kamtschatka, collected from Mr. Steller's journal 44
    its climate, soil, and produce 45
    natives of, their dress, food, and language 46, 47
American boats, a description of, 48
Americans, their behaviour to strangers, and their signs for land being near 49
Animals, domestic, none, except dogs, cows, and horses 108
    religious regard for 205
Arrows, poisoned, dangerous to be wounded with 202
Aru, a sea fowl, described 154
Atlasof, first discovery of Kamtschatka attributed to 241
    defeats the rebels, exacts tribute from the people, and builds the upper Kamtschatkoi fort ibid.
    returns with the Kamtschatka tribute 242
    is made chief of the Cossacks, returns to Kamtschatka, plunders a Chinese boat, and is imprisoned ibid.
    is freed from prison, and sent commissary to Kamtschatka 244
    cruelty of, to those under his command ibid.
    defeats the rebels 245
    is accused by the Cossacks 246
Atlasof, again imprisoned, and his goods confiscated 247
    escapes and flies ibid.
    differences between him and the Cossacks enquired into ibid.
    murdered by the Cossacks 248
Author, journal of, in his passage from Jakutski to Kamtschatka 274
    is in danger of being lost 279

B

Balagans, how built, and use of 182
Bears, fierceness of 100
    remarkable fondness of, to women 101
    how killed before the use of fire-arms ibid.
    what use made of 103
Beavers, sea, resemblance and colour of, 130
    care of, to their young, and different methods of catching them 131
Bering's island, situation and extent of 50
    its mountains and soil 51
    observations made from 53
    tides in 54
    waters of, their medicinal virtues 55
Birds, plenty of 152
    species of, sent to the Imperial Museum 153
    storm. *See* procellaria
    small, found at Kamtschatka 162
Boats, two methods of making, and management of 186
Boils, a dangerous disease, how cured 218
Bride, the difficulty and danger in obtaining 213
Brook, hot, situation and course of 75

INDEX.

C

	Page
Canoe, trouble of making, and the inhabitants esteem for	184
Cat, sea, a description of	124
a conjecture of the inhabitants concerning	125
fierceness of, in combating with each other	126
a battle of, related by Mr. Steller	127
fondness of, for their young	128
humorous tricks of, in the water	129
how catched upon Bering's island	130
Channel between Matma and Japan described	40
Japanese account of, the same as the Europeans'	41
Charetonof, John, marches against the rebellious Koreki, and is killed	257
Chiefs, appointed by her Imperial Majesty	180
Chugotchi, a chieftain, a brave defence made by, against the Cossacks	261
Cobelof, reckoned the first governor of Kamtschatka, builds a fort, and gathers voluntary tribute	242
gathers taxes from the Koreki	243
Commissaries, a succession of, from Vasili Kolesof until the great insurrection of Kamtschatka	254
murdered by the Yukageri and the Koreki	255
irregular conduct of	ibid.
Cormorants, a description of two kinds of	154
singular manner of catching	155
Cossacks, killed by stratagem	200
afraid of extraordinary caresses	201
mutiny, and murder their chiefs, and seize on their effects	249
march against the rebels, obtain a victory, bring the villages under subjection, and make the Kuriles tributary	250
their chief surprised and burnt, and the murderers punished	251
put Alexi Petroloski under arrest	256
deprive the commissaries of their authority	256
punished with death	ibid.
again mutiny	ibid.
of Kamtschatka, living and occupations of	267
differ from the natives	268
make spirits and brandy	269
Cossacks, riches of, how acquired	269
Courtship, the manner of	212
of the Koreki	232
Cow, sea. *See* manati	

D

Dead bodies, given to the dogs	220
the ceremony used at the burial of	221
superstitious notions concerning	ibid.
the Koreki manner of burning, and celebrating the memory of	233
Kuriles manner of burying	238
Deer, description of	104
Diet, its several names, and how cooked	193
Diseases, principal, what, and how thought to be inflicted	217
supposed to be incurable	218
Dogs, colour and swiftness of	106
more useful than horses for travelling	107
bred to hunt, how fed	108
description of	196
furniture of, for travelling with, and the manner of driving	ibid.
value of	197
Dreams, great regard paid to	206
Ducks, the names and an account of eleven different species of	159
stone, drakes of, particularly beautiful	160

E

Eagle, four species of	162
Earthquake, at Awatscha	68
at the Kamtschatkoi fort	70
Expeditions, sent out	257

F

Fishes, an account of	137
Sword. *See* Kasatki	
Mokoe, a description of	141
various sorts of	142
great plenty of	143
Red, different species of	145
Gorbushe, or Crookback, described	147
particular sorts of, change their colours	148
smelts, three species of	151
herrings, (the same as those in Europe) how caught by the Kamtschadales	152

Fish

INDEX.

Fish, the Samojeds' manner of treating, by Mr. Steller 194
    methods of preserving, by the different people 195
Food, a melancholy instance of the great scarcity of 141
Fort, Ochotskoy, situation of, and buildings 24
    Udeskoy, buildings and soil of 26
    Russian in Kamtschatka, an account of the present state of 263—266
Fowls, sea, where greatest plenty of 153
    fresh water 158
    land 162
Foxes, valuable skins of 95
    difficult to catch, an instance of ibid.
    great plenty of, and best time to hunt 96
    Kuriles' manner of catching, peculiar to themselves ibid.
Furniture, houshold, what it consists of 184

G

Garlick, wild, usefulness and medicinal virtues of 88
    an effectual remedy for the scurvy 89
Geese, seven kinds of 158
    method of catching, singular ibid.
Glutton, a sort of weasel, greatly esteemed by the Kamtschadales 99
    paws of, used as an ornament by the women ibid.
    dexterity of, in killing the deer 100
    gluttony of ibid.
God, extraordinary notions of 176
    opinions of 203
    feared less than the devil 204
Goods, what sorts of, demanded in Kamtschatka 271
    great profits arising from 272
    brought from Kamtschatka pay duty ibid.

H

Harchin, chief of the rebels, resolves to attack the Russian vessels 261
    meets the Russians, and makes proposals to them ibid.
    is made prisoner 262
Herbs, useful to the inhabitants 83
    kipri, its use and virtues 88
Honey, how preserved from the bears by the Russians 101

Horse, sea, where caught 110
    described by Frederick Marten, notes 124
Hunters, Vitimsky, their toil and rigorous laws 109
    enter into a company, and appoint a chief 111
    their trap-pits described 112
    their method of hunting with nets 113
    report their success to the chief 114
    acting contrary to orders punished 115
Huts, the manner of building, and a description of 181
    of the Koreki and Tchukotskoi, how made 226
    of the Kuriles 236

I

Jesso, errors of former geographers corrected in regard to 39
Inesiski, John, marches against, and brings to submission, the Kamtschadales upon the Awatscha 254
Insects, swarms of 164
    resembling a louse, Mr. Steller's account of 165
Instruments, warlike, forbid to be sold 185
Itatka, well known to naturalists, a description of 153
Iron, want of, a great inconvenience 66
    how supplied with 67
    supposed to be long known at Kamtschatka 185
    the inhabitants curious management of ibid.
Island, Shantanskoy, product of 27
    Schumtschu, the first Kurilskoy, situation, mountains, and inhabitants of 34
    Schumtschu, channel between, and the Kurilskaya Lopatka, described 35
    Paromusir, the second Kurilskoy, situation, and inhabitants of ibid.
    Sirinki, the third Kurilskoy, and Onnecutan the fourth, situations of 36
    Kurilski, Mr. Muller's account of 37
    Eturpu and Erupe, Keek-Kuriles natives of, their language and trade 39
    Matma, subject to Japan, situation of 40
    nearest to Japan, Mr. Steller's account of their product, natives, and trade 42
    Bering. *See* Bering

INDEX.

K

	Page
Kamtfchatka, situation of	9
rivers of	12
rivulets and remarkable mountains of	15
principal roads of, with their distances laid down	28—33
its soil, product, weather, and air	57—61
riches of, what	95
beasts of	ibid.
sea beasts of	115—137
natives of, their customs and manners	169
language of	171
conquest of	239
inhabitants of, rebel and murder the tax-gatherers	243
trade of, its first rise and profits	270

Kamtfchadales, divided into northern and southern people, different situations of 170
have a particular custom in giving names to things 171
the names of, some conjectures concerning 172
distinguish themselves by particular names 173
uncertain from whence they came, and when they first settled at Kamtfchatka ibid.
antiquity of, by Mr. Steller ibid.
their great knowledge of the virtues and uses of the natural product of their country 174
why thought to take their origin from the Mungals ibid.
supposed to be driven to Kamtfchatka by the tyranny of the eastern conquerors 175
employments of, in the different seasons 187
dress of 190
women, use paint 192
their method of travelling with dogs 196
have no inconvenience from cold 199
their method of making war ibid.
their barbarous treatment to their prisoners 200
their private differences useful to the Cossacks ibid.
bravely defend themselves against the Cossacks 201
a desperate resolution of, rather than submit to the enemy ibid.

Kamtfchadales, the arms of, how made 202
their manner of marching 203
have a religious regard for animals 205
instructed in the Christian faith ibid.
ceremonies of 206
their feasts and diversions 207
their manner of obtaining a friend 210
have two or three wives 215
their unconcern at being put to death 262
are converted to Christianity, and ridicule their former barbarity 263

Kamtfchatkoi fort 21
Karaginfkoy island, inhabited by the Koreki 17
Kafatki, (falsely called the Sword fish) enmity of, to the whale 139
feared by the fishermen ibid.
description of, by Mr. Steller 140
Kolefof makes the first expedition against the Kuriles 243
is in danger from the Koreki ibid.
sent from Jakutfki to enquire into the conduct of the mutineers 252
punishes the mutineers, and reduces to obedience the Kuriles 254
Koreki, where their habitations begin, and their forts described 16
two nations of, have different languages 170
language of, and manner of speaking 172
fixed resemble the Kamtfchadales 222
a description of their customs and habits 223
think themselves happy 224
more honest and industrious than the Kamtfchadales 225
in eating uncleanly 226
religion of 229
civil policy of, and punctual observance of an oath 231
courtships and marriages of 232
have great fondness for children ibid.
reduced to obedience 255
Kregezof, commissary of the upper Kamtfchatkoi fort, seizes the commissary of the lower fort, plunders it, and gives the command to Bogdan Kanafhof 252
Kuriles, two different nations of, their names and situations 170
their manner of speaking 172
manners and persons of, described 235
sacrifice to idols 236
manner of travelling ibid.

Kuriles,

INDEX.

Kuriles, how they receive and entertain visitants 237
— have aversion to twins 238
Kutchu, their god so called, reproached by them 203

L

Lion, sea, a description of 120
— fierceness of, and different methods of killing 121
— skins, use of 122
— the male's great tenderness for the female, and their care of their young ibid.
Liquor, what 195
— made from the mushroom 208
List of some plants, beasts, fishes, and birds, with their names in the English, Russian, Kamtschatka, Koratski, and Kurilski languages 163
Lizards, numerous, the natives' superstitious notions of 165

M

Manati, or sea cow 132
— eyes of, remarkably small ibid.
— love of, to each other extraordinary 134
— flesh of, its taste and resemblance 135
— a description of, found in the rivers of South-America, and at the Philippine Islands, by Captain Dampier, notes ibid.
— skin of, of great use to privateers, notes 136
Marching, to battle, manner of, remarkable 203
Marmottas, abound in Kamtschatka 98
— skins of, used for cloathing by the Koreki ibid.
— a description of 99
Marriage, how constituted 213
— feast, ceremonies at the 214
— when forbidden 215
— Koreki manner of 232
Marten, Frederick, his account of the seal, sea dog, and horse, notes 123, 124
Medicines, what they consist of 217
— used for the scurvy 218
— used in various disorders 219
Metals and *Minerals*, none found in Kamtschatka, reasons assigned for it 79

Mountain, Awachinsky, situation and fires of 67
— Tulbatchinsky, fires of 69
— Kamtschatka, its height and circuit ibid.
— burning, conjectures of, by Mr. Steller 71
— burning, the Kamtschadales' notions and fears of 76
Murder, &c. not thought sinful 204
— how punished by the Koreki 232
— self, frequent among the Kuriles 238
Mushroom, liquor made from, dangerous 208
— in great esteem among the Koreki 209

N

Natives of Kamtschatka in general 169
— three different people, their names, and boundaries 170
— ancient state of 175
— manner of living 176
— their happiness and unhappiness, what ibid.
— self-murder formerly frequent among ibid.
— are cruel and lustful ibid.
— trade of, with the Koreki, and behaviour of to each other 177
— ignorance of, in numbering 178
— their months, a table of ibid.
— laws of 179
— superstitious notions of, greatly abolished since the arrival of the Russians 180
— resolution of, to destroy all the Russians 258
— enter into open rebellion 259
— sail up the river Kamtschatka, kill all the Cossacks in their way, and set fire to their huts; take the lower Kamtschatkoi fort, massacre all the people, and burn their houses ibid.
— are opposed and thrown into confusion 260
— their chief escapes in disguise ibid.
— are defeated and killed 261
— make a brave defence ibid.
Needle, eye of, dexterously supplied 185
Nettles, the great use of 94

O

Ochotska, passage by sea to, discovered by Cosmus Socolof 256

INDEX

	Page
Offerings, manner of making	203
Otter, very common in Kamtſchatka	115
how hunted, and what uſe made of its ſkin	116

P

Paulutſkoy ſent to make diſcoveries, and defeats the Tchukotſkoi   257
Petrof, Athanaſius, with Coſſacks and the Yukageri, defeats the Olutores, and deſtroys their ſtrong places   255
    murdered by the Yukageri   ibid.
Phyſicians, (old women) their treatment of the ſick   141
Plant, ſweet, deſcription of   85
    brandy diſtilled from it by the Ruſſians   ibid.
    how gathered and prepared   86
    Mr. Steller's remarks on the brandy made of   87
    uſed for food, a deſcription of   89—91
    Kamtſchadales' knowledge of, by Mr. Steller   91
    medicinal, account of   92
    uſed for cloathing, &c. variouſly prepared   93
Procellaria, or ſtorm birds   155

R

Rams, ſtone and wild, a deſcription of   104
Rats, three kinds of, deſcribed   ibid.
    neſts and food of   105
    retiring, alarming to the Kamtſchadales   ibid.
    regularity of, in marching   106
Rebellions, an account of two   202
    of Kamtſchatka   259
    the cauſe of, enquired into   262
Rebels, number of, drowned   202
    defeated by Atlaſof   245
    puniſhed   262
Rein-deer uſed to travel with   228
Rivers, ſhores of, deſcribed   22
    Ochotſka   23
    Urak, rapid and dangerous for veſſels   25
    Ude   26
    Amur, riſe and fall of   27
Roads, deſcribed, and their diſtances laid down   28—33
    between Jakutſki and Kamtſchatka, deſcribed, with their ſituations, diſtances, and difficulty in travelling   272—280

	Page
Roots, their uſefulneſs to the inhabitants	83
of the ſaranne, how uſed	84
Ruſſia, Empreſs of, appoints chiefs	180
ſends miſſionaries	205, 265
Ruſſians give names to the different nations of Kamtſchatka	171
means uſed by, to obtain a noꞏwledge of Kamtſchatka	239

S

Sables of Kamtſchatka, properties of   97
    plenty of before the conqueſt, and little value of them at that time   ibid.
    Kamtſchadales' method of taking   98
    Vitimſky, valuable   109
    ſcarce in Siberia   ibid.
    relation of, by the hunters   110
Salmon, its uſe to the inhabitants   143
Salt, want of, inconvenient   66
    how ſupplied with   67
Saranne, five ſpecies of, reckoned by Mr. Steller   84
Seals, four ſorts of   116
    the author's relation of one taken in the Great River   ibid.
    milk of, uſed medicinally   117
    different ways of killing them   ibid.
    ſkins of, variouſly uſed   117, 118
    head of, great reſpect ſhewn to it   118
    fleſh and fat of, eſteemed delicious food   ibid.
    deſcription of, by Frederick Marten   123
Shamans, or conjurers, conjuration of   206
    Koreki, of great repute   230
    extraordinary feats of   ibid.
Sheep, why ſcarce   108
Shepetkof leaves Kamtſchatka, fortifies himſelf againſt the Olutores, and arrives at Jakutſki with tribute   252
Shrubs, ſlantza, its plenty, &c. and the uſe and quality of its nuts   82
    different ſorts of, their uſe and virtue   83
    vodinitza, Mr. Steller's account of   ibid.
Sin, mortal, what reckoned ſo   205
Sirukof, and his followers, murdered by the Koreki   242
Skins, how prepared   188
    dying and ſewing of   189
    glue made of   190
Sledges, danger of, in travelling with   197
Snow, its bad effects upon the eyes   65
    remedy for it, by Mr. Steller   66
    ſhoes, make and uſe of   197

INDEX.

Soul, notions of the immortality of 204
Spanberg, Captain, his description of the Kurilski islands, not reconcileable to Mr. Muller's 41
Spider, the women's notions of the effects of 164
Springs, hot, where found 72
   stones and clay found about the mouths of, described 73
   heat in each, a table of the different degrees of, by De l'Isle's and Farenheit's thermometer 74
   of Kamtschatka never freeze, wholesomeness of the waters of, and plenty of fish in 78
Stanovoy ridge, a description of, and the danger in passing 21
Steller, Mr. his observations of the appearance of the country about Kamtschatka 77
   accounts for the frequent earthquakes about Kamtschatka ibid.
   his account of the sea lion 122
   his description of an uncommon sea beast, which he saw on the coast of America 136
   his account of fishes 148
   his account of the Stariki and Glupisha fowls 156
Stones, &c. different kinds of, their use 80
Swan, common in Kamtschatka 158

T

Tax-gatherers, murdered, paying taxes the cause of it 243
Tcherekof, Peter, is fallen upon, has his stores, &c. plundered, and ten of his men killed 248
   remarkable event during his government ibid.
Tchukotskoi, an account of 226
   manner of living 227
   travel with rein-deer 228
   are defeated 257
Teghil, a chieftain, after a long defence, murders his wife and children, and kills himself 262
Theft, thought reputable 232
Theodot, a Russian, a tradition of 240
   murdered by the Koreki, &c. ibid
Tides, in the Penschinska sea and Eastern Ocean, observations of, by the author 165
Tides, the moon's effects on the ebbs and floods of 166
   methods followed in making observations on 167
Travellers, danger of, and how they secure themselves from storms 198
   the best time for, to travel in 199
Trees, larch, white poplar, &c. use of, and where produced 81
   birch, bark of, eat by the inhabitants, how prepared ibid.
   birch, differs from that of Europe 82
   white poplar, Mr. Steller's observations of ibid.
   fallow and alder, and their barks, use of ibid.
   hawthorn, fruit of ibid.

U

Vessel, Japanese, wrecked, and the crew murdered 258
Vice, extraordinary notions of 204
Villages, appearance of 183
Virtue, notions of 204
Volcano. See mountain.
Utensils, necessary, what they consist of 184

W

War, method of making 199
   among themselves, the end of ibid.
   carried on by stratagem 200
   the Koreki manner of making, and their arms 234
Wells, two large, waters of, &c. 76
Whales, number of, where 137
   how caught by the different people, and their ceremonies used on dragging them to shore 138
   a delicate provision, how prepared ibid.
   an engagement between them, and the kasatki, related by Mr. Steller 139
   great advantages derived from 140
   the bad effects of eating the fat of 141
   a curious chain made of the bones of 186
Widow, how obtained in marriage 214
   fins of, first taken away 215
Winds, violent, signs of 66
Wolves, numerous 100
   hurtful to the inhabitants 103
Women, shyness of, to strangers 215
   fruitfulness of, and their manner of delivery 216

INDEX.

Women use means to forward and prevent their having children   217
    treatment of, to twins and children born in a storm   ibid.
    medicines used by, to hasten delivery   218
    wandering Koreki, make themselves disagreeable   224
    fixed Koreki, adorn themselves   ibid.
    odd ceremonies used by, in naming their children   233
World, opinions of the formation of   204

Y

Yocoly, bread so called   193
Yukageri, reduced to obedience   255

Z

Zinoveef is sent chief on an expedition   242
    succeeds Cobelof as commissary, brings things into order, returns to Jakutski with the tribute, and is succeeded by Kolesof   243

Lightning Source UK Ltd.
Milton Keynes UK
UKOW06f1050101114

241333UK00006B/184/P